ENCOUNTERING THE TRANSNATIONAL

Gender in a Global/Local World

Series Editors: Jane Parpart, Pauline Gardiner Barber
and Marianne H. Marchand

Gender in a Global/Local World critically explores the uneven and often contradictory ways in which global processes and local identities come together. Much has been and is being written about globalization and responses to it but rarely from a critical, historical, gendered perspective. Yet, these processes are profoundly gendered albeit in different ways in particular contexts and times. The changes in social, cultural, economic and political institutions and practices alter the conditions under which women and men make and remake their lives. New spaces have been created – economic, political, social – and previously silent voices are being heard. North-South dichotomies are being undermined as increasing numbers of people and communities are exposed to international processes through migration, travel, and communication, even as marginalization and poverty intensify for many in all parts of the world. The series features monographs and collections which explore the tensions in a 'global/local world', and includes contributions from all disciplines in recognition that no single approach can capture these complex processes.

Also in the series

Series titles continued at the back of the book.

Encountering the Transnational
Women, Islam and the Politics of Interpretation

MEENA SHARIFY-FUNK
Wilfred Laurier University, Canada

ASHGATE

Published by
Ashgate Publishing Limited
Gower House
Croft Road
Aldershot
Hampshire GU11 3HR
England

Ashgate Publishing Company
Suite 420
101 Cherry Street
Burlington, VT 05401-4405
USA

Ashgate website: http://www.ashgate.com

British Library Cataloguing in Publication Data
Sharify-Funk, Meena
   Encountering the transnational : women, Islam and the
   politics of interpretation. - (Gender in a global/local
   world)
   1. Women in Islam - Cross-cultural studies
   2. Transnationalism
   I. Title
   297'.082

Library of Congress Cataloging-in-Publication Data
Sharify-Funk, Meena.
  Encountering the transnational : women, Islam and the politics of interpretation / by
Meena Sharify-Funk.
     p. cm. -- (Gender in a global/local world)
  Includes bibliographical references and index.
  ISBN 978-0-7546-7123-7
  1. Muslim women. 2. Women in Islam. 3. Islam and civil society. 4. Islamic
modernism. 5. Islam--21st century. I. Title.

  HQ1170.S4623 2008
  305.48'697--dc22

                          2007035683

ISBN 978-0-7546-7123-7

Printed and bound in Great Britain by TJ International Ltd, Padstow, Cornwall.

Contents

List of Figures

Series Editors' Preface

Arguably one of the more contentious arenas on the global stage concerns feminist political responses to issues associated with "Women and Islam". Debates over the range of obstacles to women's improvement in status, in wide-ranging Islamic contexts, are acquiring greater nuance as they are subjected to engaged critical scholarship. But we know far less about the consequences of transnational activism and Muslim women's public sphere agency. As series editors we are, therefore, particularly pleased to introduce this timely contribution to the burgeoning literature on Muslim women and their political diversity. In *Encountering the Transnational Women, Islam and the Politics of Interpretation,* the eleventh volume in our series (?), Meena Sharify-Funk moves beyond symbolism and rhetoric to chart variations in both the form and content of Muslim women's action, identities, and transformative outlooks. Although differences abound between Muslim women in their different geographies, cultures, and histories, the author reveals new possibilities for transnational dialogue, understanding, and even solidarities. These new affinities and developing alliances are all the more remarkable given historic divisions etched through reference to traditional Islam cast in opposition to various positions on the religiocultural continuum of Islam, including secular nationalisms, and played out in global geopolitics. A disapproving western gaze, judgmental yet at the same time fascinating, also lends form to the transnational dialogues. How remarkable and hopeful then are the new transnational intercultural conversations about women's status in Islam recorded and analyzed by Sharify-Funk.

In addition to the innovation in the research topic and findings, Sharify-Funk's carefully articulated methodology is exemplary. The project's formulation commences from reflection on the transnational activism that occurred in response to the death sentence of Amina Lawal in Nigeria. Subsequent fieldwork included a series of dialogical interviews with Muslim women activists encountered in transnational network activities in a range of countries and contexts, including international conferences. Interview data, illuminating themes related to "self", "the stranger", and "society", and to "the transnational" are then contextualized through an overview of tendencies in Islamic interpretation. Discussion of Muslim women's identity formation and how their transnational dialogues enable understandings of public agency follows. There is much to be learned about how Muslim women activists, through their transnational networks, are negotiating diversity, complexity and the contingencies attending their commonalities and differences. The constructive dialogues and collaborations revealed in this research constitute a refreshing intervention to the dissonant voices speaking to the "Women and Islam" question. The volume contributes sound research and new insights into this volatile, often ideologically fraught domain.

In particular the author challenges three types of criticism about Muslim women's activism: that it is the purview of narrowly based, elite and secular actors; that the parameters of activism are tied to a debate over "Westernization versus authenticity" rendering dialogues improbable; and, that transnational conservative networks, such as male revivalists, are more significant and influential. As Sharify-Funk demonstrates these misconceptions may well be a function of the absence of the kind of engaged, substantial scholarship into women's political diversity she offers. Her example of gendered local/global scholarship offers new insights into the Post-9/11 world of women and Islam. This book stands as a companion volume to other books in our series such as Krista Hunt and Kim Rygiel's edited collection *(En)Gendering the War on Terror* and Nüket Kardam's volume *Turkey's Engagement with Global Women's Human Rights*.

Pauline Gardiner Barber
Jane Parpart
Marianne Marchand

Acknowledgements

Despite a rapid expansion of research on Muslim women and the development of multiple research projects analyzing traditional, economic, neocolonial, and revivalist barriers to their advancement, much remains to be learned about women's activism within Islamic contexts. While there are numerous studies analyzing individual women's organizations and their efforts to achieve change in local contexts, there has been little research exploring how transnational linkages have helped women develop new activist visions suited to Islamic contexts, or investigating the implications of the accompanying forms of women's agency for the definition of Muslim public spheres. The existing literature on transnational women's activism maps the contours of emerging organizational networks, but has not yet succeeded in amplifying the voices of Muslim women who are renegotiating ideas about Muslim identity and norms that affect the lives of women. Transnational dialogue among Muslim women with diverse outlooks and cultural orientations remains a rewarding area for research into the manner in which contemporary identities and beliefs are being constructed, through a rich combination of religious, the national/cultural, and global elements.

The present study directs attention to precisely these processes, with an effort to document and analyze ways in which transnational linkages constitute Muslim women's identities as activists and affect the nature of their endeavors. While investigating the transnational aspects of Muslim women's activism, seeking to comprehend the diverse influences that shape their identities and worldviews, I have often found myself amazed and humbled at the creativity, wisdom, and generosity of the women and men I have encountered. This book would not have been possible if dozens of individuals had not opened doors for me and helped me to 'connect' across borders. I would like to dedicate this book to these courageous and remarkable people who became partners in my research, and to the many others whom I hope to encounter in future research.

In addition, I would like to thank all those at Ashgate Publishing who helped in the publishing process, especially the devoted editors of the series 'Gender in a Global/Local World.' In particular I am grateful to Donna Elliott and Margaret Younger for their support and guidance. I am also indebted to the American University's Center for Global Peace for the financial support that made my fieldwork possible, and to the American University School of International Service for a fellowship that facilitated my writing efforts. I owe the deepest gratitude to my friend and colleague, Abdul Aziz Said, director of the Center for Global Peace and the current occupant of the Mohammed Said Farsi Chair of Islamic Peace. His wisdom and guidance throughout the last ten years have continually helped me to believe in and realize my potential to serve. Quite literally, I would not be here without his support and encouragement. I must also acknowledge debts to a variety of scholars and friends who offered suggestions and advice along the way, including Mohammed Abu-

Nimer, Michel Desjardins, Louis Goodman, Peter Mandaville, Armando Salvatore, Yvonne Seng, Fereshteh Nouraie-Simone, and Diane Singerman. Their insightful critiques encouraged me to 'question the questions' and extend my understanding toward new possibilities.

Unending appreciation is due to my beloved parents, who taught me the greatest lesson in life: that love truly transcends all boundaries. They crossed many borders in order to be together. Majdiddin Sharify-Hosseini, my father, inspires me with his Shirazi spirit of kindness, and Nancy Olga Sharify, my mother, empowers me with her Viking heart and soul. Additionally, my brother, Robert Hussein Sharify, motivates me to follow his example of living life with dedication, discipline, and creative imagination.

No words can describe my love and gratitude towards my beloved husband and soulmate, Nathan C. Funk. His beautiful heart and mind continually teach me the endless ways to understanding peace. He is a true alchemist who turns thoughts into gold and encourages me to believe in the power of the written word.

Prior to the completion of this project, I lost my dear brother, Sason Sharify, who had always challenged me to dream, to believe in life's unending possibilities, and to affirm that the potential of the human soul is to be sought by continually overcoming our limited conceptions of who we are and what we are capable of achieving. As this book goes to press, I celebrate the wisdom he gave me, which I hope to pass on to my beautiful newborn son, Mikael Aziz.

Chapter 1

Introduction

'Women and Islam.' To speak these words is to evoke a rich array of images and – quite often – a range of strong emotions. Few people, it seems, have no opinion on the subject. Both in Islamic and predominantly non-Muslim cultures, the social status and public appearance of Muslim women are highly contested topics. Concern with symbolism often exceeds preoccupation with substantive issues, as the politics of the veil in countries like Turkey, Iran, and France reveals. Indeed, the image of the veil has become a cliché utilized in the titles of innumerable studies of Muslim women and Islamic societies.[1]

But what are the underlying issues defining these clashing images of Muslim modernity and tradition? What matters of concern, above and beyond norms of public dress, preoccupy Muslim women as they form their identities and their lives as professionals and activists? What does it *mean* to be a socially engaged Muslim woman in an increasingly transnational age? Is it possible for activist Muslim women to define their identities without choosing between the 'secular vs. religious' and 'Western vs. Islamic' polarities that have hitherto defined 'women's rights' as a uniquely secularist or dogmatic project? Is it possible to even discuss 'women and Islam' without evoking clichés, defensiveness, and ideological disputation?

For years – some would say decades or even centuries – far too many conversations about women and Islam have been marked by deep polarization, intellectual fragmentation, and competing agendas. The subject seems to almost immediately trigger Western accusations and Muslim apologetics, as well as a more generalized spirit of secular/religious antagonism. Given the stakes for contending parties, one would scarcely expect to encounter dialogue about women and Islam except among like-minded members of particular activist and ideological communities.

Yet this impression of unbridgeable divides is not entirely correct. Quietly, with the formation of vibrant transnational networks among Muslim women from diverse geographical locales and worldviews, new patterns of conversation are emerging. In these conversations, Muslim women who could be located at diverse points along a secular/religious continuum are seeking common ground beyond the antagonism that otherwise prevails in their social environments. These women are finding, amidst their sociological, cultural, and ideological diversity, new forms of meaning, solidarity, and belonging. Their experiences have not yet become mainstream, yet their conversations and affinities emerge from and inspire hope for future generations

---

1   Some examples of book titles are: Fatima Mernissi's *Beyond the Veil* (1990) and *The Veil and the Male Elite* (1991); Sherifa Zuhur's *Revealing Reveiling* (1992); Lila Abu-Lughod's *Veiled Sentiments* (2000); and Erqun Mehmet Carter's *Voices Behind the Veil* (2003).

of Muslim women, and for societies suspended between a traditional Islamic order and a Western world that simultaneously attracts, repels, and intrigues.

The intent of this book is to offer an introduction to exciting new forms of dialogue among Muslims – Muslim women, in particular – who have chosen to commit themselves to transnational conversations and actions about the status of women in Islam. Without downplaying the dissonance that still surrounds this topic or the high stakes for participants, I have sought to convey something of the intellectual excitement and the spirit of possibility that emerges when persons with genuine differences in worldview and conditioning come together for open and honest dialogue, and in the process enter into sustained relationships through conferences, strategic use of the internet, and collaborative projects. I have attempted to relate, both through the original words of dynamic Muslims and through my own attempts to find patterns of significance in their testimony, the rich meaning and possibility that 'the transnational' now holds for a cohort of thinkers and activists.

Until recently, questions about *transnational* trends in meaning and identity for Muslim women have received little focused scholarly or journalistic attention. Although tensions between transnational Islamic revivalism and secular nationalisms have generated considerable commentary, and the practical *utility* of transnational networking has been recognized (but not thoroughly studied), emergent trends toward transnational dialogue about the standing of women in Islamic societies remain largely unexplored. The content, meaning, and potential significance of new, boundary-crossing conversations have yet to be subjected to in-depth analysis. It is to this new domain of inquiry that I have sought to make a fresh contribution.

Transnational Connectivity: Muslim Women in Dialogue

In the face of destructive polarization and concerns about maintaining Muslim unity in the face of external pressures, increasing numbers of Muslim women are eager to encounter one another through transnational dialogue. They want to meet one another, explore differences and similarities, and find bases for working together on cooperative projects. The ability to cross boundaries through the transnational is providing them with spaces for transforming their marginal status as 'the silent other,' and for making their voices heard – as much as possible – amidst the din of geopolitical and religiocultural conflict.

The development of transnational dialogue among diverse Muslim women activists has occurred gradually, and has only recently become a subject of academic inquiry. My own interest in this topic began to form when, while initiating research on 'critical' Islamic discourse among Muslim women, I began to appreciate that the complexity of identity among contemporary Muslim women is difficult to capture with simple labels that often seem to distort as much as they clarify (for further elaboration, see Chapter 3). Who qualifies as 'critical' and who does not? How could I account for the *diversity* of the women who actually chose to involve themselves in cooperative attempts to address concrete issues that affect their well-being?

It was at this time that a prominent case of activism among Muslim women caught my attention, and piqued my curiosity about transnational dimensions of women's activism – the case of Amina Lawal. Amina Lawal is a Nigerian woman who was sentenced to death by stoning in 2002 for having a child out of wedlock. The pronouncement of this sentence, however, led to a massive protest campaign in which different women's groups from around the world came together and put aside their differences in order to participate in joint advocacy.[2] Eventually Lawal was set free, but in the process of the mobilization on her behalf, a new network had been formed – a network that included BAOBAB for Women's Human Rights (Nigeria), Sisters in Islam (Malaysia), Shirkat Gah (Pakistan), Sisterhood is Global Institute/Jordanian Office, Women Living Under Muslim Laws Network, the Muslim Women's Research and Action Forum (Sri Lanka), the Muslim Women's League (America), and the Canadian Council of Muslim Women. Such a transnational coalition of Muslim women's groups and organizations was unprecedented and, given the ideological and cultural diversity of its constituent entities, remarkable. An interview with Hauwa Ibrahim, the lawyer for Lawal and the first Muslim woman lawyer in Nigeria, confirmed my perception that this alliance had played a decisive role in the outcome of the case; Ibrahim testified that it is 'through the initiatives of a Nigerian women's group, BAOBAB for Women's Human Rights, to call for transnational joint advocacy amongst Muslim women's groups that Amina is still alive today.'[3]

While the case of Amina Lawal might have made a fascinating study in itself, mounting evidence of growth in transnational women's activism convinced me that a significant shift in the character of 'women and Islam' dialogue might be underway. Increasingly, locally and nationally based women's organizations were participating in transnational conferences, workshops, panel discussions, and tours,[4] and I wanted

---

2   For more about Lawal's case and a special interview with Lawal and Hauwa Ibrahim, see the BAOBAB website (28 November 2003): <http://www.baobabconnections.org/artikel. php?id=345>. See also the article by Asra Q. Nomani, a single mother who also had a child out of wedlock, who compares her life to that of Lawal (Nomani, 2003). It is interesting to note that Lawal's case had a strong impact on Nomani, and that it was articles like this that foreshadowed Nomani's popular book, *Standing Alone in Mecca: An American Woman's Struggle for the Soul of Islam* (2005).

3   Hauwa Ibrahim, interview by author, 20 April 2004, at the American University's School of International Service, Washington, DC. Ibrahim was invited to be a Humphrey Fellow at the American University Washington College of Law. During her stay in DC as a fellow, she presented lectures on the role of *shari'ah* (Islamic law) in Nigeria and wrote an unpublished paper entitled 'Reflections on the Case of Amina Lawal: The Woman Sentenced to Death by Stoning.'

4   One such panel discussion which I attended prior to my fieldwork was on 26 June 2002 at the National Endowment for Democracy in Washington, DC. It was entitled 'Women, Political Participation, and Democracy in the Muslim World,' and consisted of six women activists: Zainah Anwar (Executive Director of the Sisters in Islam women's organization based in Malaysia), Asma Khader (Executive Director of the Sisterhood is Global Institute in Jordan), Sindi Medar-Gould (Director of the BAOBAB for Women's Human Rights organization in Nigeria), Amina Lemrini (Director of Association Democratique du Femmes du Moroc, Morocco), Marfua Tokhtakhodjaeva (Director of the Women's Resource Center of Tashkent, Uzbekistan), and Sakena Yacoobi (Director of Afghan Institute of Learning, Afghanistan).

to know what this phenomenon meant to social actors, and how pervasive it was becoming. Was transnationalism a growing trend among Muslim women activists, or primarily an elite phenomenon? Was transnational dialogue a widely shared agenda throughout the Islamic world, or was it merely a post-9/11, America-driven project?

The more I directed my attention to transnational networking, the more I began to recognize that, despite rapid expansion of research on women and Islam and the literature's rich treatment of vital issues (legal structures, social norms, forms of abuse confronted by women, patterns of social activism, and post-colonial dilemmas surrounding identity), questions about the meaning of the transnational for Muslim women remained unanswered. I became particularly intrigued at potential contributions that could be made by exploring the validity of new ideas about the impact of the transnational on contemporary Muslim identity and intellectuality within the context of women's activism. Reading from theorists such as Mohammed Arkoun, Peter Mandaville, Armando Salvatore, and Recep Senturk piqued my interest in investigating ways in which women's identities were being reshaped by current transnational and intercultural realities. To what extent are transnational interactions such as those behind the campaign to support Amina Lawal reconstituting meaning and practice among Muslim women residing in diverse national and cultural contexts? Was this impressive display of transnational solidarity itself a product of a new type of dialogue and meaning-making? And what role was Islamic hermeneutics playing as women sought to ground their activism in the vocabularies of cultural and religious meaning that form the currency of social discourse in Muslim-majority societies?

A Journey of Encounters

These preliminary questions led me to prepare for a journey, consisting of a long series of conversations in the United States, England, Egypt, Morocco, Iran, and Pakistan from fall 2003 through fall 2004. Several of the specific countries I selected for field trips were chosen not only to meet local Muslim women activists who had become actively involved in transnational networking, but also to attend transnational conferences. These conferences afforded rich opportunities to encounter and interview activists affiliated with civil society organizations from throughout the Muslim world, including Africa and Southeast Asia. Observing the conferences also provided me with experiential understanding of the relational dynamics (including emergent alliances as well as profound personal and ideational disagreements) amongst Muslim women activists and organizations.

As I conducted my field research, I utilized an opportunistic sampling method. I started with locally prominent activists and conference attendees, and then followed up on referrals from one person to another, discovering individuals affiliated with transnationally engaged Muslim women's groups whom I had not known prior to my fieldwork. On average, my interviews were approximately one hour in length, though circumstances at times allowed for much longer discussions or required a shorter and more condensed conversation. Some of my encounters with activists took place within the context of focus groups or 'group interviews' of individuals with related interests and institutional affiliations. While some of the individuals with whom I engaged are internationally known activists, others had a much more local profile, and were relatively new to transnational conferences such as those I attended.

In approaching each encounter, I utilized the format and principle of 'active' interviewing (Holstein and Gubrium, 1995). This format enabled me to ask consistent, predetermined questions while concomitantly establishing a relation with the interviewee. It also allowed me to pursue emerging questions and share personal thoughts and experiences which became relevant for each encounter. This mixture of consistency and openness insured an atmosphere of dialogical experience wherein all the participants (at times there were multiple interviewees) were actively engaged in the conversational process. Emphasis was placed on the importance of attending to the distinctive aspects of each situation and 'establish[ing] a climate for *mutual* disclosure' (Holstein and Gubrium, 1995, 12). Because it is less rigid and provides more creative and context-sensitive conversational interactions, this active interviewing was ideally suited to inquiry, which depended on accessing personal narratives through a process of rapport based on trustful relationship (H.J. Rubin and I. Rubin, 1995, 17–51). The open nature of the format created opportunities to understand multi-faceted views on specific predetermined topics, as well as on broader or unanticipated topics. Whenever possible, I sought to tape-record these active 'encounter' interviews. At times, however, this was not possible, and interviews were documented with written notes.

During each interview, interviewees were given the option of expressing their views anonymously and without attribution, or to remove select comments from the record prior to project completion. Virtually all interviewees, however, were willing to speak 'on the record,' with the conviction that providing information about their organizations and social locations would provide added insight into contemporary dynamics of advocacy and Islamic interpretation. Though some of the interview topics are indeed sensitive, most interviewees are quite accustomed to offering outspoken commentary, and were therefore not concerned about attribution of quotations, so long as it was done faithfully and accurately (a list of interviewees and affiliations is provided in the Appendix).

Because of the manner in which my research was conducted, the writing of this book has been at least partially an exercise in 'action-research': the meanings that I 'encountered' were not simply waiting to be discovered; they were forged in dialogue through a process of mutual discovery (Greenwood and Levin, 1998). While this does admittedly impose limitations on the generalizability of my findings – some will quite rightly argue that a more tightly structured and 'distanced' approach to the subject matter can also provide valuable knowledge – I am convinced that the interactive and engaged dimension of this particular research process has provided compelling insights into the dynamic and open-ended nature of contemporary Muslim women's advocacy. To this end I have sought not only to provide a picture of social reality, but also to convey an experience of agency and 'meaning-making' in transnational networks.

During the course of my inquiry, I found that I had to some degree become not only an academic investigator, but also a 'midwife' in my interviewee's efforts to articulate some of the deepest convictions and motivating experiences behind their efforts. Operating in a maieutic or Socratic mode, I found that my pre-formulated, guiding research questions led to surprisingly deep conversations about matters of great personal and social significance. The experiences of activists whom I interviewed were remarkable both in their uniqueness and in the common threads that appeared to bind them.

The guiding questions that led to these conversations were derived from both the literature and its silences:

- How is transnationalism affecting the way contemporary Muslim activists and intellectuals – especially those engaged in conversations about the status of women in Muslim societies – perceive their identities and engage in activism?
- Is transnationalism facilitating the efforts of these Muslims to become agents of interpretation and social change?
- What aspects of transnationalism do these Muslim activists and intellectuals find most empowering or significant? What does transnationalism *mean* to them, and how does it affect their perceptions of identity and social agency?
- To what extent are Muslims who engage in 'women and Islam' debates experiencing a 'hermeneutic turn'? Are explicit ideas about Islamic hermeneutics shaping their identities and strategies?
- How do contemporary interpreters and advocates of 'progressive' reform respond to cultural and geographical dichotomies that have restricted the scope and character of Islamic identity – dichotomies that cast the Islamic and the Western in a conflictual relationship?

I started each encounter with questions about 'self' and 'other': 'How would you define the stranger?' By beginning on this note, I sought to sensitize interviewees to the encounter process: I was indeed the stranger, and we were meeting in a joint search for meaning. When necessary, I sought to clarify the meaning and intent of the question in ways that surfaced personal stories about their own ways of encountering strangers. This theme of 'strangeness' was also quite relevant to my research project insofar as contemporary Islamic interpretation is eminently concerned with questions about the relationship of 'traditional' Islamic beliefs with belief systems and philosophies that appear foreign or inauthentic. With remarkable consistency, female interviewees connected the 'self,' 'other,' and 'stranger' theme to their own experiences as Muslim women whose status as self-defining agents was often unrecognized.

Subsequent questions dealt with 'self' and 'society': How did my interviewees perceive their own relationship with society and its social norms – particularly with respect to the influence of Islam on the role of women. I was particularly struck by the degree to which many women, though not 'theorists' in the academic sense, are dealing with issues of Islamic interpretation and identity at a high level of subtlety and sophistication. Encounters in diverse locales revealed conscious and reflective agents, working in accordance with their own tacit theories and evolving conceptions.

The third general topic of my encounters was 'the transnational': How did my partners in the interview process define and experience the transnational? How did they experience relations between their own *cultural* self and the wider world? What problems were they experiencing in this domain, and to what extent did they see gaps in meaning as reconcilable? To what extent did they perceive the transnational not only as a *challenge* for Islamic societies, but also as a *resource* – a resource, perhaps, for women's empowerment or transformation?

After extensive interviewing (dozens of interviews in each country), I turned to my interview transcripts as texts in need of interpretation. I 'reencountered' my interviewees through the artifact of my notes and transcripts, and sought to trace emergent themes that linked the testimonies of multiple interviewees. As distinct and striking themes emerged, I developed the structure upon which this book is based.

Though their levels of concern about external manipulation varied, many of my interviewees were highly articulate about the ways in which their efforts have captured the interest of diverse parties and interests. In Chapter 2, 'Mixed Messages and Multiple Agendas,' I explore these issues and their implications for protagonists of social change in Muslim-majority societies. As many of my interviewees noted, all publicity is not necessarily good publicity, especially if the fate of Muslim women is linked to foreign actions that are regarded by most Muslims as imperialistic in nature.

Chapter 3 provides additional context for interpreting the testimony of my interviewees and dialogue partners, by offering an overview of tendencies in Islamic interpretation, a review of scholarship on Islamic transnationalism, and a description of insights and gaps that may be found in the existing 'women and Islam' literature. With respect to the 'women and Islam' literature, I note the impact of transnational feminist research projects exploring traditional, economic, neo-colonial, and revivalist barriers to the advancement of women, while pointing to the need for further research on ways in which sophisticated critiques of imbalanced gender relations have begun to emerge among Muslim women who chose engagement with religious hermeneutics as a means of improving the status of women.

The remaining chapters of this book analyze the results of extensive field research with activists and thinkers from Afghanistan, Algeria, Canada, Egypt, England, France, India, Indonesia, Iran, Jordan, Lebanon, Malaysia, Morocco, Nigeria, Oman, Pakistan, Israel/Palestine, Syria, Tunisia, Turkey, and the United States. Chapter 4 relates competing paradigms for Muslim meaning and identity, and describes the strong ambivalence of most interviewees about past labels that equate religiosity with tradition and modernity with secularity, and describes varying perspectives on the epistemological and practical uses of dialogue. Chapter 5 explores ways in which the transnational is shaping how Muslim women define their identities and formulate their approaches to activism and social engagement. Chapter 6 investigates how transnational and local dialogues among Muslim women are facilitating their efforts to define themselves as 'civil society' actors. Attention is given to traditional as well as innovative ways of constructing identity and social norms, with particular reference to 'public–private' dichotomies, roles in the family and in society, and the potential emergence of 'transnational civic Islam.' Chapter 7 addresses a major challenge in contemporary discourse about women and Islam:

the problem of 'othering,' through which women are deprived of (or deprive one another of) legitimacy as social agents. It examines efforts by Muslim women to reclaim 'selfhood' and agency in the face of traditional as well as modern forms of marginalization. The conclusion of this study, Chapter 8, proposes that transnational dialogue among Muslim women from diverse contexts and social strata is playing a significant role in contemporary activism, by helping activists as well as intellectuals to imagine new ways of identifying themselves, interpreting Islamic texts, and engaging in social conversations. Transnational engagement appears particularly consequential in stimulating dialogue across secular/religious divides in ways that are simultaneously reinforcing a shared Muslim identity and generating hermeneutic strategies which provide religious legitimacy for 'progressive' positions on gender issues.

A Note about the Author

This introduction would be incomplete without a brief note concerning my own status as the researcher and author. Throughout the course of this study, I found it fascinating to reflect not only on increasing transnational connectivity among Muslim women, but also on my own identity as a product of modern transnationalism. Like so many of my interviewees, I am not the product of a single culture, nor am I the possessor of a single collective identity. I am a dual citizen, politically as well as culturally – a carrier of two passports (American and Iranian), and an inheritor of two cultural/religious legacies (Islamic-Sufi and Judeo-Christian-Secular-Scandinavian). My father and grandfathers provided me with a deep connection to the Islamic world, while my mother's abiding connection to the Judeo-Christian-Secular West determined the culture in which I was raised, and to which I am also indebted. I consider it a great privilege to accept these gifts of the transnational – gifts which may perhaps have influenced me to search for new opportunities and new meanings in a world of collapsing distances.

Chapter 2

Mixed Messages and Multiple Agendas: The Politics of 'Women and Islam'

The Enterprise of Interpreting 'Women and Islam' in a Post-9/11 World

Since the tragic events of 9/11, the diverse voices claiming to speak with authority about Islam, and about women and Islam, have become increasingly cacophonous. Few contemporary topics are more controversial than Islamic interpretation, and controversies have a way of becoming especially acute when interpreters announce an intent to define Islamic guidelines for the status of women. When 'women and Islam' is the question, answers become dissonant.

In the West as well as in the Muslim world, interpreting Islam has become a virtual 'cottage industry.' The ranks of interpreters are incredibly diverse, including terrorism experts, government policymakers, and journalists, as well as religious studies scholars, political scientists, Muslim *'alims* and religious fundamentalists of varied confessional backgrounds. Though many interpreters' views would not be recognized as authoritative by traditional religious leaders, interest in how Islam is understood and practiced has expanded dramatically in recent years. A survey of language used in prominent North American and European newspapers and magazines reveals an extensive list of labels categorizing Muslims based on their postures toward Western culture and politics as well as towards one another; the titles of articles reveal not only real disputes within Muslim communities, but also the interests and preoccupations of those inquiring. Journalists, editors, and academics alike are inquisitive about the extent to which 'conservative' Muslims can be integrated within mainstream Western culture ('For Conservative Muslims, Goal of Isolation a Challenge,' 'Progressive Muslims Challenge Tradition,' 'Why I Am Not a Moderate Muslim: I'd Rather be Considered Orthodox'), and dissuaded from adopting radical stances vis-à-vis current political issues ('The Quest for a "Moderate Islam",' '"Muslim Refusenik" Incites Furor with Critique of Faith').[1]

Among non-Muslims as well as among Muslims, it seems that everyone has become a stakeholder in the future of Islam, and that everyone is attempting to frame or reframe the discursive categories within which Islamic interpretation and politics are discussed. Each label for categorizing 'desirable' types of Muslims and Islamic interpretations (whether defined by self-identified groups of Muslim interpreters or by non-Muslim observers) seems to have a ready counterpart category

---

1   These titles come from the following articles: see Murphy, 2006, A01; Scrivener, 2004, A01 and A26; Khalid, 2007; Haddad, 2004; Brown, 2004, A14.

for branding adversaries as 'undesirable others.' 'Conservative Muslims' compete with 'progressive Muslims' for air time, as 'traditionalist' Muslims denounce 'self-hating Muslims' and 'Islamophobes.' Meanwhile, 'moderate Muslims' challenge 'militant Muslims,' putative 'Muslim refuseniks' denounce 'Muslim extremists,' and would-be reformists repudiate 'apologists' who refuse to embrace the for change. There are too many binaries: 'liberal vs. conservative,' 'moderate vs. militant,' 'orthodox vs. heretical.' Everyone, it seems, has a party line about who the 'good Muslims' and 'bad Muslims' are, and everyone seems ready to monopolize public discourse, whether in predominantly 'Western' or 'Islamic' worlds. Sadly, many of these dichotomies distort as much as they reveal, shrouding the complexities of human opinions, beliefs, and sentiments in superficial preconceptions and over-simplifications.

From the multiple agendas of Islamic 'interpreters' emerge mixed messages on a wide range of subjects. Awareness of these agendas is important for critical reflection on the dynamics of contemporary Muslim societies, and essential for comprehending the politics of women and Islam. No responsible study of Muslim women's activism can afford to ignore the political context within which debates about the subject transpire, or to overlook that fact that those who speak for Muslim women often fail to consult them when formulating rhetoric and programs. Too many 'projects' for changing Muslim women's lives carry heavy political and ideological baggage – baggage that becomes a burden to those who are its intended carriers.

The Troubled Discourse of Muslim Women's Rights: Liberation or Co-optation?

A quick survey of official, state-sponsored literature and propaganda reveals that Western as well as Islamic governments almost universally claim that their policies have the best interests of Muslim women in mind. Remarkably, almost every official pronouncement about the status of Muslim women proclaims a desire to help, or points to progress, achievements, and solutions. Post-9/11 publications of more secular Muslim governments (for example, Morocco, Egypt, Tunisia) trumpet evidence of women's advancement as proof of their march towards modernity and progress. Ideologically Islamic governments (for example, Iran and Pakistan) argue that their efforts to promote Islamic values are actually better for women, protecting them socially while also providing avenues for professional advancement.

Governmental proclamations in support of women's rights often appear quite ironic when actual practices and social conditions are taken into account. Contradictions between word and deed are especially evident in Muslim-majority states (for example, Egypt, Syria, Saudi Arabia, Iran, Indonesia), where claims to support reforms providing 'equal treatment for women' contrast unfavorably with conditions in which reformists advocating political and economic change (both men and women) are imprisoned, harassed, and sometimes tortured or sent into exile

(Gedda, 2004).[2] Even as more women are entering prominent political positions (for example, as presidents, prime ministers, foreign ministers, and judges) and even religious leadership roles – that is, advisors to imams in Turkey (Schleifer, 2005), and 'muftias' in India (Lancaster, 2003) – Muslim women who seek to enter the *authoritative* realm of 'imam' (prayer leader) or 'interpreter' are characterized as 'infidels' and ostracized. For example, a Muslim woman who led prayers for mixed congregations of men and women aroused ire throughout the Islamic world, prompting a group of Muslims to sue her in a court of law, with the argument that she must be stripped of the title of 'Muslim' (see the section on Amina Wadud in Chapter 3). In the Middle East, prominent gatherings of male and female reformist thinkers in Doha, Qatar[3] and in Egypt were denigrated by traditional religious authorities as deviant undertakings. Even though religious scholars from al-Azhar University were invited to participate in the Egyptian event, Grand Mufti Tantawi rejected those assembled as a group of 'outcasts.'[4] Despite claims by many autocratic governments to promote liberalism, participation, and progress, books by genuine reformists are often banned (Schemm, 2004).[5]

---

2   Many articles have come out in 2004 and 2005 that analyze this increase in governmental support for 'democratic' reform in these countries and the actual treatment of non-governmental reformists. For some examples, see Ambah, 2004a, 1 and 7; Ambah, 2004b, 6; Mackinnon, 2005, F8; Shadid, 2005, A1; Malinowski, 2004, A17; and Hughes, 2004, 10.

3   Over 100 Arab advocates of democratic reform (representing most of the Arab countries) participated in the Doha conference on Democracy and Reform in Qatar, on 3–4 June 2004. From this conference the Doha Declaration for Democratic Change was created and distributed throughout the Arab world. For more about the Doha Declaration, see the Center for the Study of Islam and Democracy (CSID) Bulletin, (18 June 2004). Also available on the CSID website: <www.islam-democracy.org>.

4   See Macfarquhar, 2004, A29–A30. This article describes the encounters of Mohammed Shahrour (a Syrian reformist thinker) and other reformist intellectuals calling for a reinterpretation of Islamic holy texts at a conference in Cairo entitled 'Islam and Reform.' In this article, Mufti Muhammad Sayed Tantawi of al-Azhar (Egypt's most well-known religious institution), in reaction to the ideas shared by Shahrour and the other reformist intellectuals, 'labeled them as a "group of outcasts".'

5   One example is articulated in Schemm, 2004. This article is about the conservative practice of religious authorities in Cairo, Egypt to blacklist and prohibit the sale of reformist books (that is, *The Responsibility for the Failure of the Islamic State* and *Towards a New Jurisprudence*) by Gamal al-Banna (a reformist thinker living in Cairo, Egypt). In the article, SaadEddin Ibrahim, another well-known reformist thinker, argues that Gamal al-Banna is 'becoming increasingly important' in areas of legalistic reinterpretation and societal reform. Here are some of Gamal al-Banna's controversial statements: 'We must open the doors for the freedom of thought without any restrictions at all … Even if one wants to deny the existence of God,' and 'We can read and learn more from European culture and history – from all human culture … Islam is the last of religions, but it must not be a closed box, it must be a kind of open road.' It is interesting to note that Gamal al-Banna is the great uncle of Tariq Ramadan, another reformist scholar based in Switzerland, who since the beginning of 2004 has been

Western governments too have redoubled their rhetorical commitment to the subject, often with disappointing or counterproductive results. Representatives of the Bush administration in the United States (that is, First Lady Laura Bush, Karen Hughes, and Condoleezza Rice) have argued quite forcefully that the promotion of women's rights is part of the solution to terrorism, and an essential basis for freedom, democracy, and development.[6] Indeed, the United States government has declared the liberation of Muslim women to be one of the central goals of its military campaigns in Afghanistan and Iraq (United States Department of State's Bureau of Democracy, Human Rights and Labor, 2001 and Wolfowitz, 2004). For the first time in US history, an American president has used the subject of 'women and Islam' as a means of justifying war. Unfortunately, such universal governmental endorsement of women's liberation as a goal of policy does not appear to be having uniformly positive effects, nor have governmental proclamations of support been embraced by Muslim women activists – particularly when conjoined with military activity. To the surprise of newcomers to the topic (and especially to 'quick study' terrorism experts), many longtime advocates of Muslim women's rights are highly skeptical about foreign declarations of support for their efforts. Discourse has become increasingly divided, with some scholars of women and Islam expressing concern that the subject of 'women and Islam' has been hijacked, while others claim that finally it is gaining the attention it deserves.

At the turn of the twenty-first century, it is ironic that prominent scholars like Fatima Mernissi and Leila Ahmed, who opened new frontiers in the scholarship of 'women and Islam,' would demonstrate a noticeable silence towards the subject. Why? After the horrific events of 11 September 2001, as Ahmed pointed out in a lecture at the Library of Congress, the subject of 'women and Islam' became an overnight sensation for the American media and scholars alike.[7] From *Time*

---

banned from America (see note 22). It is ironic how both Tariq Ramadan and his great uncle Gamal al-Banna are 'outcasts' because they advocate how Muslims can better integrate into non-Muslim societies, as well as how Muslims need to be more engaged with the development of democratic practices and civil society.

6   As stated by First Lady Laura Bush during a trip to Afghanistan in which she was representing the Bush administration, 'the fight against terrorism is also a fight for the rights and dignity of women.' See Whitehouse.gov, 2001; and Condoleezza Rice's endorsement and promotion of the US State Department first international 'women of courage' awards (see note 19).

7   After 9/11, Mernissi posted a new message on her personal website: 'Please do not address any questions on women and Islam.' Her position would influence Ahmed who, at an address to the US Library of Congress, felt compelled to ask her audience why, in their opinion, distinguished 'feminists' such as Mernissi and herself now felt the need to state such a position. Ahmed's lecture, entitled '"Women in Islam" and America: Reflections on Where We Are Today' (presented on 4 February 2004) was the first in a series entitled 'Giving Voice to Change: Muslim Women in the Era of Global Communication,' co-sponsored by the Middle Eastern Division and the Kluge Center of the Library of Congress and the American University Center for Global Peace. It is interesting to note that Fatima Mernissi had also been asked to give a lecture in this series, but had refused to participate as a form of protest against

magazine's special report entitled 'Lifting the Veil,'[8] to many articles about the plight of secular Muslim women exiles now living in the Muslim diaspora,[9] popular writings increasingly portrayed the status of Muslim women as a 'wedge issue' between Islamic and Western cultures (Haddad, Smith and Moore, 2006). Ahmed, as well as many other scholars of women and Islam, started to perceive a pattern in American government and media: the co-optation (as well as misappropriation) of the discourse of women and Islam as a justification for policies driven by other concerns such as counterterrorism, access to oil resources, maintenance of political hegemony, and nuclear non-proliferation (Zine, 2006; Falah and Nagel, 2005; Barlas, 2007; Shahnaz Khan, 2007a). In their view, the subject of 'women and Islam' had become a means for legitimizing American wars with countries such as Afghanistan and Iraq, as well as a justification for efforts to enforce political, economic, and social reform in other Muslim countries like Iran and Syria. Ahmed experienced this 'neo-colonialist'[10] and 'neo-Orientalist'[11] ideological agenda for women's liberation as a force that had obscured genuine historical progress ('what has been right') through an exclusive preoccupation with continuing problems ('what has gone wrong'). It has silenced voices such as her own (despite her status as a prominent Harvard scholar), by effectively 'taking over' the project of reform for Muslim women:

> We have been critics – fierce, moderate, and mild – of Islam for years. Even though we have been and continue to be invisible to the America media. The media notoriously has no sense of history, working always in the now. In their defense, I shall observe that it is

---

what she perceived as America's political agenda. Mernissi did, however, submit a paper for the final edited volume from the series, entitled *On Shifting Ground: Muslim Women in the Global Era* (2005).

8   See *Time: Special Report* (2001) 3 December, Vol. 158, no. 24 (NY: Time Inc.).

9   Some articles: 1) Jennifer Frey, 'Thinking Outside the Burqa,' *The Washington Post*, 30 November 2001, C1 and C4; this article describes the life of Nasrine Gross, an Afghani exile who became an official advisor on women and Islam to the State Department and Bush administration after 9/11. 2) Nora Boustany, 'A Beacon, Even in the Darkest Hours,' *The Washington Post*, 20 February 2004, A21; this article describes the challenges faced by Farida Azizi, a leading peace advocate and special advisor for Vital Voices Global Partnership, who introduced President Bush at a signing ceremony for a bill aimed at improving the life of Afghani women.

10   In her talk at the Library of Congress, Ahmed observed that America was engaged in resurrecting an 'old script' written by the European colonialist powers who had also sought to morally justify invading Muslim countries (for example, Algeria) in order to 'save women from Islam.'

11   'Neo-Orientalism' is a term that has been increasingly used by many post-colonial scholars. As mentioned by Ahmed in her talk at the Library of Congress, what has happened to the great debates between Bernard Lewis (from the old Orientalist school of Middle Eastern Studies) and Edward Said (one of the greatest opponents of Orientalism)? Who is going to fill the gap of Edward Said in an age of neo-Orientalism? For other scholars using such language, see Moghissi, 1999, Qureshi and Sells, 2003, and Malik, 2006.

my distinct impression that although we have been outspoken in our criticism for years, since 9/11 our voices have grown more muted … and for myself I have felt silenced.

For two years after 9/11, Ahmed – who for the last 30 years had advocated Muslim women's rights – felt compelled to remain silent about problems facing Muslim women, so as not to reinforce what she regarded as a neo-colonialist, neo-conservative agenda. Given Ahmed's considerable status and privilege, and her position at one of the world's most prestigious universities, this perception of newfound powerlessness is particularly striking. In many respects, it symbolizes a much more widely felt dilemma experienced by 'moderate' Muslims in Western as well as Islamic contexts: if they criticized the West, they might be mistaken for 'enemies,' and if they criticized practices of Muslim communities, they might inadvertently reinforce a spiral of armed confrontation (a dilemma to which we will soon return).

After breaking her silence about the current state of affairs, Ahmed concluded her talk by arguing that 'women and Islam' as a subject has become too politicized in the Western public sphere:

'Women and Islam' has become enmeshed in and captured by the politics of our day. Unless we manage to extract it from the political meanings from which it has become silently charged, we too will inevitably project narratives of oppression of women and Islam.

For Ahmed and for many other scholars, the present climate of politicization can be seen in: 1) the rise of Muslim women exile literature encouraging hard-line stances toward countries and cultures of origin;[12] 2) the misuse of media images, especially concerning veiled Muslim women, to heighten political antagonisms;[13] and 3) the absence of educational programs about the diversity of Islam. Ahmed's personal frustration with these trends became unmistakable when, during the 'question and answer' period of her talk at the Library of Congress, she agreed with an audience member who proposed that perhaps the subject of 'women and Islam' should be 'dissolved,' for it has become (and might always have been) a 'deeply problematic category.'

In contradistinction to Muslim women scholars and activists who would like to make a Heideggerian erasure[14] of 'women and Islam,' there are other scholars of

---

12 For more information about this literature, see the section at the end of this chapter on 'Emancipation of Women from Islam.'

13 In major newspapers, images of veiled women are usually accompanied by titles that reflect oppression and segregation of Muslim women; however, images of unveiled Muslim women (or images with a Muslim woman and veil lifted) are depicted with titles that suggest liberation and freedom. For a good example, see Banerjee, 2004, A12. This article depicts in an image two Iraqi veiled Muslim women, Ibtisam Ali and Faten Saleh. Unlike what the title suggests, the article is about these two women and how they are leading a petition demanding that 40 per cent of the national assembly seats should go to women.

 14 A Heideggerian erasure is when one has drawn a line through a word or phrase in order to imply that it has been erased; however, like all erasures, there will always be evidence that it was there.

'women and Islam' (for example, Mahnaz Afkhami, Director of Women's Learning Partnership[15]) who would argue that the subject of women and Islam has greatly benefited from the attention of post-9/11 discourses. As can be seen in the numerous governmental as well as quasi-governmental activities that have blossomed since 9/11, these scholars and their initiatives have <u>gained greater financial</u> as well as <u>political support</u>. Some of the more well-known activities were:

- immediately after 9/11, the State Department produced a policy document on 'liberating' Afghani women entitled 'The Taliban's War Against Women' (November 2001);[16]
- the United States Institute of Peace held its first panel on 'Women and Islam' on 17 June 2002;
- the National Endowment for Democracy (NED) sponsored a conference on 'Women, Political Participation and Democracy in the Muslim World' on 26 June 2002, and then for its annual Democracy Award in 2002, the NED invited First Lady Laura Bush to honor the 'Outstanding Democratic Women of the Muslim World';[17]
- the 2003 Nobel Peace Prize was given to the first Muslim woman, Shirin Ebadi, for her activism for women and human rights in Iran;[18]
- in March 2007, the US State Department gave out awards for the first international 'women of courage,' of whom seven of the women were from Muslim countries (Afghanistan, Indonesia, Iraq, Maldives, and Saudi Arabia) and were praised by Secretary of State Condoleezza Rice for 'combating attempts to dehumanize women;'[19]
- the National Film Board of Canada (NFB) launched a 'Women and Islam' film series featuring prominent 'progressive' Canadian Muslim women and

---

15   Women's Learning Partnership is a non-governmental organization that promotes women's leadership and empowerment. See their website: <http://www.learningpartnership. org/>.

16   See United States Department of State's Bureau of Democracy, Human Rights and Labor, 2001. Also, after November 2001, the State Department would form a committee on 'Women and Afghanistan,' initiated by Charlotte Beers, the former Under Secretary of Public Diplomacy and Public Affairs, which would spark other initiatives by the same office.

17   Laura Bush has also pledged that 'the United States government is wholeheartedly committed to the full participation of women in all aspects of Afghan society, not just in Kabul, but in every province,' as stated in Kazem, 2005. Additionally, Laura Bush's tour of the Middle East (May 2005) was to not only better the image of America to the Muslim world but also advocate for women's rights. See VandeHei, 2005, A20.

18   There are numerous articles about Shirin Ebadi and her activism that came out after she won the prize. Some are: Sadri, 2003; Vick, 2003, A19 and A22; and Kennicott, 2004, C1 and C4.

19   See the article 'Muslim Women Can Reshape Islam,' in *The Christian Science Monitor*, 14 March 2007. Also see the press release on 6 March 2007 by the US Department of State: <http://www.state.gov/r/pa/prs/ps/2007/mar/81433.htm> (accessed 29 May 2007).

their advocacy through film, 21–27 May 2007.[20]

The aftermath of 11 September 2001 raises challenging questions about the 'women and Islam' discourse. Many scholars are beginning to recognize that they must move beyond traditional questions – whether they are hindering or benefiting women in Muslim societies – to address broader political questions as well:

- Are they becoming agents of a neo-colonial project and – in the process – tacitly supporting efforts to replace one form of patriarchy (traditional Islamic) with another (conservative Western)?
- Are there nonetheless opportunities for a 'breakthrough' to a new level of Muslim self-reflexivity and self-critique?
- What might be done to encourage a genuinely 'Islamic' reformation that is not merely an externally driven intellectual project?

Within this context of suspicion, simply raising the issue of 'women and Islam' can result in distrust and misunderstanding, even among those who are directly engaged with substantive issues. Suspicions abound: Whose side are you on? What is your agenda? Are you a functionary of the Bush administration?

As disconcerting as such questions may be, there are many legitimate reasons for suspecting that official professions of support for progressive change in Muslim societies – both those of Westerners and those of Muslim governments anxious to establish a 'moderate' reputation – are externally motivated or overstated. When rhetoric about women's liberation becomes associated with policies of military confrontation or political repression, governments send mixed messages about their intentions.

With respect to the United States, many observers – and not just Muslims – find it rather ironic that the first Muslim woman recipient of the Nobel Peace Prize, a progressive lawyer named Shirin Ebadi, was initially denied permission to publish her book in America, despite proclamations of support for 'moderate Islam.'[21] They were even more puzzled when a leading, self-proclaimed 'reformist' Muslim scholar, Tariq Ramadan, was denied a visa to enter the United States and accept a Peace Scholar position at Notre Dame University, and a widespread outcry among prominent American scholars and media commentators failed to prompt

---

20   See the press release on the NFB's website: <http://www.nfb.ca/communique/communique.php?nav=2&lg=en&id=18038&v=h> (accessed 29 May 2007).

21   See Shirin Ebadi, 2004. This article describes how, after winning the Nobel Peace Prize and touring America as well as Europe, Ebadi wanted to publish a memoir of her travels and distribute it in America; however, she soon found out that, like many other Iranian scholars, American publishers would decline publishing her book in fear of not adhering to the American Treasury Department's regulations and America's trade embargoes with Ebadi's homeland of Iran. The 'official banning' of Ebadi's book with the 'official praising' of her activism by President Bush has raised even more skepticism and, according to some, has 'fann[ed] the flames of antagonism between the two peoples [Americans and Iranians].' See Milani, 2004. After long deliberations, Ebadi's book was finally published in May 2006.

reconsideration of his case.[22] With respect to women's rights, activists also find it troubling that the United States government will not ratify an international women's treaty to ban discrimination,[23] despite First Lady Laura Bush's active public advocacy for women's rights and development in the Muslim world, as a representative of the United States government.[24]

Cause for concern about the impact of Western policies and proclamations can also be found in reports on the status of Afghani and Iraqi women (Pollitt, 2007). In Afghanistan, post-invasion conditions vary widely; gains in the capital city of Kabul contrast starkly with minimal changes throughout the rest of the country, and newly empowered warlords have demonstrated commitment to discriminatory practices (Hunt, 2006; Shahnaz Khan, 2007a; Constable, 2006). In Iraq, that status and well-being of women has declined precipitously since the March 2003 invasion. Pervasive insecurity, sectarian rivalry, and the political mobilization of Islamist parties have generated conditions that, in the view of most women's activists, compare unfavorably with previous Ba'athist order.[25]

Though concerns about co-optation of 'women's rights' discourse for purposes of warfare are less pronounced in Canada and continental Europe, the status of Muslim women remains a potent symbolic issue. In France and Quebec (as well as in Great Britain), discussions of the *hijab* and *niqab* have generated considerable political controversy, and have often reinforced polarization between secular ('assimilated') Muslims and their more culturally conservative counterparts, while marginalizing efforts to address more substantive issues such as domestic violence and engagement in the public sphere.[26] Paradoxically, efforts to 'help' Muslim women by banning

---

22   See Lampman, 2004, 16. This article describes the controversy over Homeland Security's decision to revoke the visa of Tariq Ramadan, who had been offered the position of the Henry R. Luce Professor of Religion, Conflict and Peacebuilding at the University of Notre Dame's Joan Kroc Institute. There were many other articles by concerned scholars demonstrating their support for Ramadan's scholarship, such as Donnelly, 2004, A25 and Eck, 2004. Tariq Ramadan also wrote in petition an op-ed article, entitled 'Too Scary for the Classroom?' in *The New York Times*, 1 September 2004. Although Ramadan has been critical about the position of the US towards war in Iraq and the US–Israeli policies in Israel/Palestine, many of these American scholars state that there is no justification for denying Ramadan entry into America, which upholds the right to freely express and criticize; especially when one's intention is towards efforts of reform and dialogue. As this book goes into print, Ramadan is still banned from traveling to the United States.

23   This treaty has already been ratified by over 169 countries; see Kristof, 2002.

24   See note 17 in this chapter.

25   For a nice summary, see al-Ali, 2007a. For a more detailed account, see al-Ali, 2007b.

26   In the last few years, anti-sentiment for Muslim women covers, such as the *hijab*, *niqab*, and *burqa*, has been prominent within the headline news of many Western countries, especially France, Great Britain and Canada. Such intolerance in Quebec in particular is reaching its zenith, as reflected in a statement by Sheema Khan, 'the growing intolerance for reasonable accommodation of religious practices in Quebec seems to be reaching a tipping point' (Sheema Khan, 2007a, A21).

women's head-coverings in schools (France) and sports competitions (Quebec) have increased barriers to participation in public life.[27]

More encouraging trends are not absent, however; the Canadian Broadcasting Corporation's new series, 'Little Mosque on the Prairie,' has heightened the profile of Muslim Canadians, providing an impetus to dialogue within as well as beyond the boundaries of the country. 'Little Mosque' invites viewers to consider Muslims – represented as an internally diverse yet still cohesive community – as 'normal' members of Canadian society and small-town prairie life, and has been interpreted by some as a challenge to the notion that cultural and religious markers such as the *hijab* are impediments to full engagement with Western social life.[28]

'Western Muslims': Hybridity, the Politics of Moderation, and the Search for Non-Cooptated Emancipation

Analysts of multiple agendas surrounding women's rights and the war on terrorism have become increasingly adroit in their characterizations of the 'camouflaged politics' inherent in much commentary on Muslims (Hunt and Rygiel, 2006). They have convincingly argued that much journalistic and even academic writing is predicated on essentialized notions of 'Islam' and 'the West,' and posits a need for Western humanitarian intervention – hence the diverse array of popular voices calling for an 'imperial rescue' of Muslim women (Hunt, 2006). In response, they argue for nuanced commentary that resists totalizing discourses and self-congratulatory moralism. Provocatively, they frame 'West versus the rest' discourse as residue of the colonial era or as a manifestation of hidden Islamophobia.

This critical literature provides an important corrective to commonplace misconceptions and to one-sided preoccupation with Muslim faults, and provides the backdrop against which many Muslims – especially but not exclusively in the West – are seeking to redefine their identities. Muslims seeking to avoid simplistic anti-Western or anti-Islamic identities face a difficult task of embracing cultural

---

27 Although the French *hijab* debate began in 1989, when school administrators objected to Muslim girls wearing hair covers to school as a violation of secularism, a law was passed in 2004 that barred conspicuous religious apparel (for example, Muslim headscarves, Jewish skullcaps, and large Christian crosses) in public schools. For more reading, see Bowen, 2007. In a similar fashion, Muslim girls who wear the *hijab* are being banned from sports activities in Quebec. Asmahan Mansour was expelled from a soccer tournament in Laval, Quebec, for refusing to remove her headscarf, and then later Jean Charest (recently elected Premier of Quebec) condoned the expulsion (Seguin and Scoffield, 2007, A11). In Montreal, five Muslim girls were prevented from participating in a tae kwon do competition due to their headscarves (Marotte, 2007, A1 and A6). In response to the headscarf controversy, another article featured Tyseer Aboulnasr, a *hijab*-wearing black belt of tae kwon do, who 'noticed that it was an ideal sport for devout Muslim women because it allowed them to be athletic while remaining modestly covered' (Thanh Ha, 2007, A3).

28 Many newspaper articles have come out about the new TV series, 'Little Mosque on the Prairie;' see Doyle, 2007, R1 and R2; Sheema Khan, 2007b, A19; and MacDonald, 2007, R1.

hybridity, critiquing dominant categories of understanding, and reframing debates about social change in the Muslim world.

Embracing Hybridity

Despite misgivings about media representations, recent world events have spurred many Muslims living in Western countries to engage in self-critical reflection. Increasingly, they are asking questions that challenge the conventional wisdom of insiders and outsiders alike, and that invite new thinking about what it means to be Muslim in the twenty-first (CE)/fifteenth (AH) century. The following questions are illustrative:

– origin?

- How can individual Muslims – who cannot look to a unified church for authoritative guidance – remain true to their individual responsibility for seeking the Muslim ideal?
- Is it possible to 'push the boundaries' of traditional Islamic thought while remaining authentically Muslim? Can Islamic thought be progressive?
- What role can Muslims outside of the 'Muslim world' (Muslims in Western societies) play in redefining the current Islamic discourse? Is there a role for non-Muslims in discussions about the meaning of Islam? Who is willing to come to the table for dialogue about contemporary Islam?
- What adjective – if any – should be placed before 'Muslim' by those who seek to counteract Western stereotypes and radical misconceptions? To what extent do labels such as 'moderate Muslim' help or hinder these efforts? Does not the use of such a label imply that most Muslims are 'immoderate'? Is there a viable alternative?

Such questioning is connected to what some may call a 'shift,' 'transformation,' or 'new synthesis' in contemporary Muslim identity, especially among Muslims living in Western societies. Both in their emerging literature and in their daily lives, Muslims are seeking to redefine the sense of difference associated with Muslim identity markers in the Western public sphere. Many Muslims are rejecting the notion that they must choose whether it is more important to be a good Muslim or to be a good Canadian/American/European (Ramadan, 2005; Barlas, 2007; M. Khan, 2002), and are affirming hybrid identities in which multiple loyalties are mutually reinforcing rather than mutually exclusive. In such formulations, being Canadian or American need not detract from Islamic identity, and vice versa. The following titles of books are particularly interesting for what they tell us about the contemporary phenomenon of a hybrid identity: *Western Muslims and the Future of Islam* (Ramadan, 2004a), *American Muslims: Bridging Faith and Freedom* (M. Khan, 2002), *What's Right with Islam is What's Right with America* (Abdul Rauf, 2005), *To Be a European Muslim* (Ramadan, 2002), *American Muslims: The New Generation* (Hasan, 2001). As will be further discussed in the next chapter, these 'new voices of Islam' are products of transnational/transcultural/translocal conversations in which more Muslims are attempting to transcend the bifurcation of the world based on purely 'Islamic' or 'Western' options. Such voices reflect the development of new constitutive transnational spaces for debates, discussion, and dialogue amongst diverse individuals on issues of women's rights, identity, society, nationalism, and hermeneutics.

The Project and Problem of a 'Moderate Muslim' Label

Unfortunately, the complexity of 'hybrid' Muslim identities is seldom reflected in popular media representations, in part because of presumptions about reader interest. Given the elevated security concerns of the post-9/11 era, non-Muslims in Western society tend to be more curious about the intensity of patriotism and extent of acculturation among Muslim citizens than about Muslim efforts to formulate coherent worldviews and complex understandings of political affairs. It should come as no surprise, then, that in defining desirable characteristics for the 'Western Muslim,' a growing community of scholars, policymakers, and media professionals have defined labels such as 'moderate Islam' and 'moderate Muslim' in ways that are instrumental to the goal of winning a fight against the narrow militant, political, and/ or radical Islam. As a predictable result, many Muslims feel frustrated or ambivalent about these labels.

One concern about the 'moderate Muslim' label is that it appears to mark its bearer as an 'uncritical ally' of 'the West,' at a time when Muslim alienation and disaffection is increasing. While the connotation of being 'against violence' still appeals, there is an additional undesirable implication: being indifferent to policies that fail to address root causes of Muslim militance. As some scholars have observed, labeling Muslims as either 'moderate' or 'immoderate' tends to silence a majority of Muslim voices, and reinforces illusive 'good Muslim' versus 'bad Muslim' dichotomies. In the Summer 2005 special volume of *The American Journal of Islamic Social Sciences* that was dedicated to 'Debating Moderate Islam,' Asma Barlas, a prominent Muslim feminist, offers a sharp critique:

> The official view of Islam as a pair of good and evil twins conjoined at the hip performs two crucial political functions. On the one hand, by portraying 'militant Islam' as the real threat to global security, Washington is able to deflect critiques of the US's role in underwriting injustice and oppression on a global scale. On the other hand, by shifting the burden of 'defeat[ing] and eradicat[ing] militant Islam' onto 'moderate Islam,' the US is absolved of the responsibility to rethink its own injurious policies (Barlas, 2005, 161).

For Barlas, the project of supporting 'moderate Muslims' comes then at a high cost for both non-Muslims and Muslims. Non-Muslims misread the sources of Muslim resentment, while genuine Muslim voices go unheard.

According to Barlas and other critics, terms such as 'moderate Muslim' provide little insight into the actual beliefs and policies of those who bear the label, and are primarily used in a strategic manner. At the same time, the 'moderate Muslim' label implies (however subtly) that most Muslims are *not* moderate:

> If calling oneself a moderate at a time when there is such pressure to 'toe the official line' can thus 'easily become too much a badge of mindless loyalty,' refusing to call oneself a moderate can just as easily become a sign of disloyalty. Either way, the state's advocacy

of 'moderate Islam' is a kiss of death for Muslim critics abroad, wary of the US's agendas, and of non-Muslim critics at home who are convinced that a moderate Muslim is merely a militant in denial or in disguise (Barlas, 2005, 162).

As a quick internet search can reveal, there is a diverse range of Muslims who are being labeled 'moderate.' Some Muslims are regarded as 'moderate' by some and as 'radical' by others. This raises many questions: Who is doing the labeling? And who is supporting the one labeled? For instance, are there differences in how the Rand Corporation, the American Enterprise Institute (neo-conservative/anti-multiculturalism), the Brookings Institution, and Harvard University (just to name some institutes who have used this label) define 'moderate Muslims'? Is a consensus definition of 'moderation' possible? Is moderation the hallmark of a particular epistemological or interpretive tendency, or can it be found among diverse varieties of Muslims – not only among 'ex-Muslims,'[29] Muslim secularists, and reformists, but also among traditionalists and revivalists?

Emancipation 'from' Islam vs. 'in' Islam

Significantly, some of the most widely read writers on 'women and Islam' are individuals who have either claimed or received the 'moderate voice of Islam' label. Many write for the popular market, and represent themselves as 'feminist exiles' from Muslim lands who have found *freedom* in the West. In recent years these authors – Ayaan Hirsi Ali, Irshad Manji, Azar Nafisi, and Asma Hassan, to name a few – have sold an impressive number of books in multiple languages, often topping North American and European bestseller lists (Hirsi Ali, 2006 and 2007; Manji, 2004; Nafisi, 2003; Hasan, 2001). Although their narratives differ in significant ways, it is interesting to note commonalities in the themes they explore. First, they seek to inform the Western lay reader about the challenges facing Muslim women, often with a special emphasis on atrocities and negative personal experiences. Second, they manifest a concern for emancipating Muslim women from patriarchal practices, and acknowledge significant debts to Western culture for shaping their views. Third, they link the agenda of women's rights to broader reforms of Muslim communities and societies. Fourth, they tend to bypass academic literature and theoretical debates about the politicization of feminism in a time of war. Fifth, they tend to represent the resources for transforming the Islamic world as personal or Western in nature, rather than indigenous.

Though it may be unrealistic to expect more nuanced or scholarly writings on 'women and Islam' to reach a wide audience, the absence of diverse voices in the bestselling literature is disconcerting. Unfortunately, popular writing on the subject does much to reinforce suspicion among Muslim communities about 'hidden agendas'

---

29 In Germany, a group of secularists from Turkish, Iranian and Arabic backgrounds have formed the Central Committee for Ex-Muslims as a form of protest against being automatically identified as Muslim by the German government. This committee was also formed in opposition to the Central Committee of Muslims, which is Germany's most prominent Muslim organization. For more, see Saunders, 2007, A01 and A20.

and – despite the authenticity of many narratives and the significance of problems they describe – is only experienced as empowering by a minority of 'elite' Muslim women, even in a Western context. Many Muslim readers perceive these books as calls for women's emancipation *from* Islam rather than for women's liberation *in* Islam. Regardless of authorial intentions, leading paperbacks reflect intercultural polarization and often reinforce preconceptions.

Conclusions

The subject of women and Islam is intensely politicized, both in the Islamic world and in the West. In addition to obvious political reasons for concern about this state of affairs, it must also be acknowledged that the existence of 'outsiders' who hope to assist in the cause of liberation is not an unalloyed blessing for Muslim women. The perception of a combined military and cultural assault on Islamic culture reinforces emotional and intellectual defensiveness, hardening patriarchal attitudes among Muslim men in particular. When many Muslim women – even highly educated women who regard themselves as inclined toward openness and progressive thought – read from the Western literature on women and Islam, they encounter arguments that address some of their legitimate concerns, while placing them in a context that is deeply polarizing.

But what are the voices and concerns of Muslim women who are compelled to work for change within predominantly Islamic cultural milieus? How do they address themselves to traditional religious as well as cultural barriers to the advancement of women? How do Muslim women seek to make their voices heard, and from what indigenous sources do they formulate their views about Islam? For answers to these and other questions, we must address ourselves to the subject of contemporary Islamic hermeneutics.

Chapter 3

Trends and Transformations in Contemporary Islamic Hermeneutics

There are many reasons for Western interest in the subject of women and Islam. Many Western women find themselves drawn to the subject out of a genuine sense of curiosity, and perhaps also concern. Anthropologists and students of comparative religion are motivated by habits of questioning that are specific to their respective disciplines, and to their efforts to understand distinct ways of being human. Though the interest of politicians and strategists in this topic is the most suspect for contemporary Muslim communities, most of the reasons for external interest differ from those that are commonplace among Muslim women. For Muslims, Islam is both a religion and a culture – a source of spiritual ideas and of social norms. To be interested in Islam is, for Muslim women, to seek an engaged understanding of beliefs that affect one's entire way of life.

For many Muslim women, knowing Islam is a means of knowing one's own culture. While many Muslim women experience the facts of their religion as settled and are willing to grant authoritative status to the Islamic teachings that prevail in their given social milieu, others find themselves questioning the manner in which religiously informed social values have been constructed. Who, they ask, is doing the interpreting? According to what intellectual standards? Who is willing to include Muslim women in the interpretive conversation? And where can Muslim women turn when the gates of authoritative conversation are closed?

As Muslim women attain to higher levels of education and become better equipped to participate in the world beyond their family networks and neighborhoods, increasing numbers are engaging in conversations that are simultaneously preoccupied with religion, with hermeneutics, and with the status of women in society. With surprising frequency, their conversations are taking place in transnational space, both 'real' and 'virtual' (internet mediated). Many are finding that dialogue across borders provides them with an empowering point of entry into broader conversations about contemporary Islam.

Islamic Transnationalism – and Islamic Identities – Reimagined

Any serious study of women, Islam, and transnationalism should be careful not to overstate the 'novelty' of transnationalism or interculturality in relation to Islam. Islamic thought throughout history has been shaped by cultural exchanges. In this respect contemporary developments are qualitatively distinct yet continuous with a larger historical process. A 'spirit of encountering the other' is not foreign to Islam, for Islamic civilization has always been a product of exchanges between multiple cultures and intellectual traditions.

It is unfortunate that, in contemporary intellectual discussions, the words 'Islam' and 'transnationalism' are most often conjoined in the context of security threat analysis. It is undeniably true that transnational connectivity, expedited by modern communications technology, has played a significant role in the constitution of Muslim networks inspired by a desire to confront the West militarily as well as ideologically. The basis for this radicalized Islamic transnationalism has taken many decades to form, and it is now a significant force in global affairs. But militant networks are by no means the only face of transnational Islam. In many respects, transnationalism has become 'the new normal' in Muslim lands, just as it has in the rest of the world.

A substantial literature suggests that transnational cultural flows have unsettled traditional Muslim self-identity, with particular respect to gender relations and their attendant norms. A number of studies go so far as to suggest the emergence of a 'new hermeneutic field': Islamic identity and intellectuality are being reshaped by current transnational and intercultural realities in profound ways, and not merely through reactionary rebuttals of 'foreign' ideas or reflexive imitation (Salvatore, 1997). An increasingly prominent school of thought views Muslim women not only as passive objects of change, but also as change agents who are deeply involved in processes of reinterpretation and social advocacy.

The ever-growing literature on women and Islam attests to profound challenges to and changes in the ways that Muslims encounter one another and their world. A major branch of this literature deals with the cultural and structural realities of patriarchy, with particular emphasis on socioeconomic factors. This literature has been heavily influenced by Western literature on transnational feminism (for example, Mohanty, Russo and Torres, 1991; Grewal and Kaplan, 1994). While it is not a primary emphasis, writings in this genre have recently begun to touch upon the relationship between transnationalism and identity (Moghadam, 2005; Badran, 2002; Bayes and Tohidi, 2001).

Rather than view Muslim women only as objects of transnational forces, the emerging literature on Muslim women and transnationalism seeks to underscore opportunities that transnationalism provides for social agency (Tohidi, 2002; Moghadam, 2005; Badran, 2002; Cooke, 2001). This literature breaks new ground in the study of how Muslim women activists, in their search for adequate responses to the gender-polarized worldviews of Islamic traditionalists and revivalists, have utilized transnational spaces to challenge dominant conceptions of Islamic norms by projecting their own understanding of Islamic identity. Such explorations of Muslim women's activism, however, manifest greater concern with the activism and agency than with questions of worldview, meaning, and textual interpretation. The hermeneutical process of reconciling women's rights with Islam is not a primary focus of analysis.

A more recent branch of the women and Islam literature addresses precisely these interpretive issues, albeit without direct concern with the transnational (Wadud, 1999; Barlas, 2002). This emergent literature focuses its critique not only on social practices, but also on the hermeneutical methods through which Islamic social norms are derived and legitimized. A common argument among authors who choose to engage Islamic hermeneutics is that Western feminist approaches to women's liberation are unlikely to prove adequate to the tasks associated with women's advocacy in Muslim cultures; an indigenously rooted approach that recognizes possibilities for an empowering reading of religious texts is more likely to counter patriarchal religious discourses than an approach that appears foreign and secular (Wadud, 2006).

Though the literature on women and Islam raises a number of timely questions about social change in the Muslim world, there is considerable room for creative new approaches that can contribute to a fuller understanding of contemporary Muslim realities. Questions about the relationship between transnationalism and women's participation in Islamic interpretation are particularly inviting: How do critiques of patriarchy and of authoritative patriarchal hermeneutics relate to transnationalism? How are we to understand the origins and character of new Muslim discourses and self-critiques? Are changes in Muslim discourse on women 'exogenous,' and best understood through transposition of 'Western' labels such as 'modern' or 'progressive' Islam? Or are these changes manifestations of an emergent, transnational hermeneutic field that blends different cultural influences in unexpected and sometimes unpredictable ways?

In this chapter I will argue that it is possible to conceive of Muslim identity and intellectuality in terms that transcend the conventional labels, and that do not simply transpose Western categories or posit continuities with reactionary forms of 'Islamism.' Contemporary Islam is a transboundary, pluralistic phenomenon characterized by constant renegotiations of sacred meaning. In these exchanges, many Muslim women are finding increasing opportunities to act as catalysts of creative thought, and are at the same time reimagining their identities within the context of a new, pluralistic hermeneutic field. While their readings of Islam are by no means the dominant constitutive forces in Muslim politics, the growing involvement of Muslim women in transnational interpretive dialogues has significant implications for the study of Islamic interpretation and activism. It suggests a need for direct engagement with contemporary Muslim intellectuals – for this study, women in particular – to explore how cultural encounters are shaping their Muslim identities and approaches to the hermeneutics of Islam. Contemporary Islam contains a wide variety of interpretive possibilities from which Muslim women can draw as they reshape their self-understandings in light of new experiences.

Trends in Islamic Interpretation

Commentators focusing on contemporary tendencies in Islamic interpretation are by no means of one mind in their efforts to classify thinkers who are receptive to new understandings of Islamic ethics and morality, particularly with respect to the status of women. In addition to the hostile labels that are placed on 'innovative' interpretive tendencies by Muslim protagonists of 'traditional' social roles, a number of differing labels have also been applied by Western scholars and media analysts. Drawing on nineteenth-century usage of the classical Islamic concept of *islah* ('reform') some Muslim and non-Muslim scholars construe 'pro-woman' interpretations as 'reformist Islam.' In contrast, those who see open-mindedness with respect to women as a counterpoint to a broader phenomenon of Islamic extremism use the language of 'moderate Islam.' Others, believing gender equality to be an essentially modern phenomenon, speak of a 'modernist Islam,' while still others use such terms as 'liberal Islam,' 'critical Islam,' or 'progressive Islam.' Even though the media tend to use all of these labels interchangeably,[1] each of them is laden with implicit theoretical as well as strategic or rhetorical content.

The lack of consistency in terminology used by interpreters and those who study their efforts should not deter analysts seeking to make sense of significant trends in contemporary Islamic thought. Despite differences, those who are called reformists, moderates, modernists, liberals, critical thinkers, progressives, often shared a number of distinctive motivations. Their interpretive practices include: *too definitive?*

- acts of questioning traditional interpretive practices and legalistic structures;
- acts of engagement in critical debate by revisiting the historicity of traditional analysis;
- acts of deciphering and elucidating new meaning through processes of reinterpretation, often in relation to new contexts of experience (for example, temporal, hermeneutical, cultural, political, and so on).

Due to the inherent pluralism and the diverse influences motivating contemporary reinterpretive projects, all interpretive labels are best understood as approximations of dynamic, variegated, and fluid processes. Moreover, broad labels for diverse social phenomena can never be more than 'ideal-types':[2] they are only approximations capturing general tendencies, or lenses that disclose specific categories of meaning while downplaying others. The various labels applied to 'new' schools of Islamic interpretation – especially those that Western scholars are inclined to view as 'positive,' such as 'reformist,' 'moderate,' 'modernist,' 'liberal,' 'critical,' 'progressive' – tend to overlap to a considerable extent, in implied content if not always in semantics. This is suggested in Figure 3.1.

Although the boundaries implied by terminology about Islamic interpretation cannot be rigidly defined, words that are chosen for 'favorable' trends implicitly invoke other categories of Islamic interpretation from which they have been differentiated. The existence of a 'moderate' Islam necessarily presupposes the existence of an

---

1   A good example is an article by Karim Rasian, 'Indonesia's Moderate Islamists,' in *Foreign Policy* (July–August 2002), which uses most of these terms (that is, 'progressive Muslims,' 'liberal Islamists,' and 'moderate Muslims') to define a new breed of Muslim thinkers.

2   The notion of an 'ideal-type' was initiated into the context of social sciences by Max Weber in his chapter entitled '"Objectivity" in Social Science and Social Policy,' in Edward A. Shils and Henry Finch (eds), *Max Weber on the Methodology of the Social Sciences* (IL: Free Press, 1949), 49–112. According to Weber, an 'ideal-type' is a processual representation of 'revealing concrete cultural phenomenon in their interdependence, causal conditions, and their *significance.*'

Reformist

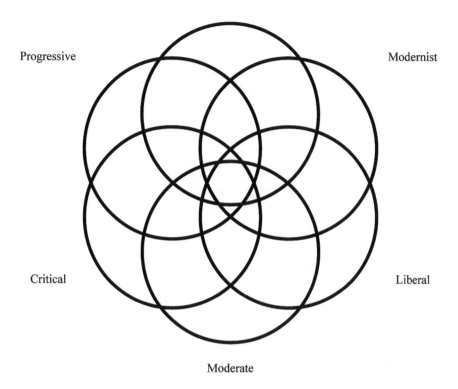

Progressive   Modernist

Critical   Liberal

Moderate

Figure 3.1 Labeling 'positive' Islamic interpretive tendencies

'immoderate' or even 'extremist' Islam.[3] 'Modernist' Islam requires a 'premodern'

---

3   After the tragic events of 11 September 2001, you find numerous articles and reports, as well as initiatives, supporting the project of 'moderate Islam,' all of which share a common objective: the prevention of terrorism by Muslim extremists. For examples, see Yankelovich, 2004, 9, and Masmoudi, 2004. Other examples of supporting a 'moderate Islam' agenda are found in the mainstream American institutions like the RAND Corporation's project and subsequent report, 'Civil Democratic Islam: Partners, Resources, and Strategies' (Reynolds, 2005, and Haddad, 2004, 8–12). The Carnegie Council on Ethics and International Affairs also sponsored a program entitled 'The War for Muslim Minds' (September 2004) in which Gilles Kepel, a French Arabist, argued with Ian Buruma, author of books dealing with radical Islam, that moderate Muslims (especially those living in the Muslim diaspora found in Europe) may be more powerful than previously perceived. There are also Muslim organizations, like the Center for the Study of Islam and Democracy (CSID), which advocate the project of 'moderate/liberal' Muslims. However, as pointed out by Radwan Masmoudi (Executive Director of CSID), to be labeled 'moderate Muslim' may benefit a Muslim in a Western context (that is, backing as well as funding from Western political institutions) and

Islam,[4] while 'liberal,'[5] 'critical,'[6] and 'progressive'[7] labels presuppose 'illiberal/

---

simultaneously delegitimize a Muslim in an Islamic context (that is, all your projects are seen as Western conspiracies). For more, see Masmoudi, 2003, 40–44. This thought is shared by many other Muslim scholars and activists who promote the modernization of Islam but know they are stereotyped as being less authentic, less committed, and less solidly established in communal faith and doctrinal truth.

4   Charles Kurzman views the first wave of reformists from the last century as 'modernist' Muslims (for example, Muhammad 'Abduh, Muhammad Rashid Rida, Sayyid Jamal al-Din al-Afghani, Sayyid Ahmad Khan), distinguished by distancing themselves from the secularists who downplayed the importance of Islam while 'privileging nationalism, socialism and other ideologies,' and by differentiating themselves from the revivalist Muslim brotherhoods who advocated modern values but downplayed modernity by 'privileging authenticity and divine mandates' (Kurzman, 2002, 4). These Muslim individuals started some of the great modern debates, such as 'Should the Islamic faith use traditional scholarship or reimagine Islam in modern contexts?' and 'Should the Islamic faith be engaged in original precepts or in modernizing original precepts to meet today's changes?'

5   Kurzman regards the second wave of reform ('or subset of modernist Islam' or 'neo-modernist') from the last century as 'liberal' Islam. In his view, a number of Muslim thinkers (for example, Ali Shariati, Fazlur Rahman, Mahmoud Muhammad Taha, Abdullahi an-Na'im, Fatima Mernissi, Amina Wadud, Muhammad Shahrour) revived as well as extended the modernist Islamic discourse by providing new methodological frameworks of interpretation concerning Islamic scripture and law. They also began to reconcile Islam with the precepts and practices of Western liberalism, especially in the subjects of individual liberties, democratic processes, pluralism, civil society and gender equality (Kurzman, 1998).

The National Endowment for Democracy (NED) has hosted many discussions on the 'concerning prospects for Liberal Islam'; one conference was held on 25 September 2002, in which the keynote speaker, Nurcholish Madjid, as senior researcher at the University of Paramadina in Jakarta, Indonesia, and who also ran for the presidency in 2003, 'explained how concepts of modernity, pluralism, and human rights do exist within Islamic tradition. He [also] argued that even when Muslims use modern secular institutions, their behavior can still be governed by Islamic ethical principles' in *NED Newsletter* (Fall 2002), 5.

6   Peter Mandaville, in *Transnational Muslim Politics: Reimagining the Umma* (2001), analyzes an emerging trend comprised of men and women throughout most of the Muslim world who are negotiating the processes for meaning of Muslim identity in modern contexts through critical reflexivity and activity. These critical Muslims (for example, Mohammad Arkoun) are 'increasingly willing to take Islam into their own hands, relying on their own readings and interpretations of the classical sources or following 'reformist' intellectuals who question traditional dogmas and challenge the claims of the *'ulama* to be privileged sources of religious knowledge' (178). One Muslim thinker who has used the label of 'critical Islam' is Ebrahim Moosa (in Safi, 2003, 111–27).

7   Many new Muslim virtual as well as non-virtual organizations, especially found in North America, have emerged in the last five years, with their identity being linked to 'progressive Islam' or 'progressive Muslims.' Such formal virtual organizations are 'The Muslim Meet-Up' (<www.islam.meetup.com>), 'Progressive Muslim Network' (<www.progressivemuslims.com>), and 'Muslim WakeUp!' (<www.muslimwakeup.com>); and a non-virtual organization which is called the 'Progressive Muslim Union of North America.' According to Saadia Yacoob, a founder of the Progressive Muslim Network in Washington, DC, these Muslim individuals particularly advocate 'a radical reinterpretation of societal structures and ideals, rather than proposing reforms that do not question the inherent

conservative,' 'uncritical,' and 'reactionary' Islamic counterparts respectively. While each linguistic approach highlights different aspects of Islamic intellectual thought and bears within itself distinctive conceptual as well as rhetorical advantages and disadvantages, the 'reformist' label has been most consistently applied by Western scholars of Islam because it is perceived as carrying less cultural baggage than alternative labels. As conventionally used by scholars of Islam, 'reformism' (in

Traditionalism

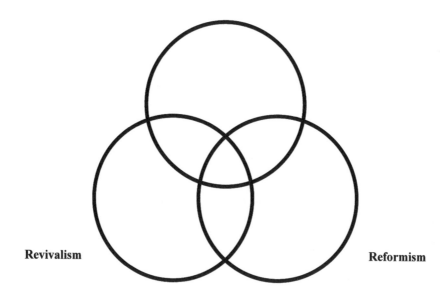

Revivalism   **Reformism**

Figure 3.2 Three interpretive tendencies

---

oppressive foundations upon which the societal structures were built' in a conference paper entitled 'Developing Identities: What is Progressive Islam and Who are Progressive Muslims?' for the 33rd Annual AMSS Conference, 24–26 September 2004. Additionally, a colleague of Ms Yacoob, Sanjay Bavikatte, defines progressive Islam, in an on-line paper entitled 'Allah is in the Details: Towards a Theory of Progressive Islam,' found in *Qalandar* (an on-line journal which specializes in Islam and Interfaith Relations in South Asia at <http://www. islaminterfaith.org/issue.html>, accessed 1 July 2003):

… as an ideology [which] emerges at the node of [a] complex matrix of reflexivity, relativization, and trans-nationalization. More specifically, Progressive Islam is a process of self-examination that results in attempts at cultural legitimization and assertion within Islam of specific 'progressive' ideas. These ideas may be both the result of absorption of elements of other cultures and a resurrection of previously marginalized ideas/fragments of belief within Islam itself.

See also insightful articles such as Eisenberg, 2004; Scrivener, 2004a, A1 and A26; and Scrivener, 2004b, F7. See also Safi, 2003.

Arabic, *islah*) presupposes not only a 'traditionalist' project (*taqlid*) that seeks to maintain past precedents and forms, but also a more populist phenomenon of 'revivalism' or 'renewalism' (*tajdid*) – a movement that involves change in the character and content of Islamic concepts, but not necessarily along a trajectory that leads westward.[8] Even the reformist–traditionalist–revivalist paradigm has limitations, however, for it is arguable that many if not most Muslim individuals are dwelling 'in between labels,' as represented in Figure 3.2.

As interpretive tendencies found in Islamic societies, 'traditionalist Islam'[9] is also known among Western scholars as 'conservative Islam' or 'customary Islam.' Reformist Islam sometimes includes secularist tendencies, whereas 'revivalist Islam' correlates with such phenomena as 'Islamist brotherhoods,' as well as with much of what Western observers refer to as 'fundamentalist Islam,' 'political Islam,' 'radical Islam,' and 'Muslim extremism.' Each of these ideal-typical tendencies refers to Islamic intellectual orientations toward Western culture, as represented in the following 'stereo-typical' equations:

Retrench	=	Traditionalist
Reject	=	Revivalist
Reflect	=	Secularist
Relate	=	Reformist

Even though all of these tendencies have their own stories, with historically key figures and significant moments, there is an absence of scholarship that traces *how* and *why* each have emerged in relation to one another, constructing and (re)constructing one another's boundaries of meaning. Ultimately, such research would add to the process of understanding the diverse trends of interpretative identities in the Islamic world and their impact on relations between Islamic and Western cultures, Muslim society and the public sphere, authoritative politics, and women.

Imagining Muslims and the Muslim Ummah in 'Trans-' Formation

Trans-national, Trans-cultural, Trans-local

During the last decade, a growing group of scholars has attempted to understand the transnational or transcultural dimensions of Muslim public experience. This emerging literature is ushering in new ways to imagine Muslims (both men and women) and Muslim public spheres (from 'sub-Ummahs' to the larger global 'Ummah,' or community of Muslims) as being constituted in a variety of negotiations that transcend national, cultural, and community boundaries. Whether they focus on the space of

---

8   For a good comparison of *tajdid* and *islah*, see Voll, 1983.

9   This interpretive tendency will be discussed in more detail later in this chapter, in the section entitled 'Persistence of Traditional Certitude: The Power of Patriarchal Consensus.'

relations amongst nations ('the transnational'), the space amongst cultures ('the transcultural'), or the space amongst different localities ('the translocal'), scholars of Islam are emphasizing the border-crossing processes of identity formation – ways in which Muslim identities emerge from the experience of encountering multi-faceted and pluralistic contexts.

For these scholars, the lived realities of the world cannot be accommodated by a two-dimensional map with definitive borders and boundaries; only a multi-dimensional map of conglomerated, fluid, intercontextual realities can capture the authentic nature of contemporary human experience. Within such a complex densely networked world, 'Islamic' and 'Western' (as well as other) spheres cannot exist in isolation, as monolithic realities, and each of the world's geographic zones is seen as a composite of overlapping religious, cultural, and political as well as ethnic contexts. It is through the interaction of these contexts that individual identities are formed. Because the contexts are dynamic rather than static, identities are constantly subject to change, as individuals relate to others and interpret texts governing relations within and between communities. Changes in technology, as well as global economic and political organization, have made it virtually impossible for any human community to live in isolation, or to maintain past beliefs and values without reference to markedly different ways of life. For contemporary Muslims (whether laity, academicians, clergy, or political figures), this means that there is no escape from conversations with – or about – 'others.' No-one can avoid encounters with otherness, and these encounters challenge individuals and communities to reimagine both themselves and others in ways that support either a solipsistic or dialogical orientation.

One of the most well-known and senior Western-Islamic thinkers offering ideational alternatives for rethinking Muslim identity in the twenty-first century is Mohammed Arkoun. In his work, *The Unthought in Contemporary Islamic Thought*, Arkoun presents a multi-faceted critique of solipsistic tendencies both in Islamic thought and in political and social practice. He encourages Muslims to think the *unthinkable*, to transcend the impasse of what he calls 'institutionalized ignorance' and to embrace the full range of intellectual and cultural resources that are openly available to Muslims in the modern world today. For Arkoun, Muslims cannot *disengage* or be *disembedded* from the modern construction of Islam: they cannot and should not create hermeneutic enclosures that bound interpretive experience to past 'untouchable' discursive corpuses. Rather, Muslims need to live in creative *disclosure*: dynamic as well as transparent interactions within unlimited pluralistic spaces.

However, according to Arkoun, in order to think the *unthinkable*, Muslims also need to understand processes that have bound themselves to 'fixed' texts and contexts, and therefore to static conceptualizations and ideological 'totalizations.' Cognitive errors associated with static thinking negate new cultural experiences and insist that contemporary realities can only be understood within a past frame of reference that forms a limiting cultural enclosure. In Arkoun's view, this 'totalized' viewpoint (which claims comprehensiveness and closure) results in dichotomous thinking, logocentrism, and the monopolization of truth itself (Arkoun, 2002, 170–203).

Dichotomous thinking accepts the Aristotelean principles of contradiction and identity: a proposition is true or false, teaches good or evil. But pluralist logic is more flexible, offering a variety of ways and possibilities for expressing religious values and spiritual experiences through secular, political institutions or philosophical postures. In such a civil society, different cultures and world visions are not juxtaposed without significant appropriate interactions in the sane space of citizenship, as has been the case so far in many democratic societies in which communities are situated in specific urban locations; *intercreative* activities are made possible, even postulated, by the new style of thinking, the new political and legal concept of citizenship and the human subject (Arkoun, 2002, 324).

Arkoun beseeches Muslims to encounter a new methodological and epistemological attitude that successfully strives to depart from historically constituted 'logocentric enclosures' and, concomitantly, to extend their scope as a 'trans-individual subject[s]' (Arkoun, 2002, 179). The prefix 'trans,' according to Arkoun, implies a subject not only in motion but in metamorphosis: a process of perpetual fluctuation and 'trans-'formation. Therefore, experiences of 'trans-'action/'trans-'formation are inescapable in knowledge construction and (re)construction of textual and contextual realities. Arkoun's favored attitude would encourage new epistemological as well as methodological processes for studying the hermeneutic conversations between Islam, politics, and modernity. It would also usher in a new age of what Arkoun calls a 'worldwide space of solidarity and citizenship' (Arkoun, 2002, 311).

Two scholars of Islam who believe Arkoun is a pioneer in rethinking the construction of Muslim identity from a 'trans-'formational perspective are Armando Salvatore and Peter Mandaville. In *Islam and the Political Discourse of Modernity*, Salvatore, a Research Fellow in Sociology at Humboldt University in Berlin, Germany, locates the work of authors such as Arkoun in broader theoretical as well as genealogical contexts. He insightfully notes that intellectual and cultural *interactions* between the 'West' and 'Islam' are driven not so much by political, military, and economic factors as by interpretive practices within 'transcultural spaces.' In positing the existence of these spaces, he underscores continual, complex interactions between a non-essentialized 'West' and a similarly non-essentialized 'Islam'; neither civilization's character or identity can be 'fixed,' yet processes of 'essentialization' and 'othering' – insisting on a pure 'self' and a pure 'other' – nonetheless sustain adversarial cultural interactions. By denying the existence or legitimacy of transcultural (or intercultural) realities, the practices of culture-specific hermeneutic circles generate confrontation.[10] Salvatore argues that political discourses which deny the existence of significant interaction at the cultural level are revisionist in nature. Insofar as cultural realities are represented as monolithic and normatively exclusionary through what he calls 'monodimensional hermeneutics,' political options for accommodation are ruled out. With respect to Islam, revivalist tendencies seek to predicate politics on the presumed qualities of a pure religious culture:

---

10 To clarify this thought, imagine two overlapping circles whose outer limits are sustained by the beliefs of those who stand within them in a pure, unadulterated, perfect circle that exists (or should exist) separately from all other circles.

[L]inear, monodimensional hermeneutics [is] primarily centred on an essentialized view of Islam 'as such', where the political is considered derivative of religion, to the opening of a bidimensional hermeneutic field, where the political acquires the status of an additional and autonomous dimension grounded on a concern of the observer (Salvatore, 1997, 117).

Consequently, any attempt to reconstruct a 'pure culture' or normative past originality results in 'essentialist discourses' and 'monodimensional hermeneutics.'

For Salvatore, what Muslims experience today is a simultaneous existence of one world and many worlds – of an emergent, transcultural frame of reference for Islam and its multiple conversations with modernity and politics. In this new frame of reference, there are many Muslim intellectuals who are reconceptualizing the frontiers of the Muslim public sphere and who understand that the search for a common binding culture leads not to a master formula that is acceptable to all, but rather to encounters with the irreducible uniqueness of others. Once again, as with Arkoun, the 'trans' outlook, narrative, or culture cannot be imposed or created by a consensual committee; rather, it is expressed in dynamic disclosures linked to new ways of experiencing the world.

Peter Mandaville, Director of the Center for Global Studies at George Mason University, in his timely and insightful book, *Transnational Muslim Politics: Reimagining the Umma*, also provides a compelling portrait of 'new' and 'critical' transcultural, or what he calls 'translocal,' trends within Islam. These trends are comprised of new 'imagined' public spaces wherein men and women are freely practicing their innate Muslim right of *ijtihad*, which in turn creates an agglomeration of these disparate public spaces that form spaces of translocality.

New intellectuals, university students and lay Muslims – men *and* women – can to some degree all be seen as sources of ijtihad and purveyors of authentic Islam. Their debates and critiques, I want to argue, constitute a dramatic widening of the *Muslim public sphere*. Furthermore, its emergence can be explained to a large extent as a consequence of translocality – in other words, the traveling theories, hybrid/diasporic identities and media technologies which Muslims are embracing. This public sphere also fulfills a crucial political function insofar as it offers a discursive space in which Muslims can articulate their normative claims (i.e., 'Islam') from a multiplicity of subject positions. As we have seen, though, this is not a space devoid of hegemony ... The nature of this arena is such, however, that dissenting voices will always be heard (Mandaville, 2001, 186).

This global Islamic 'public sphere' or civil society represents an increasingly visible as well as virtual critical mass of Muslim intellectuals, laity, and clergy (*'ulama*), men and women from Morocco to Indonesia. These widely scattered yet interacting voices have contributed to the emergence of what Mandaville calls a 'critical' Islamic translocality:

New explorations in what we might term a 'critical Islam' are emerging through a reassessment and re-interpretation of traditional textual sources. Going back to the early traditions is hence not a throwback to 'fundamentalism,' but, in the case of these new Muslim discourses, an attempt to critically re-read the ethical core of the founding texts directly into contemporary contexts without the mediation of centuries of dogmatic theology. The emergence of a new Muslim public sphere has also meant a significant change of personnel in terms of who is authorized to undertake this critical renewal of Islam … [D]ebates over the political imperatives of translocal Islam – and also over who can legitimately set this agenda – serve to create new Muslim public spheres in which formerly disenfranchised voices (e.g. 'deviants', 'moderates', and women) are empowered to articulate alternative interpretations of Islamic authenticity (Mandaville, 2001, 4).

Mandaville notes the emergence of 'a new breed of Islamic intellectual,' and observes that many of these intellectuals are women. Though some of Mandaville's critics have contended that these tendencies of critical thinking are confined to an intellectual elite, my own studies suggest that this is not necessarily the case (see Chapters 5 and 6). Mandaville's contentions concerning the need to 'rethink Islam' in reference to politics, gender, and community provide an intriguing point of departure for further investigation.

These three authors are 'breaking ground' in contemporary Muslim identity in new and profound ways; however, there are some silences in their arguments that need to be addressed. First, all three authors, Arkoun, Salvatore, and Mandaville, are theoretically articulating ways to interpret Muslim identity in more complex perspectives; however, how are they helping to bridge the gap between theories and practices of Muslim politics? Second, all three emphasize the role of rethinking or reimagining ideological as well as geographical landscapes, yet all three dilute the importance of national identity and its meaning for contemporary Muslims (especially Muslim women activists – see Chapters 5 and 6). Finally, Salvatore and Mandaville, in particular, focus on the formation of 'transculturality' and 'translocality,' but do not clarify or develop the relationship of these formations with the ideational as well as structural realities of the 'transnational,' which requires negotiation among national identities and efforts to cope with the policies of nation-states.

Embracing the 'Both/And'

In an article entitled 'The Coming Transformation of the Muslim World,' Dale F. Eickelman, a cultural anthropologist at Dartmouth College, proclaims that Muslims are, indeed, living in a 'profound era' of intellectual, social, and political transformation of their world:

> What distinguishes the present era from prior ones is the large numbers of believers engaged in 'reconstruction' of religion, community, and society. In an earlier era, political or religious leaders would prescribe, and others were supposed to follow. Today, the major impetus for change in religious and political values comes from below … These transformations include a greater sense of autonomy for both women and men and the emergence of a public sphere in which politics and religion are subtly intertwined … In changing the style and scale of possible discourse, [Muslims engaged in such a discourse] reconfigure the nature of religious thought and action, create new forms of public space, and encourage debate over meaning (Eickelman, 1999).

As suggested by Eickelman, as well as Mandaville, more Muslims are expanding their perceptions of themselves and others, moving beyond premodern consensual thinking towards more self-reflexive thinking. These authors are suggesting that there is no one definitive discourse of Islam that can definitely label or shape Muslim identity. Rather, Muslims, through transnational as well as transcultural conversations/negotiations, are becoming interpretive agents of multi-faceted textual and contextual realities.

This 'trans-'formational nature of Muslim public experience has been described in a variety of ways, and some of the recurring characteristic tendencies include movement towards symbiosis in intercultural relations, notions of dynamism, and a 'both/and' attitude of openness toward differences. Whereas discursive frames for discussing authentic identity have previously underscored the necessity of choosing between pure 'Islamic' or 'Western' options – presenting the intellectual with an 'either/or' option – emergent approaches to interpretation underscore possibilities for reconciliation.

As pointed out by Farish A. Noor, a Malaysian human rights activist and academic, the new voices of Islam are products of this 'symbiotic' relationship between tradition and modernity, between global and local, between West and East (Noor, 2002, 1).[11] This relational symbiosis is the act of living together in a more intimate association or close union of dissimilar otherness, whether temporal or spatial. Transcending the bifurcation of the world based in static, separated pre-conceived concepts of self and other, symbiotic thinking encourages – what other scholars have pointed to – more organic awareness of 'hybrid' or 'creolized' identity as an ever-changing whole with endless frontiers (Williams, 2004, A15; J. Anderson, 2001). In an article entitled 'Muslims Need Creative Pluralism,' Tariq Ramadan[12] states a similar argument: Muslims (especially Canadian Muslims) need to embrace the multiplicity of their identity as well as their common humanity.

> Muslims must reform themselves; it is not for others to change … It is a complex and difficult challenge that requires knowledge and analysis of traditional Islamic sources as well as the Canadian environment, its history, its institutions, and its culture. We are only at the beginning of this process, but evolution is much more significant and tangible among younger generations of Canadian Muslims, particularly women. Society cannot disregard new realities transforming it from the inside … What should bring us together today is our common citizenship: We live in the same society, we share the same challenges and future (Ramadan, 2005, A23).[13]

---

11   Noor edited a volume entitled *The New Voices of Islam*, when he was a Visiting Fellow at the International Institute for the Study of Islam in the Modern World (ISIM). For more information about ISIM and its research projects, go to: <http://www.isim.nl>. Noor was also the Secretary General of the International Movement for a Just World (JUST) and has taught at the Centre for Civilizational Dialogue at the University of Malaya.

12   See more about Tariq Ramadan in Chapter 2, note 22.

13   In another article, Ramadan also stated, 'Muslims living in Europe have an opportunity to reread our [religious] source … We are going through a reassessment and the most important subject is women. Our experience in Europe has made it clear we must speak about equality' (Ford, 2005). A friend and colleague of Ramadan on various projects, Azizah Al-Hibri, a Professor of Law at the T.C. Williams School of Law in Richmond, VA, stated a similar argument, applied not to Canadian or European Muslims, however, but to American Muslims:

An attitude of symbiosis between tradition and modernity, as well as between culturally and geographically defined identities (for example, Islamic/Western), creates space for relation, enabling all Muslims (whatever their walks of life) to openly discuss the complexity of being Muslim in the new contemporary contexts while simultaneously embracing the context of humanity as a whole. Such symbiosis is opening new constitutive spaces of debate, discussion and dialogue amongst different individuals on issues of identity, society, nationalism, and hermeneutics.

Contemporary Muslim commentators who argue for new conceptions of Islamic identity seek to ground their calls for change in basic reconceptualizations of Islam and Islamic tradition. Their approaches to communal values underscore dynamic relativity and the importance of context. As Abdul Aziz Said, the current occupant of the Mohammed Said Farsi Islamic Peace Chair at the American University in Washington, DC, eloquently suggests:

> Islam may be likened to a 'river' rather than a 'lake'. Islam is in motion through history, and has never been static. Like a river, Islam has sometimes picked up sediments that are not particularly Islamic, yet the soils over which Islam has flowed have sometimes enriched Islam by providing new, culturally diverse ways for the universalism of the tradition to manifest. Islam is dynamic rather than static, and can be reconciled with modernity.[14]

Said's metaphor helps interpreters to conceive of Islam as something other than a static set of theological propositions. Interpreters must view Islam in living, historical contexts, as a tradition that is flexible and adaptive, yet continuous across time. Encounters with new cultural and historical realities may sometimes 'compromise' core Islamic notions, yet they also present opportunities for new discoveries and angles of vision.

In his exploration of emerging tendencies in modern Islamic thought, Sanjay Kabir Bavikatte, a Professor of Law and Development at the University of Guyana in Guyana, South America, extols the importance of relativization:

> [Globalised culture] links together previously encapsulated and formerly homogenous cultural niches forcing each to relativize itself to others. This relativization may take the form of either reflexive self-examination in which certain principles (projected as

---

In order to be good Americans in this country, first of all you have to be good Muslims … We need to be psychologically bound to this land, because this is where we are going to live and die. We need to understand that we are engaged in nation-building … We also need to understand that democracy is a work in progress. There are still a lot of defects in this democracy, and certainly Muslims have suffered from some of these defects … but that is no reason to despair. That is a reason to start a civil rights movement.

How do you start a civil rights movement for Muslims, or for Arabs, or other groups? First you have to know the history of the civil rights movement in this country. You have to know what Martin Luther King, Jr. and Malcolm X and others did. We need to rediscover our history, rediscover America's history, redefine it and redefine ourselves …

For more of Al-Hibri's speech see Al-Hibri, 2005.

14   This statement was made by Abdul Aziz Said in an opening speech entitled 'Toward a Contemporary Islamic Synthesis,' for the international conference, *Contemporary Islamic Synthesis* at the Library of Alexandria in Egypt, 4–5 October 2003.

fundamental) are reasserted in the face of threatening alternatives or the absorption of some elements of other cultures. Second, it allows for development of genuinely trans-national cultures not linked to any particular nation-state-society that may be either novel or syncretistic.[15]

The process of relativizing is connected to another tendency: an attitude of openness and rediscovery – an affirmation of 'both/and' possibilities inherent in contemporary cultural encounters and interpretive processes. More specifically, it becomes possible to conceive one's own authenticity as emerging from a rediscovery and affirmation of – rather than a negation of – the other, or to imagine tradition and modernity as realities that can be reconciled with each other. It also becomes possible to imagine the essence or ideals of a religious tradition as emergent and potentially dynamic, rather than as static and rooted in a distant historical reality.

Another contemporary Muslim thinker whose writings affirm such interpretive possibilities is Recep Senturk, Chair of History of Science at the Center for Islamic Studies (ISAM) in Istanbul, Turkey. In 'Toward an Open Science and Society: Multiplex Relations in Language, Religion, and Society,' Senturk argues for an 'open ontology' as well as a 'multiplex epistemology' – that is, a more complex vision of the world that can accommodate different kinds of truths, including the truths of modern physical, social and human sciences, as well as those of premodern metaphysical speculation:

> ... [T]he essentialist and the relational approaches can coexist and complement if they are combined in a stratified image of the world and applied simultaneously. For such an inclusive approach we need to operationalize what I term an 'open ontology,' which postulates an 'open world,' a multiplex structure with multiple layers complementing each other ... Our world view becomes 'open' when we discontinue excluding layers and dimensions that are accessible to different perspectives and intellectual communities (Senturk, 2001, 101).

For Senturk, contemporary identity in any context needs to be approached with an all-inclusive, open-ended worldview. Ideally, such thinking promotes dialogical understanding and egalitarian cultural engagement. Epistemologically, it demands a broad and participatory process in which members of estranged cultures rediscover their respective traditions and come to respect one another's deeper cultural values and motivations. While gaining access to empathetic understandings of other cultural systems, they also begin a process of broadening and reconstituting the cultural as well as intellectual foundations of their own identities.

---

15   Sanjay Kabir Bavikatte, 'Allah is in the Details: Towards a Theory of Progressive Islam,' on the *Qalandar* website: <http://www.islaminterfaith.org/issue.html>. For more on Bavikatte's thoughts on the competing visions within Muslim thought, see 'Promises of a Brave New World,' in *CHOWK On-Line*: <http://www.chowk.com/show_article.cgi?aid=000 01418&channel=university%20ave&start=0&end=9&chapter=1&page=1>.

Women as Catalysts for Muslim 'Trans-' Formation

No topic other than Islam's relation (or lack thereof) to political violence has caused more ink to be spilled than the status of women in Islamic culture. The mere existence of this literature is testimony to contemporary transnationalism: it has been composed by women in the Muslim world and women in non-Muslim countries; many of the authors claim Islamic identity or heritage while others do not; and the Muslim norms under scrutiny may be found in countries of immigration as well as in countries of origin. Regardless of their heritage, cultural background, or spatial location, scholars who write on 'women and Islam'[16] participate in a common discursive space that is thoroughly transnational, demonstrating that no cultural space can be insulated from 'otherness.'

The literature on women and Islam contains many controversies and disagreements, but its principal themes testify to ongoing transformations, cultural exchanges, frictions, and negotiations. It provides evidence of hermeneutical and philosophical revolutions and counter-revolutions – of the secular revolution that gave rise to secular nationalist/socialist feminism, of counter-trends celebrating 'Islamic authenticity' in the face of 'foreign' ideologies, and of a more recent rise in 'Islamic' feminism(s). Despite all of this ideational ferment, much of the literature on women and Islam – especially the literature critiquing Islamic forms of patriarchy – maintains a curious silence on matters of hermeneutics, in favor of a predominantly structuralist account of social change and contestation. This absence of hermeneutics prevents this literature from directly addressing the idea of a 'new hermeneutic field' constituted by transnationalism.

Before the resurgence of Islamic social movements, several generations of Muslim intellectuals were trained in the framework provided by a secular revolution, in which epistemology was separated from traditional religious ontologies. With the emergence of postmodern thought as well as new popular ideologies, more Muslim intellectuals have felt inclined to reclaim Islamic identities and ontologies. They have sought to harmonize modern critical epistemologies with premodern religious epistemology. In the process, they are beginning to think that which was unthinkable – or not permissible – for previous generations, which sought to avoid asking questions about Islam, through a secular bypass of religious reasoning or a traditionalist aloofness to modernity.

What follows is a summary of insights which can be derived from the increasingly voluminous literature on hermeneutical debates and the ongoing processes of textual and contextual contestation, reinterpretation, and reimagination. A number of emerging voices are seeking to enact a 'trans-' formation of traditional ideas and corresponding authority relations through their written word and activism. In particular, it is

16   When studying the subject of women and Islam, one encounters the intersections of many hermeneutical circles, based on discipline of study (scholars of women and Islam specialize in a variety of different disciplines – for example, religious studies, philosophy, sociology, anthropology, literature, and political science) and on the epistemological positioning (that is, socialist, modernist, postmodernist, post-colonialist). Therefore, the subject of women and Islam is very multi-/inter-disciplinary in nature.

important to critique two major tendencies that are relevant for an understanding of women and transnationalism: 1) a critique of 'authoritative patriarchy' in Muslim public experience, and 2) a critique of patriarchal hermeneutics.

Critique of Authoritative Patriarchy in Muslim Public Experience

Persistence of Traditional Certitude: The Power of Patriarchal Consensus

The problem of authority has long been a fundamental issue for Muslim societies. From the conflict over succession after the death of the Prophet Muhammad to the conflict over interpretation of the Qur'an and the Sunnah, as well as codification of *shari'ah* (the canonical Islamic law), Muslims have fought, debated, and argued about *whose Islam* is to be given consensual authoritative power over the Muslim Ummah.

In early Islamic history, acts of consensus among culturally legitimate authorities validated the definitive, canonical version of the Qur'an as well as the codification of the Hadith and the Sunnah, and the codification of *shari'ah* as it was developed by Sunnite and Shi'ite legalistic schools. Claims of social consensus also validated the authoritative influence of the *'ulama*. Key foundations for authoritative power over the Muslim Ummah then could therefore be seen in: 1) the 'consensus' of the Muslim community which ultimately gave power to the *'ulama* to codify Muslim norms and laws; 2) the consensus of the political (state) male leaders who favored particular *'ulama* and consequently established the institutionalization of theological as well as legalistic schools through the state; and 3) the consensus of male scholars, *'ulama*, and all the shared scholarship derived from the processes of interpreting the Qur'an, the Sunnah, and the historical *shari'ah* (Abou El Fadl, 2001; Mernissi, 1996; Ahmed, 1992).

Out of these *'ulama* emerged a group of scholars who were known as the *mutaqlidun* or the traditionalists. They were entrusted with the responsibility of upholding the act of *taqlid* – strict adherence to past interpretive identity.[17] These *mutaqlidun* would not only create persistence of traditional certitude as concretized in Islamic theology and law and reinforced by the political achievements of an ever-

---

17 *Mutaqlidun* – 'traditionalist' or 'customary' interpreters – remain the dominant interpreters of the Islamic texts in present-day Islamic societies. Although they would influence many different fields of knowledge (theology, philosophy, science, theosophy, jurisprudence, just to name a few), the most prominent examples would become known especially for their efforts in developing legalistic traditions. For instance, the *Mujtahid al-Mutlaq* (Abu Hanifah, Malik ibn Anas, Muhammad ibn Idris ash-Shaf'i, and Ahmad ibn Hanbal – the four founders of the Sunni legalistic schools of thought – and their interpreters, *Mujtahid al-Madhhab*) are classical examples of traditionalist interpreters. It is interesting to note that the word *mutaqlidun* is a plural Arabic active participle that comes from the verbal noun *taqlid*, meaning 'tradition' and 'imitation.' *Taqlid* is derived from the second verbal root, *qallada*, which means 'to imitate,' with the connotation 'to follow blindly another's opinion.' In addition, it is interesting to note that *taqlidi*, the adjective that means 'traditional,' is also associated with the notion of 'uncritical faith' (Cowan, 1980, 786).

expanding Islamic empire. They also fortified traditions of pride in such certitude, and allegiance to authoritative examplars.

While traditional authoritative tendencies of the *mutaqlidun* cannot realistically be represented as monolithic, patterns exist which, when compared, give understanding to a general traditionalist perspective.[18] Generally speaking, *mutaqlidun* culture was strongly patriarchal (women were extremely rare among their ranks), and contained an inherent preference for patriarchal authoritative rule. From this *mutaqlidun* perspective, authority was a distinctly male prerogative, and delegation of authority was limited to specialized (male) scholars of Islam. Such a gender-selective approach to authority has restricted the access of women to intellectual, religious, and political institutions, limiting opportunities for women to participate in social, moral, economic, political, and educational activities that define the character of cultures and societies. Therefore, as argued by many scholars of women and Islam, knowledge systems and political ideologies have almost invariably been composed, interpreted, and applied by men.[19] In recent years more scholarship has emerged to demonstrate how a variety of Muslim women have historically played a more prominent role in scholasticism and politics than given credit for by the legalistic schools of thought.[20]

Even with the waves of secular reformation and revivalism (and their influence in the fields of education and political participation) in the twentieth and twenty-first centuries, the traditional patriarchal certitude still persists through the allegiance and pride represented by contemporary *mutaqlidun*.[21] Basically, women are increasingly being educated and entering into political activism; however, they are still subjugated to neo-patriarchal structures that reinforce traditional patriarchal cultural norms from the public to private spheres. Such subordination on all levels in Islamic societies is reflected in Amina Wadud's article, 'Muslim Women as Citizens?':

---

18   As stated previously, it is important to recognize the diversity and complexity of not only Muslims but also the *mutaqlidun*. There have been and are many traditionalists who have upheld more 'reformist' or 'moderate' beliefs. For a good comparative analysis of contemporary traditionalists, see Zaman, 2002.

19   Some of the most influential women and Islam books include, but are not limited to: Mernissi, 1991; Ahmed, 1992; Wadud, 1999; Afkhami, 1995; Mir-Hosseini, 1999; Barlas, 2002; Mahmood, 2005.

20   Some good examples of such scholarship: 1) Mohammad Akram Nadwi, a Sunni religious scholar based at the Oxford Center for Islamic Studies in Britain, is producing a biographical dictionary of female *hadith* scholars that rediscovers the 'long-lost tradition of Muslim women teaching the Koran, transmitting *hadith* … and even making Islamic law as jurists' (Power, 2007, 22); 2) Rkia E. Cornell, Professor of Arabic Literature at Duke University, has translated *Dhikr an-Niswat al-Muta'abbidat as-Sufiyyat*, a book on early Sufi women saints by Abu Abd ar-Rahman as-Sulami (d. 1021) which was lost and only found in1991; 3) Fatima Mernissi, a Professor of Sociology at the Mohammed V University in Rabat, Morocco, wrote *The Forgotten Queens of Islam* (1993), a book about a variety of historical Muslim women as prominent politicians of their times.

21   More scholars are distinguishing the differences between 'premodern' traditionalist characteristics and 'modern' traditionalist characteristics, by utilizing the labels of classical traditionalist and 'neo-'traditionalist. See Armajani, 2004, 11–12.

In the Islamic state as imagined in conventional thinking, women are second-class citizens enjoying no right to self-determination. In historical *shari'a* [Islamic law], Muslim women are simply appendages to their men, first their fathers and brothers, later their husbands (and possibly, at the end of a long life, finally their sons). Within historical *shari'a*, the situation is one where Muslim men exercise domination over women and enjoy a monopoly of political power and force ... [Historical *shari'a*] cannot now be appropriately implemented because of its inability to accommodate modern understandings of gender relations and the status of women. Because it is male biased, a new interpretation needs to be arrived at – which it readily can – through a new methodology of Qur'anic interpretation (Wadud, 2000, 207).

Most contemporary traditionalists claim that they view women as equal with men on the level of piety, and state that there is no contradiction between their attachment to separate gender roles and the Qur'anic norm that affirms righteousness as the single most important standard for defining the dignity and worth of a person.

O Humanity! We created you from a single pair of a male and a female, and made you into nations and tribes, that Ye may know each other. Verily the most honoured of you in the sight of Allah [God] is the most righteous of you ... (Qur'an 49:13).

In other words, women are spiritually and morally equal, but they have separate roles in society, usually defined by their status within the family unit as mothers, wives, sisters, and daughters (Stowasser, 1994, 6). This 'equal before God, unequal before man' interpretation leads to complete division in society and labor (Othman, 1997, 1). There are some traditionalist reasons for this division: 1) it follows the natural, divinely revealed order of labor: women are the nurturers and men are the providers. Therefore, genders only mix in specific contexts, limiting the interface between men and women; 2) this limited interface between genders also protects men and women from sexual temptation and exploitation; 3) such division also protects Islamic communities from succumbing to the Western, 'unisex' societies – in which there is no distinction of the roles and functions of women and men in society.[22]

One of the most prolific leading contemporary *mutaqliduns* based in the West is Seyyed Hossein Nasr, who holds the Chair of Islamic Studies at George Washington University. Nasr, who held many distinguished positions under the last Shah of Iran, is a critic of Islamic revolutionary doctrines and practices. His worldview is comparative to the monarchal political order that resembles the past and present Middle Eastern states (for example, Gulf monarchs, Morocco, Jordan, and pre-revolutionary Iran). In his well-known book, *Traditional Islam in the Modern World*, Nasr articulates the character of traditionalist Islam, its current condition, and its message to the modern world.

In his chapter entitled 'The Male and Female in the Islamic Perspective,' Seyyed Hossein Nasr, like other contemporary *mutaqlidun*, proposes that the idealized, 'complementary' roles of men and women are upheld by selected verses of the Qur'an (that is, 2:233, 2:240–241; 4:34, 7:89). He asserts an argument in favor of compartmentalized cooperation in which men and women have distinctive,

---

22 For more about the problem of 'unisex' societies according to Muslim traditionalists, see al-Faruqi, 2001.

separated duties in society, but a unified purpose of preserving moral and social order, and supports this claim by stating that the Qur'anic view of complementarity 'was rooted in equity rather than equality' (Nasr, 1987, 54). Both claims for equity and equality are based in the Qur'anic command for justice; however, Nasr stresses that equity – that each man and woman should be treated according to their duty and contribution to Muslim society – is a fundamental precept in Islam; whereas equality – that each man and woman should be treated equally no matter what is his or her situation – is more of a modern, foreign construct. For Nasr and other traditionalist scholars, equilibrium of the world as a whole is created by the male and female working together, but only in a gender-polarized way. Unfortunately, many contemporary *mutaqlidun*, like Nasr, do not directly address the issues of power within these polarized relationships, while affirming the decisive role of male authority in the public realm, where he serves as vicegerent of God. Important questions are not raised: Can power be associated with the feminine? If the Prophet Muhammad focused so much energy on balancing the male and female,[23] does that not imply that all humans, male and female, are the vicegerents of God, righteous in authority?[24]

It is interesting to note that, no matter how positively contemporary *mutaqlidun*, like Nasr, view the importance of a balanced, yin-yang world (Nasr, 1987; 2004), such a perspective may be misused to discriminate against women whose roles in such a world are perceived as passive and pre-defined. Nasr, himself, while advocating traditionalist norms, almost admits that the exclusive, categorical positions derived from the traditionalist argument can be seen in fundamentalist actions towards women:

> Traditional Islam insisted upon women dressing modestly and usually wearing some kind of veil or head-dress which would cover their hair. The result was an array of female dresses from Morocco to Malaysia, most of these dresses being of much beauty and reflecting femininity in accordance with the ethos of Islam, which insists upon conformity to the nature of things and therefore the masculinity of the male and the femininity of the female. Then came the modernist changes which caused women to remove the veil, uncover their hair and wear Western dress ... Now there appears that 'fundamentalism' or revivalism, which in some areas has placed a handkerchief on the head of women and a machine-gun in their hands with total disregard for the beauty of the rest of their dress as a reflection of their female nature as always envisaged by Islam. One wonders which is more pleasing to the eyes of God, the Western-clad Muslim woman ... or a gun-wielding Muslim woman whose Islamicity is summarized in a handkerchief to hide her hair while the fire of hatred hides all the gentleness and generosity that Islam has traditionally identified with womanhood ... (Nasr, 1987, 24).

---

23 As pointed out by many scholars of women and Islam, in various parts of the Qur'an both men and women are addressed. To know more about the historical context of this hermeneutic discourse, see Wadud, 1999; Stowasser, 1994; Murata, 1992.

24 The absence of the feminine and the importance of femininity are recurring themes in many of Fatima Mernissi's works. See Mernissi, 1990; 1991; 2001.

Ironically, in this footnote Nasr, for the first time in his traditionalist argument, seems to make concessions towards modernity in lieu of the revivalist's mistreatment of traditional norms. However, it is only a footnote.

The Emergence of Muslim Feminist Critique

Muslim scholars and activists who concern themselves with 'women and Islam' issues (being dissatisfied with both the traditionalist and revivalist gender-polarized solutions), have initiated intellectual and social trends marking a significant discontinuity from traditionalists' tendencies to monopolize the (re)construction of Islamic culture. With the influence of Islamic modernism, many of these voices have developed a 'Muslim' feminist critique. As pointed out by many scholars of women and Islam, there are many differences between Muslim feminism(s) and Western feminism(s), as reflected in the multi-faceted contextual influences of the twentieth century which ultimately had residual effects in the twenty-first century on Muslim societies (that is, colonialism, nationalism, revivalism/Islamism, secularism, imperialism, and cultural triumphalism); however, there are also many commonalities as seen in the protection of rights (divorce, inheritance, civic participation), the process of socio-historical contextualization, and the reform of legalistic structures and cultural norms (Yamani, 1996; Fernea, 1998; Moghissi, 1999; Badran, 2002). Although 'Islamic feminism' is not a monolithic methodology for questioning the effects of the patriarchal monopolization of authority – whether in the public sphere (for example, being the primary interpreters of Islamic texts, being the only Islamic jurists, being the political leaders) or the private sphere (for example, being the provider) – Islamic feminism, in general, is resistant to the subordination of women by conservative, traditionalist men.[25] If Islamic modernist reformism ushered in intellectual, ideational equality (modernism is often more of an academic than activist enterprise), it was Islamic feminism that called for the construction of egalitarian communities.

Gleaning (as well as emerging) from the 'pioneering' secular feminist activism and literature found throughout the Muslim world, Muslim feminist activism and literature is an increasingly 'global' reality, as pointed out by Margot Badran, a Research Fellow at the American Research Center in Egypt, Cairo:

> Islamic feminism is a global phenomenon. It is not a product of East or West. Indeed, it transcends East and West. As already hinted, Islamic feminism is being produced at diverse sites around the world by women inside their own countries, whether they be from countries with Muslim majorities or from old established minority communities. Islamic feminism is also growing in Muslim diaspora and convert communities in the West … Islamic feminism transcends and destroys old binaries that have been constructed. These include polarities between 'religious' and 'secular' and between 'East' and 'West' (Badran, 2002, 4).

---

25 Although the concept of 'Islamic feminism' has been used and defined by many scholars of women and Islam, most authors would agree on this point.

In the advocacy for both ideational and structural equality, Muslim feminist critique seeks the enablement or empowerment of Muslim women. The foundation of this 'empowerment' is a call for *women* to return to and *interpret* the primary Islamic textual sources (the Qur'an and the Hadith) as well as subsequent sources (that is, *Usul al-Fiqh* – the intellectual and scientific structure of *shari'ah*, Islamic law – from their own womanly perspectives. By claiming the right to interpret texts, women challenge existing hermeneutical understandings (textually and contextually) of Islamic history, authority, social structures, and gender relationships. Two women who have become bona fide champions of Muslim feminist critique from a transnational perspective are Fatima Mernissi and Leila Ahmed.

Fatima Mernissi, a Moroccan sociologist, is one of the foremost feminist interpreters of Islam and has been recently appointed to work with the new monarch of Morocco, King Mohammed VI, to help in the development of a discourse on human rights and civil society. In her well-known book, *The Veil and the Male Elite: A Feminist Interpretation of Women's Rights in Islam* (1991), Mernissi shares her own intellectual journey and discusses the obstacles in reinterpretation of textual as well as contextual discourses. She addresses both traditional biases within Islamic cultures and newer misunderstandings that reflect the influence of Western 'propaganda' on cultural identity.

In this hermeneutically oriented investigation, Mernissi questions traditions of misogyny within Islam. She meticulously examines the historical context of various controversial Qur'anic verses and Hadith sayings that encourage discrimination against women. She then compares and contrasts those verses or sayings with other verses and sayings that contradict them, and raises provocative questions about the intentions and reliability of some transmitters of traditional sayings.

While critiquing problems of deprivation and discrimination that affect women, Mernissi also demonstrates through hermeneutical analysis of the traditions and sayings that the Prophet Muhammad supported the empowerment of women to fully participate in the process of social reconstruction, banishing the pre-Islamic, discriminatory cultural and tribal traditions. She illustrates this point by describing the participatory roles women held at the time of the Prophet, especially focusing on the female figures who lived in the Prophet's household. Thus, her main argument can be summed up that Islam was created to usher in the construction of an egalitarian society based on the notion of individual responsibility. However due to the male elite's preoccupation with pre-Islamic tribalism, the Prophetic idealism of human rights and, in particular, women's rights was subsumed.

Sequels to her journey with the male elite continue as Mernissi develops recurrent themes of women and Islam in such works as *The Forgotten Queens of Islam* (1993) (a book about 15 female rulers and their influence for women in political Muslim public spheres), *Women's Rebellion and Islamic Memory* (1996) (a compilation of essays which explores the contemporary construction of Muslim sexual identity and its influence on the status of modern Muslim women), *Scheherazade Goes West: Different Cultures, Different Harems* (2001) (a complementary post-script to her autobiographical *Dreams of Trespass: Tales of a Harem Girlhood* (1994) which unveils the 'fatwas and harems' of the civilized West). In all of these writings, emphasis is placed on women's empowerment in and participatory engagement with Muslim society.

Although Mernissi received fame and recognition for her work on women and Islam, it is interesting to note that in the last four years she has been gradually changing her focus from supporting just women and Islam projects[26] to nurturing more civil society projects which encourage pluralistic debate and dialogue.

> Regardless of sex, the winners of the 21st century are definitely the dialogue-nurturers. Educated women armed with computers have defeated extremists by denying them monopoly to define cultural identity and interpret religious texts. Armed with information technology, women have engineered a pluralist reading of both religion and culture, highlighting humanist verses of the Koran which deny sacredness to violence (Mernissi, 2000).

Mernissi, in her booklet *The New Cheherazads: Women and Civil Society in Digital Islam* (2000), goes on to argue that these public dialogues are vital for the well-being of any civilized society because they provide a secure, distinctive space for confronting and eliminating discriminatory as well as violent religious and cultural traditions rooted in tribalism (as reminiscent of her earlier work, *The Veil and the Male Elite*). Ultimately, for Mernissi, these public dialogues support the empowerment of all individuals to fully participate in the processes of the Muslim public experience.

If Mernissi began a revolution in reclaiming women 'into' Islamic patriarchal history, it was Leila Ahmed who initiated a thorough critique of authority, women and Islam. Ahmed is an Egyptian-American Professor of Women's Studies and Islam at Harvard University. Her definitive work, *Women and Gender in Islam* (1992), is an historical analysis of the construction and (re)construction of conceptual as well as social meanings of women in Islamic social contexts. By tracing the Islamic formulations of gender as a social construction in both classical and contemporary periods, Ahmed sheds light on significant contextual patterns of gender subordination as well as alienation.

This intriguing exploration, which seeks to identify discursive formulations of androcentric behavior in early Islamic societies, provides an understanding of the complexity found in exchange between social contexts. According to Ahmed, this complex contextual exchange (especially Arab, Babylonian, Zoroastrian, Hellenic) ushered in new tendencies of patriarchal privileging. Basically, pre-Islamic Arab culture which demonstrated habits of privileging women became overwhelmed by 'other'/'outside' male-dominated norms and practices from the lands of Mesopotamia, Persia, and Byzantium. One particular practice that interested Ahmed (and has consequently influenced numerous scholars of women and Islam) was the emergence and persistence of the *hijab*, the veil. Quite controversially, Ahmed

---

26 As mentioned in Chapter 2, Mernissi literally states on her official website (<www.mernissi.net>) that 'as an academic researcher, I stopped working on women's issues since the Gulf War and switched to civil society as my major topic. Therefore, don't invite me anymore to speak on women's issues, I am the wrong person. Invite, instead, my colleagues, both men and women who are busy building women's studies units in Moroccan universities.'

argues that the veil only became mainstream in Islamic culture as a result of cultural diffusion from non-Islamic sources.

Not only did this authoritative work open new frontiers to question the limited access to and/or absence of women in all realms of Muslim public spheres, it also opened new ways of thinking about women and Islam as 'trans-'boundary constructions of pluralistic exchange and negotiation. Therefore, it is no wonder that Ahmed's latest work, *A Border Passage* (1999), focuses on her own border-crossing journey from Cairo to America. In it she explores the interpretive influences of her own identity and how she has been molded by a multiplicity of discourses. Her personal narrative provides a fascinating, reversed mirror-image account of her own historiography. Where her previous works emphasized historical analysis of the manner in which transnational influences on Arab-Islamic culture reinforced the patriarchal character of Islamic norms and introduced many new and stifling social institutions, the reflections contained in *A Border Passage* reveal how modern transnational realities opened her world to new ways of thinking about gender and equality.

Critique of Patriarchal Authoritative Hermeneutics

> The silent majority of Muslims want to find a voice and not leave the voice of Islam only to the conservative, so-called observant Muslims. We have arrived at the moment when there's enough people who have not spoken who feel it's time to speak, that I think we'll see quite the transformation, and we'll hear a whole variety of issues (Ahmed, 2000)[27]

> We're in the early stages of a major rethinking of Islam that will open Islam for women. [Muslim scholars] are rereading the core texts of Islam – from the Koran to legal texts – in every possible way (Ahmed, in Armario, 2004).

Hermeneutics, the art of interpretation, has defined and regulated the development of Islam, both as a theological doctrine and as a historical and cultural force. Traditional approaches to interpretation have favored an outlook of theological and normative stasis or 'crystallization,' whereas contemporary, modernist approaches tend to conceive of Islam in historical and dynamic terms. Through these two diametrically opposed viewpoints, Muslim scholars operating within the frameworks of established creedal schools of thought (Sunni and Shi'ite as well as Sufi Islam) have articulated and debated the intellectual, cultural and political implications of religious precepts for women.

Although the historical schools of Islamic thought differed and rare reformist examples can be identified, scholars operating within these schools generally adhered to and propagated the dominating traditionalist, patriarchal interpretation of Islamic precepts and practices, or else were silenced by it. However, with the rising

---

27 See the Ford Foundation Project's Religion and Culture: Meeting the Challenge of Pluralism website: <http://www.religionandpluralism.org/LeilaAhmed.htm>. In addition to her support of pluralism, Leila Ahmed has also been a leading voice in encouraging dialogue among civilizations, as reflected in her activism in bringing together over 100 scholars to sign an 'Open Letter to President Khatami' on 1 January 2000. See Ahmed, 2000.

influence of a multiplicity of factors related to social change (that is, modernization, globalization, industrialization, and so on), the last century has ushered in waves of secularism, revivalism and reformation throughout the Muslim world. Out of these waves, a variety of Muslim intellectuals and activists (with different labels as mentioned previously in the literature review) – both women and men – are now challenging the predominant, conservative interpretive practices by revisiting the historical, social, and cultural contexts of the 'traditionalist' interpretations, as well as analyzing the interaction of these interpretations with contemporary revivalist usages of the religious texts.

Particular effort has been made by a variety of Muslims to integrate the spatial and temporal dimensions of interpretation and to bring into focus the manner in which forces, historical and modern, are articulating with each other within bounded space. Many of these individuals seek to reframe the debate on Islamic cultural norms by creating new hermeneutical methods in order to present a viable alternative to patriarchal, conservative traditionalism. In doing so, although these Muslims may have different techniques for hermeneutical analysis, there is one distinctive characteristic in the Islamic modernist and postmodernist approaches to interpretation: the construction of sustainable ideational as well as structural equality for women and men.

Hermeneutical Traditionalist Tendencies

In the 'modern' traditionalist literature, scholars give particular attention to the role of interpretation, in which they generally reject and denounce the revivalist/ fundamentalist and modernist reinterpretations while upholding a premodern synthesis of hermeneutic practices and normative conclusions (Nasr, 1966, 93–118). Even though traditionalists accept that there are varying traditional interpretive tendencies, they advance the thesis that a coherent and generalizable 'traditionalist' model provides an ideal, comprehensive model for understanding and emulating the teachings of the Qur'an (holy scripture of Islam), Hadith (sayings by the Prophet), the Sunnah (traditions of the Prophet) and Fiqh (that is, early Muslim jurisprudential scholarship). These teachings, as traditionalists propose, can and should be applied to contemporary society, through adherence to specific historical practices. The traditionalist model then presents Islam in its classical form, and is therefore a more authentic expression of normative Islam, as reflected in the Qur'an and the example of the Prophet, than modernist, postmodernist, and revivalist/fundamentalist approaches. Although traditionalist arguments vary, they all have two hermeneutical methods in common: 1) reconstructing 'past originality'; and 2) a minimalist hermeneutics in which the interpreter suppresses textual ambiguities while claiming that the text 'speaks for itself.'

Traditionalists defend Islamic Law as interpreted by the five classical schools of Islamic thought (Hanbali, Maliki, Shafi, Hanafi, and Jafari), and maintain that its historically derived forms are completely providential – Divine. The Law (for traditionalists, this is not 'law' but 'Law') is the concretized Divine Will, and is *not* open to casual debate or pragmatic reform. This belief that the practice of the earliest believers and the interpretations of early generations of jurists provides the ideal model for contemporary society, especially for relations within the family and the community, reinforces an inevitably 'crystallized' view of the Law and the traditions supporting it. Emphasis is placed on the 'perceived' virtue of past Islamic communities, while modern Islamic communities are evaluated pejoratively for their failure to live up to the standards of their forebears. Therefore, present-day contexts, whether religious, social, political, cultural, or economic, are reconstructions of early Islamic communities.

This normative stasis as prescribed by traditionalist beliefs is best illustrated in the restrictions placed upon one controversial Islamic concept, *ijtihad* (independent juristic interpretation). Although most Sunni traditionalists believe that the 'doors of *ijtihad*' closed after the schools of thought were formed and fully institutionalized (approximately 700 or 800 years ago), there are others like Nasr who acknowledge the possibility of *ijtihad*, but only under the constraints of other traditional legal principles such as *qiyas* (analogical reasoning as defined by the intellectual elite), *ijma* (consensus of the intellectual elite), and *istihsan* (application of discretion in a legal decision). Unfortunately, these constraints severely undermine the potential of *ijtihad* by emphasizing obedience to deterministic concepts. However, the traditionalist argues for these constraints due to a strongly felt obligation to preserve authentic religious forms. 'Complete' knowledge is transmitted from generation to generation, with a priority placed on memorization and fidelity to the wisdom of great synthesizers of the past, resulting in a 'locked-in' mentality that penalizes innovation and prizes the legacy of past male scholarship and the heritage of received wisdom.

Many critics of the traditionalist approach particularly critique its 'atomistic' nature (Rahman, 1982; al-Hibri, 1982; an-Naim, 1996; Wadud-Muhsin, 1992). These critics suggest that traditionalism tends to universalize the particular (that is, to selectively generalize from specific historical practices, injunctions, and utterances) while offering no consistent methodological principle to justify the absence of contextualization, the suppression of textual richness, and the selectiveness that this approach entails (Wadud-Muhsin, 1992a, 2). By universalizing the particular, traditionalist interpretive practices have locked Muslims into narrow, rigid, and inflexible ways of defining their values and their identity. This absence of flexibility in interpretation has been cited as a core cause of the identity crisis that Muslims are experiencing today, particularly in relation to the role and status of women (Esack, 1997b; Abou El-Fadl, 2001; Barlas, 2002).

Tendencies of a New Hermeneutic Field

Such adherence to atomistic as well as fatalistic tendencies was deeply unsatisfying for one of the influential thinkers of modern Islamic hermeneutics, Fazlur Rahman (1919–88). One of the many positions Rahman held was on the Advisory Council of Islamic Ideology, a religious policymaking body in Pakistan which proposed policies for implementation by the Pakistani government. Although he met with great opposition and finally had to leave Pakistan in 1968, it was this practical experience of initiating political and legal reforms that encouraged Rahman, for the rest of his life, to advocate the transformation of a whole intellectual tradition.

In the decades since Rahman began his reinterpretive project, his works have become a major touchstone for emergent, transnational trends in Islamic interpretation. What draws many to Rahman is his ability to emphasize the need for a new opening of sacred texts, and for pluralistic exchange of opinions among scholars. By engaging Western as well as Islamic sources in a dynamic and innovative manner, Rahman provided an example that has given inspiration to many 'reformist' thinkers, especially but not only among women and educators. As in all of his books, Rahman poses his life-long question: 'How does Islam as a religious, cultural, political, and ethical heritage deal with a modernizing and rapidly changing world?' (Rahman, 2000, 4). This explicitly stated question relates closely to Rahman's other implicit preoccupations, which might be formulated in the following terms: 'How do Muslim scholars develop a viable Islamic humanism without becoming vulnerable to delegitimization by adherents of traditional fatalism?' 'How can a dialogic hermeneutics and historical method be developed wherein one can reevaluate the past and differentiate those practices which advanced Muslim society from those which resulted in stagnation?'

An important summation of Rahman's re-evaluation of Islamic methodology and hermeneutics, *Revival and Reform in Islam: A Study of Islamic Fundamentalism* (2000), was composed at the end of his life and reflects his most important contributions to scholarship. In this study of intellectual ferment within Islam, Rahman investigates, dissects and confronts the main tendencies of revivalist thought, which can be found at various stages of Islamic history and, more recently, in the period dating from the late 1800s, when scholar-activists such as Jamal al-Din Afghani, Muhammad Abduh and Qasim Amin sought to rethink Islam to make it a more relevant force in the modern world. Noting that the term 'fundamentalism' can apply to adherence to basic principles as opposed to haphazard affirmation of historically contextualized injunctions, Rahman seeks to reframe the debate on Islamic norms and hermeneutical methods and present a viable alternative to traditionalism.

Rahman rejects the revivalist tendency to superficially and selectively 'Islamize' externally derived knowledge systems. Revivalists, Rahman notes, are preoccupied with the dilemmas of reflecting or rejecting dominant Western cultural powers and corrupt secularized Muslim regimes. Although their interpretations resemble traditional tendencies (that is, static, atomistic, and selective practices), their approach is defensive in nature, populist in style, and often lacking in scholarly discipline. They aim to protect Muslim society against encroaching Western cultural and political power and attach specific symbolic importance to a reaffirmation of selected traditional interpretations and practices, which uphold a moral social order (for example, the appearance and role of women).

Although Rahman does not explicitly focus on women in this book, he does implicitly denounce the revivalists' view of the woman as a politicized symbol that represents both authentic, traditional Islamic values with contemporary socio-moral order. Unfortunately, instead of being a bridge between tradition and modernity, the woman is utilized as a political tool and manipulated in the struggle for cultural hegemony or political influence. His groundbreaking ideas would inspire generations of scholars, including many women interpreters, to challenge the status quo for women under Islamic traditional norms.

The approach advocated by Rahman aims at a comprehensive but internally derived overhaul of the Islamic intellectual tradition, not piecemeal adaptation or defensive maneuvering. Citing medieval sources and such influential philosophical thinkers as al-Ghazali and Ibn Taymiyya, Rahman challenges the static notion of *irja*, or predestination, as seen in both traditionalist and revivalist thought. He believed *irja* created a sense of moral apathy and degradation of Islamic intellectualism which in turn nurtured fatalistic doctrines of 'predeterminism' as well as 'concrete' (static, formalistic) attitudes of conformism. This 'uniformism' of Islam presented a monolithic ideal, effectively disregarding de facto Islamic diversity in thought and practice. Ultimately, such thinking impoverished theological and philosophical constructions of *tawhid* (unity of God or, from a philosophical perspective, the unity of existence), and reinforced both metaphysical absolutism and political docility in the form of 'unconditional obedience to the ruler, no matter if he be a tyrant, a transgressor against the law and usurps power' (Rahman, 2000, 80). Rahman, unlike contemporary traditionalists like Nasr, challenges the traditional fixation on authority and fatalism by demonstrating how the thoughts of two philosophers, al-Ghazali and Ibn Taymiyya, were terribly misconstrued and 'miserably truncated,' to such a point that their works were used to legitimize tyrannical practices (Rahman, 2000, 132).

Rahman claims that due to the lack of a comprehensive understanding or 'whole-text' learning, especially on topics of political authority, many political, fundamentalist, movements (for example, the Wahhabi movement in Saudi Arabia) have dangerously misrepresented certain philosophers' thinking by 'piecemealing' the philosopher's argument to their own political agenda. For instance, even though there are strong *irja* (deterministic) elements within the thought of Ibn Taymiyya (1263–1328), there are also counterparts to these elements, such as his extensive thought on free will. In his argument against the religious leaders of his day, Ibn Taymiyya pointed out how scholars tended 'to affirm the divine will but [did] not affirm wisdom and [affirmed] only [God's] all-compelling will (*mashi'a*) without affirming mercy (*rahma*), love (*mahabba*) and no gratitude [contentment] (*rida*)' (Rahman, 2000, 149). God's transcendent, omnipotent, qualities of commandments and prohibitions were emphasized, but immanent qualities were overlooked, resulting in a denial of human freedom. However, Rahman also stresses the fact that Ibn Taymiyya did not dismiss the concept of *irja*; rather, he was warning about the misuse of *irja*, that is, 'put[ting] determinism forward as an excuse for one's errors.' In summary, Ibn Taymiyya's ideal scenario was the synthesis between Divine responsibility and human responsibility.

Rahman argues that it is the duty of the philosophers to struggle with paradoxical realities, concepts, and sources within Islam. An attitude of passivity, as manifested in traditional master–student relationships, had no claim in the pursuit of knowledge and the development of the Islamic intellectual tradition. Therefore, Rahman reclassifies Islam in the twentieth century as 'neo-fundamentalist' Islam, a reconstruction of 'fundamental' or original precepts and practices within Muslim traditions in order to meet the challenges of contemporary Islamic societies.

In another famous book, *Islam and Modernity: Transformation of an Intellectual Tradition* (1982), through the process of reinterpretation, Rahman advocates a renewal of Islamic intellectualism as it relates to the moral improvement of humankind. In his historical investigation, which utilizes a *longue duree* approach, Rahman points out that traditional Islamic models of juristic reasoning, such as *qiyas* (analogical reasoning), greatly restricted the ability of Muslim intellectuals to apply Islamic values. These models were very atomistic in their hermeneutical approach (giving priority to injunctions without context, and without an integrated philosophical sense of underlying principles), preventing comprehensive analysis of the whole text of the Qur'an and resulting in the equation of Islamic values with specific historical practices. In other words, Muslims have long lacked a well-developed 'Qur'anic *Weltanschauung*' that might help them differentiate that which is essential and relevant to the demands of a situation from that which is not.

Rahman's reinterpretive hermeneutical process depends upon a 'double' intellectual movement: 1) formulating an understanding of the Qur'anic *Weltanschauung* (in terms of general principles) within its historical context; and 2) reevaluation of contemporary social and moral context(s) within which Islamic values may be applied. First, one must move from the concrete case treatments of the Qur'an – taking necessary and relevant social conditions of that time into account – to the general principles upon which the entire teaching converges. Second, from this general level there must be a movement back to specific legislation, taking into account the necessary and relevant social conditions (Rahman, 1982, 20).

Gleaning from the insights of Western hermeneuticists, in particular Hans-Georg Gadamer's principle of 'effective history,' Rahman stresses the importance of knowing our pre-determinations and questioning our self-awareness of historical influences. However, he also questions the reliability of 'whose' effective history is being asserted:

> This means that the process of questioning and changing traditions – in the interests of preserving or restoring its normative quality in the case of its normative elements – can continue indefinitely and that there is no fixed or privileged point at which the predetermining effective history is immune from such questioning and then being consciously confirmed or consciously changed. This is what is required for an adequate hermeneutical method of the Qur'an ... (Rahman, 1982, 11).

By pointing out the impermanent, ever-changing, nature of reality, Rahman challenges traditional, static tendencies and stresses the need for the development of an Islamic dynamism or an Islamic theory of social evolution. Such a theory would be based in his 'double' reform movement of historical context analysis and social and moral context analysis. One traditional belief was that if you cannot define a religious concept concretely and operationally (in terms of specific behavior demanded from it), it would tend to be avoided in practice, vanish from intellectual debate, or permit excessive scope for individual idiosyncracies. The concept of *ijtihad* ('the effort to understand the meaning of a relevant text or precedent in the past, containing a rule, and to alter that rule by extending or restricting or otherwise modifying it in such a manner that a new situation can be subsumed under it by a new solution'), independent juristic interpretation, provides a notable example (Rahman, 1982, 8). Due to its potentially boundless, individualistic nature, *ijtihad* could have been impossible to regulate. It contradicted the 'absolute authority' of the consensus of learned male elders, *ijma*. Rather than give free rein to individual interpretive efforts, jurists sought to restrict them and eventually proclaimed that the 'doors of *ijtihad*' had been closed. Rahman notes that, ironically, closing the doors of *ijtihad* implied closing the doors of intellectual *jihad* (striving) for both men and women. Ultimately, historical reflection and open debate were sacrificed to the fear of abandoning historical authenticity.[28]

According to Rahman, the obvious solution for reconciling tradition with modernity would result in the reformation of traditional educational practices that in turn – to use Gramscian terminology – becomes the reformation of the 'traditional' Islamic intellectual into the 'organic' intellectual. In his analysis, Rahman distinguishes between two directions of orientation for reform: 1) Islamizing modern secular education; and 2) modernizing Islamic education. The first movement he describes as 'classical modernism,' which can be viewed as a 'defense of Islam' against Western ideas, and the second movement he characterizes as 'contemporary modernism,' which is the rise of secular thought within Islam. Rahman favors the second orientation of the 'organic' intellectual, as a vehicle for meeting the changing needs of Islamic societies (that is, impact of globalization, modernization, secularization, industrialization, and cultivation of science and technology).

Interesting insights emerge when we juxtapose Rahman's project with the social and political thought of Antonio Gramsci. Antonio Gramsci's conceptions of political contestation, ideology, and 'organic intellectuals' have influenced many Muslim feminists (once again demonstrating the transnational character of 'Islamic' intellectual space). Although Antonio Gramsci stated that 'all *men* are intellectuals,' he also stated that 'although one can speak of intellectuals, one cannot speak of non-intellectuals, because non-intellectuals do not exist' (Gramsci, 1971, 9); hence, *men* may imply human (this, of course, could be a result of a translated oversight). Given his experiences in Pakistan, Rahman might agree with Gramsci that intellectuals are 'subaltern functionaries' of Islamic superstructures: they can either form and maintain a hegemonic state or construct and sustain a counter-hegemonic movement. Rahman and most reformist thinkers promote the idea that 'organic' reformist intellectuals play a key role in developing critical awareness, as well as actively engaging in the formation of political and ideological consensus. In addition, followers of Rahman's initiatives would go one step further and reinforce what was stated by Edward Said, who is greatly inspired by Gramsci's insights:

> … the intellectual is an individual with a specific role in society that cannot be reduced simply to being a faceless professional, a competent member of class just going about her/his business … [Instead,] the intellectual is an individual endowed with a faculty for representing, embodying, articulating a message, a view, an attitude, philosophy or opinion to, as well as for, a public (E. Said, 1994, 11).

---

28   There have been many individuals to follow and further develop Rahman's arguments about *ijtihad* debates (for example, Abdullahi An-Na'im, Azizah Al-Hibri). One of the more recent public discussions about *ijtihad* was at the United States Institute of Peace's workshop entitled 'Ijtihad: Reinterpreting Islamic Principles for the Twenty-First Century.' For a summary of this discussion, see the Special Report 125 on the USIP's website: <www.usip.org/pubs/specialreports/sr125.html> (accessed 26 February 2005).

Said clearly beseeches intellectuals to avoid the assimilated traps of 'subaltern functionaries' and give their active consent to counter-hegemonic movements by representing the 'weak and unrepresented' (E. Said, 1994, 22). This 'art of representing' in a critical manner is crucial for the emancipation of Muslim women. As stated by Said, 'the purpose of the intellectual's activity is to advance human freedom and knowledge' (E. Said, 1994, 17). Gleaning from the analysis of the intellectual by Gramsci and Said, other questions to explore in further research are raised: How organically developed are the intellectual strata of Islamic societies? What is the degree of connection that reformist intellectuals have with fundamental, traditional social groups? And how established are the gradations of their functions and of the gender-hegemonic superstructures?

Muslim Women as Contemporary Interpreters

A variety of Muslim reformist scholars of hermeneutics, under the influence of Fazlur Rahman's initiatives, are also challenging dominant contemporary traditional interpretive practices by revisiting the historical, social, and cultural contexts of the traditionalist interpretations, as well as analyzing the interaction of these interpretations with the contemporary revivalist intent of the religious texts. Their intent is to interpret by utilizing old and new hermeneutical techniques, to comprehensively understand divergent approaches to similar issues, and eventually to influence a 'reconstruction' of Islamic values and precepts that can be translated into contemporary Islamic social norms.

Despite the fact that dominant interpretive practice is based on traditional interpretations that for hundreds of years were regulated under the guidance of male scholarship, Muslim women interpreters are discovering that areas of traditional consensus do not exhaust the richness and potential range of interpretations that can be derived from core religious sources. Among the leading modern Muslim women interpreters are Amina Wadud and Asma Barlas.

If Rahman ushered in a new hermeneutic methodological framework, it is Amina Wadud who took his initiative and seriously applied it for women. Wadud, a Professor of Religious Studies at the University of Virginia, in the same spirit as other Muslim women intellectuals,[29] promotes the right for women to be 'an autonomous spiritual and intellectual human being who can effect a change in history' (Barazangi, 2000). However, spiritual and intellectual equality is only in its beginning phase as stated by Wadud:

> When Muslims grapple with the notion of equality for women here, the historical silencing of the female voices creates a gap. Understanding both effects of this gap and the nature of the missing female voice are useful to any consideration of how to correct the gender

29 Wadud, in a variety of ways, follows in the footsteps of one of the first modern women interpreters, Nazira Zein ad-Din, who was a strong advocate for women's rights and equality. In an article by Bouthaina Shaaban, she addresses the scarcity of women's voices in the realm of interpretation and discusses the contributions of a small number of Muslim women interpreters, like Nazira Zein ad-Din, who opened the 'unthinkable' for women as religious authoritative figures.

imbalance in Muslim practices … Considering the female voice within the Qur'an and female responses to the text … are in their initial stages (Wadud, 2000, 13 and 16).

In her well-received book, *Qur'an and Woman: Re-Reading the Sacred Text from a Woman's Perspective* (1999, second edition), Wadud – through the utilization of a hermeneutic methodology – argues for an 'holistic'/'*tawhid*' interpretation as an alternative approach to interpreting Islamic teachings on the role of women in society and gender equality. Reflecting Fazlur Rahman's idea of a Qur'anic *Weltanschauung*, holistic interpretation 'reconsiders the whole method of Qur'anic exegesis with regard to various modern social, moral, economic, and political concerns' (Wadud, 1999, 3).

In addition to her hermeneutical model based on a continuous aspiration to understand 'the whole-text' or 'worldview,' Wadud concentrates on historical context as well as grammatical composition and syntactical analysis. One example she utilizes on the topic of gender equality is the Qur'anic concept of *taqwa* (Islamic piety). As stated in the previously quoted Qur'anic verse 49:13 ('We created you male and female … that you may know one another. Indeed the most noble of you from Allah's perspective is whoever (he or she) has the most *taqwa*'), Wadud points out that distinctions between males and females are of little significance due to the fact that 'the distinguishing value from Allah's perspective' lies in the concept of *taqwa*, Islamic piety, or God-fearingness, or mindfulness of God:

> It is … important to understand how the Qur'an focuses on woman as an individual because the Qur'an treats the individual, whether male of female, in exactly the same manner: that is, whatever the Qur'an says about the relationship between Allah and the individual is not in gender terms … Allah does not distinguish on the basis of wealth, nationality, sex, or historical context, but on the basis of *taqwa*. It is from this perspective then that all distinctions between woman and woman, between man and man, and between woman and man, must be analyzed (Wadud, 1999, 34 and 37).

Through her analysis of *taqwa*, Wadud builds her argument against the traditional delineation of roles between men and women and the hierarchal, pre-ordained patriarchal intellectual system. She demonstrates that emphasis should be placed on 'human dignity, equal rights before the law and before Allah, mutual responsibility and equitable relations between humans,' rather than on the complementarity of men and women, which can be easily misconstrued (Wadud, 1999, 63). In defense of her arguments, Wadud shares her 'hands-on' experience of enabling women with the right to interpret the scripture for themselves while working with an organization called the Sisters in Islam (SIS) in Malaysia. SIS began to practice interpretation for themselves; interpretation became the basis for advocating reform and challenging the existing social structure of gender relationships (see Chapters 5 and 6 for more on SIS).

Additionally, in advocating an 'effective history' methodology, Wadud emphasizes the importance of reflexivity in advancing knowledge claims. In particular, she challenges the tendency to exalt past interpretations of holy texts, and notes that '*tafsir* [historical and contemporary commentary] is (hu)man-made and, therefore, subject to human nuances, peculiarities, and limitations' (Wadud, 2000, 11). She then goes a step further by advancing a dynamic rather than static concept of the divine principle, stating that, '… divine will is always in the process of becoming, humankind can only hope to gain direction toward that will by likewise being in process, never complete' (Wadud, 2000, 11). Therefore, Wadud not only challenges the methodological underpinnings of traditionalist Islam but also the ontological and epistemological foundations.

Wadud also not only advocates reform of traditional interpretive theory but also practice. In August 1994, Wadud was the first female invited to give a *khutbah*, a Friday sermon, at the Claremont Main Road Mosque in Cape Town, South Africa. The title of her sermon was 'Islam as Engaged Surrender' (Wadud, 2006). This experience of being an *Imam*, a leader of Muslim prayer, would foreshadow another 'groundbreaking' event on 18 March 2005. On this day, Wadud led a *khutbah* of the first formal mixed-gender congregation (about 80–100 Muslim women – both wearing the veil and not – and men) at the Cathedral of St John the Divine in New York City. According to many newspapers and on-line resources, this event has 'caused quite a stir' among Muslims around the world (Lampman, 2005; El-Tablawy, 2005; Amanuallah, 2005). Some Muslims view it as 'heresy,' while others applaud it as 'positive reform.' Unfortunately, Wadud's activism for gender equality came with grave personal consequences, such as: Wadud's teaching contract with the Department of Islamic Revealed Knowledge at the International Islamic University was not renewed as a result of her activism with Sisters in Islam in Malaysia; Wadud has been threatened by some members of the Muslim community in Virginia to have her fired from her position at the Virginia Commonwealth University; and, recently, there are some Muslims who want to sue her and strip her of her title as a 'Muslim.'[30] These extreme reactions beg the question, 'Whose Islam has the authority to place in exile any one individual or group?'

Wadud's reinterpretive work has influenced many Muslim women; some of the more prominent women, who are also authors and activists, are Asra Nomani, Raheel Raza, Farzana Hassan, and Asma Barlas.[31] As stated by Wadud in an interview, these women are furthering her work in new ways, and she particularly noted that Barlas' book, *'Believing Women' in Islam: Unreading Patriarchal Interpretations of the Qur'an*, is extending her hermeneutical scholarship of gender equality to new levels.

---

30   There were many reactions, especially toward the event in New York City. One individual is quoted as saying:

We American Muslims in New York should sue in court for libel and slander, to force them to stop calling themselves 'Muslims'. If this lady and her troupe were to do this whilst calling themselves 'Jehovah's Witnesses', just watch how fast they would be slapped with a lawsuit!'

For more reactions, see <www.altmuslim.com> and <www.muslimwakeup.com>.

31   In particular, Nomani, Raza, and Hassan have been strong and more controversial voices for reform of Muslim women's role in the religiously authoritative sphere, especially when it comes to women leading prayers to mixed congregations. For more on their individual projects, see <www.asranomani.com>, <www.raheelraza.com>, and <www.farzanahassan. com>.

Barlas, a Professor and Chair of Politics at Ithaca College, is another Muslim woman intellectual who has paid a high price for raising her voice and challenging patriarchal authority. As stated on the Center for the Study of Islam and Democracy's website:

> Barlas was born in Pakistan, where she was one of the first women to be inducted into the Foreign Service. Her career was cut short, however, when General Zia ul Haq fired her for criticizing his military regime. She then joined an opposition paper, *The Muslim*, as assistant editor but was forced to leave the country for the US in 1983 where she later got political asylum.[32]

In *'Believing Women' in Islam*, Barlas offers even more historical analysis than Wadud of the patriarchal enterprise of Qur'anic interpretation as framed within intertextual discourses (that is, the Sunnah, the *shari'ah* and the state).[33] By arguing for not only a *holistic* (*tawhidi*), but also a post-patriarchal, reading of the Qur'an, Barlas implicitly asks, 'What is patriarchy and how does it influence Qur'anic interpretation?' 'What can women offer to new interpreted Qur'anic models?' 'Is a Muslim woman's experience of the Qur'an different and/or how is this difference valued?[34]

Whereas the traditional hermeneutical approach directs all attention to the authoritative text while ignoring questions about *who* is interpreting and under what circumstances, Barlas' approach balances the claims of the text with consideration of the needs and existential circumstances of the Muslim society and its interpreters. She, like many of her colleagues, focuses on the interaction between text, interpreter, and context.

Gleaning from many contemporary Muslim thinkers (for example, Mohammad Arkoun and Abdol Karim Soroush) who emphasize subjective pre-understandings, Barlas calls for the reflexive contextual understanding of one's place in the world. By understanding oneself through self-reflexivity, one becomes able to penetrate how others see the world, and to open up ways of understanding the crises confronting the

---

32   See <http://www.islam-democracy.org/barlas_bio.asp>. Currently, Asma Barlas is also a member of the board for the Center for the Study of Islam and Democracy (CSID). For more about her background and writings, see Barlas' personal website at <http://www.ithaca.edu/faculty/abarlas/index.htm>.

33   To understand how Wadud's scholarship and activism has influenced Barlas, see Barlas, 2004, 97–123.

34   These questions are reminiscent of Wadud's experience:

Mercifully, the more research I did into the Quran, unfettered by centuries of historical androcentric reading and Arabo-Islamic cultural predilections, the more affirmed I was that in Islam a female person was intended to be primordially, cosmologically, eschatologically, spiritually, and morally a full human being, equal to all who accepted Allah as Lord, Muhammad as prophet, and Islam as *din*. What remained was to advocate the details of this research as legitimate grounds for contesting the unequal treatment that women have experienced historically and continue to experience legally in the context of Muslim communities ... It will also be my task to emphasize how a Qur'anic hermeneutics that is inclusive of female experiences and of the female voice could yield greater gender justice to Islamic thought and contribute toward the achievement of that justice in Islamic praxis (Wadud, 1999, ix–x).

other (Barlas, 2002, 1). Being conscious of one's own contextual relativity is a basis for understanding the pluralism of contextual particularisms.

According to Barlas, the Qur'anic text must be continually interpreted but in accordance with the interpreter's present situation, both textually and contextually. This dynamic, intersubjective, as well as intertextual, approach allows for the interpreter to mediate his or her own customary 'pre-understandings' of a text (for example, patriarchal prejudices) with present-day contexts. This intersubjective process is elaborated by a colleague of Barlas, Khaled Abou El-Fadl, the Omar and Azmeralda Alfi Distinguished Fellow in Islamic Law at UCLA in California:

> To what extent do I, as the reader, decide the meaning of the text? To what extent are my sensibilities and subjectivities determinative in constructing the text's meaning? ... Should the reader focus on the intent of the author and consider the author's intent determinative as to the meaning of the text? Isn't this more respectful towards the author, especially when the author is divine? ... Does it make sense to talk of the author's subjectivities in the case of a divine authorship? ... If God chose to communicate through an objective linguistic medium how will this medium interact with human subjectivities or even idiosyncrasies? ... Am I bound or limited by the communities of meaning that have been generated around the text? (Abou El-Fadl, 2001, 4).

Barlas, like Abou El-Fadl and many other young scholars evoking reform in Islam, such as Farid Esack[35] and Omid Safi[36] (to name just a couple), is utilizing a critical Islamic interpretation to seek answers that are contextually appropriate, fulfill individualistic human needs, and enable the human being to reach his or her full potential. Whereas traditionalist interpreters manifest interest in bringing dialogue to a close through arrival at an authoritative male consensus or ruling, these critical interpreters agree with Amina Wadud that interpretation can never be over.

Through their questioning, a common pattern is developing: each is searching and promoting a new reflexive methodology. They seek to reinterpret religious traditions *holistically*, in terms of overarching as well as overlooked textual and

---

35 South African scholar and former Commissioner for Gender Equality, Farid Esack, in *Qur'an Liberation and Pluralism: An Islamic Perspective of Interreligious Solidarity Against Oppression* (1997b), agrees with Wadud and Barlas that 'one cannot escape from the personal or social experiences which make up the sum of one's existence' (Esack, 1997b, 12). However, Esack adds to Wadud and Abou El-Fadl's questions by implicitly asking, 'What is an "authentic" understanding of the Qur'anic message in present-day realities?' 'What creates and shapes "authenticity"?' 'How legitimate is it to produce meaning, rather than extracting meaning, from Qur'anic texts?' (Esack, 1997b, 13). In the case of women, Esack beseeches women to undertake a 'gender jihad,' encouraging women to not succumb to the aggregate consequences of traditionalist thinking (Esack, 1997b, 239). It is interesting to note that Esack's idea of 'gender jihad' would re-emerge in Amina Wadud's latest book, entitled *Inside the Gender Jihad: Women's Reform in Islam*.

36 Omid Safi is a Professor of Religious Studies at Colgate University and is the current Director of the Progressive Muslim Union of North America. His edited publication, *Progressive Muslims: On Justice, Gender and Pluralism* (2003), is a definitive work in the understanding of the new Muslim epistemic community of 'progressive Muslims.' For more information about this community, see note 7 in this chapter._

contextual values, in order to articulate understandings that promote not only the empowerment of women, but also the initiation of reflexive change of Muslim societies. Such reflexivity encourages open dialogue among Muslims in search of forms of present-day originality that do not reduce the meaning of Islam to specific historical practices.

For Barlas and Wadud, Muslims must reformulate their understandings of early and medieval Islam, extract essential Islamic values, principles, and goals from the root sources, and move beyond legalistic reduction towards a more integrated, systematic, and reflective methodology. Basically, Muslims must carefully examine relations between the sacred text and the contemporary, experiential contexts in which precepts must be translated into practice. Articulating the role of hermeneutics through which the Qur'anic ethos could be grasped as a dynamic whole, these scholars provide a compass for the application of Islamic values to modern problems. In these efforts, a new hermeneutic field is beginning to emerge and challenge both the traditionalist and revivalist persistence of patriarchal certitude.

Conclusions

Though reformist and philosophical approaches to Islamic interpretation are still struggling for popular recognition and religious legitimacy, an increasing number of lay Muslim thinkers are finding 'academic' reasoning about Islam relevant both to their own social change efforts and to their personal search for meaning – for an 'open' Islamic identity that can be reconciled with strongly felt needs for change and contemporary relevance. As will be demonstrated in subsequent chapters, complex philosophical arguments – about reason and revelation, principle and form, and the relevance of time, context, and place to religious practice – are informing the activities of activists and thinkers in many corners of the Islamic world. The politics of Islamic reform, like Islam itself, is a transnational process, in which both ideas and actions matter.

As Muslim women seek to come to terms with the many tensions and oppositions that shape their cultural and intellectual landscapes, many are finding transnational engagement to be a powerful source of inspiration and strength. The remainder of this study will seek to illustrate the significance of 'the transnational' for a remarkable and internally diverse sample of dynamic Muslim activists – most of whom are women – by exploring the following questions:

1. How are Muslims who concern themselves with reformist approaches to the status of women conceiving of transnationalism? What does transnationalism *mean* to them, and how does it affect their perceptions of identity and social agency?
2. Is transnationalism facilitating the efforts of these Muslim activists and intellectuals to become agents of interpretation and social change? What aspects of transnationalism do these Muslims find most empowering or

significant?

3. To what extent are Muslims who engage in 'women and Islam' debates experiencing a 'hermeneutic turn'? Are explicit ideas about Islamic hermeneutics shaping their identities and strategies? Does transnational dialogue play a constitutive role in the formation of their ideas?

4. How do contemporary interpreters and advocates of 'progressive' reform respond to cultural and geographical dichotomies that have restricted the scope and character of Islamic identity – dichotomies that oppose the Islamic and the Western?

The search for answers to these questions requires direct interaction with contemporary interpreters, in a manner that elicits personal narratives as a basis for analyzing the impact of experiences with transnational dialogue.

Chapter 4

Identity and Interpretation: Dialogue and the Negotiation of Meaning

In the previous chapter, our discussion ended with a series of questions about the manner in which transnational encounters are shaping the identity and hermeneutics of Muslim women activists. To what extent are the identities and ideas of these women *transnationally constituted*? Does transnational dialogue facilitate their efforts to become effective advocates for Muslim women? To what extent are transnational conversations about Islamic hermeneutics relevant to the work of these activists? Can participation by otherwise 'isolated' Muslim women in these conversations increase their capacity to overcome traditional cultural and geographical dichotomies that have opposed 'authentic' Islamic identities to 'alien' ways of being, and thereby limited possible ways of understanding and interpreting Islam?

In the present chapter, I will use testimony from interviewees to discuss key dilemmas pertaining to *identity formation*, *intellectual outlook*, and *social values* as perceived by public intellectuals and activists with whom I met during the course of my research. Recollections and observations of my interviewees suggest that:

- Though Muslim women's activists (a category which is not exclusive of men) in a wide range of settings are all struggling with competing 'Islamic' paradigms of traditionalism and modernism, a surprising number articulate strong ambivalence about this and other dichotomies. Almost all of my interviewees expressed personal resistance to being labeled in relation to popular categories.
- With respect to identity and worldview, there is a tendency to reject 'either/or' choices and oppositions in favor of various 'both/and' reformulations. Many see themselves as 'living between "isms,"' through participation in dialogical relations with 'others' of many varieties.
- Most interviewees reported that transnational conversations were not important to them for 'instrumental' reasons alone; dialogue across borders had been constituted of their respective outlooks and identities.

Though there are obvious limits to the generalizability of conclusions generated from my encounters, it is undeniable that many Muslims engaged in transnational conversations about the status of women are coming to view dialogue not only as a mundane basis for conversation and networking, but also as an *ethos* that has profound implications for *epistemology* (hermeneutics) and *identity*.

Before offering testimony from interviewees, I will first discuss 'normative systems' that are shaping the values and identities of contemporary Muslims. I will focus particular emphasis on a tension to which contemporary Muslim intellectuals often attest, between traditional/religious outlooks and those which might be characterized as modern/secular. After noting <u>bases</u> within the <u>Islamic intellectual tradition for dealing with such clashes of social vision</u>, I will proceed to explore commentary from my encounters on the *meaning* of the 'dialogues' with which they are engaged – dialogues that, as it turns out, are very much concerned with traditional–modern tensions, and within which many interpreters are seeking new answers. These answers include a search for paradigms that might potentially transcend or reframe the traditional–modern dichotomy and provide a basis for an 'open' or 'dialogical' identity, as well as for more dynamic and pluralistic bases for engaging in social relations – beyond the confines of established categories.

The Construction of Muslim Meaning:'In-Between' Tradition and Modernity Competing Paradigms

To understand <u>contemporary</u> Muslim intellectualism, it is essential to develop a clear understanding of <u>tensions</u> between <u>two competing worldviews</u>: the 'traditional/ religious' worldview and the 'modernist/secular' worldview. Each perspective may be characterized as a normative system or 'paradigm' that shapes Muslim identities and values, and that provides standards for authority, authenticity, and societal norms.

The traditional/religious <u>normative</u> system is <u>basically</u> a past-oriented system of meaning that <u>appeals</u> to historical conceptions of Muslim identity – historical conceptions that are conceived as both authentic and as authoritative for today's world. In this traditional/religious paradigm, which I will henceforth describe as 'traditionalist,' standards of meaning and value derive from 'past originality' – that is, from understandings of cultural and religious texts that have been passed down from authoritative past exemplars. <u>Proud obedience</u> to rulings derived from historical consensus is the <u>basis</u> for one's authenticity as a Muslim, and hence for one's standing in Muslim communities and families. As contemporary Muslim women interpreters frequently note – and as many traditionalist interpreters are not hesitant to acknowledge – authoritative standards reflect a patriarchal ethos and accentuate traditional 'male' virtues, particularly in the public sphere (see Chapter 3 for a more detailed exploration of Muslim feminist perspectives).

Figure 4.1 provides a schematic representation of the interlocking core premises of the traditionalist paradigm: patriarchal authority, as projected by male political and religious leaders, delineates an *a priori* normative consensus about revealed and inherited Muslim standards of value and virtue, together with an ideal of Islamic historical identity that seeks to determine the basis for contemporary authenticity. The existence of a historically transmitted normative consensus, in turn, provides reinforcement for patriarchal authority and for the narratives upon which authentic Muslim identity are based. Finally, the existence of a putatively fixed sense of historical Muslim identity provides support for the idea of unproblematic, revealed standards and for conceptions of leadership and authority. Each element in the

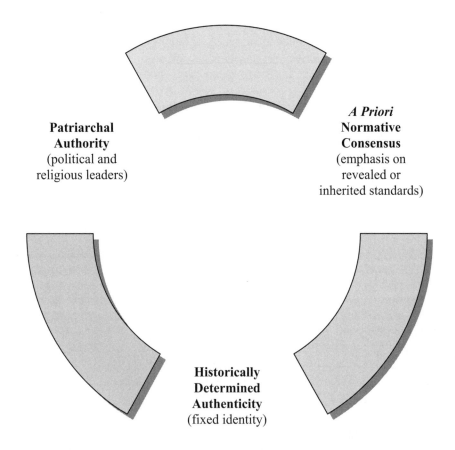

**Patriarchal
Authority**
(political and
religious leaders)

***A Priori*
Normative
Consensus**
(emphasis on
revealed or
inherited standards)

**Historically
Determined
Authenticity**
(fixed identity)

Figure 4.1 Identity, authority, and norms: the traditionalist paradigm

authority–consensus–authenticity triad reinforces and co-constitutes the other elements.

Traditionalist hermeneutics has emphasized tradition as a stabilizing mode of being in the world.[1] The task of the traditionalist interpreter is to preserve, transmit, and police a sense of bounded identity and political community. He (and, in some cases, she) must seek to attain and maintain consensus on a set of authoritative texts, and on definitive interpretations of their meaning. A principle of bounded interdependence – which conceptualizes and regulates notions of 'authenticity' as the aspiration to maintain independence vis-à-vis adversary groups – is maintained by efforts to delimit a 'canon' whose meaning cannot be enriched through dynamic engagement with the texts of other cultures, especially those of the modern West.

---

1 It is important to acknowledge the complexity of 'tradition' and how it has been defined by different scholars. For more on the function of tradition as 'a stabilizing force,' see Berkey, 2002.

In contrast, the modernist paradigm is a largely future-oriented system of meaning that highlights the agency of the individual in the negotiation of normative standards and in the construction of social identity and meaning. Identity and value are constructed rather than inherited or revealed. Historical conceptions and standards are subjected to tests of rationality, expediency, and contemporary relevance, regardless of their past status or prestige. Authority, in turn, is contested and polycentric, with intellectual difference and plurality perceived as inevitable and, in some cases, desirable: there is greater scope for individual subjectivity, at least with respect to non-scientific, non-technical matters such as the derivation of textual meaning and the definition of individual preferences and values. Social values, however, are expected to correspond with an increasingly secular ethos, in which progress and productivity in the material world are prized far more than personal religious values and metaphysical beliefs. Professional accomplishment and educational credentials become important bases for the definition of individual identity, and for achieving status in society. As many Muslim feminists are aware, the modernist ethos erodes traditional patriarchy and seeks to homogenize gender roles within the context of civil society. Like traditionalism, it is a paradigm that is both transnational and localized in its manifestations.

Figure 4.2 offers a schematic representation of core premises within the modernist paradigm: polycentric authority, derived from multiple and contending sources, develops a negotiated and approximate sense of normative consensus within society – a set of basic rules and behavioral expectations. Because authority is more diffuse than in the traditional paradigm, authenticity becomes more fluid and contextualized. Society's negotiated normative consensus, in turn, is expected to reinforce the principle of intellectual pluralism (within disciplinary boundaries established by various fields of technical or expert competence) and to provide overarching templates for individual political loyalties, such as nation-states and political parties. Ethnic and cultural identities, though not erased, are subjected to greater scrutiny by the individual. Finally, recognition that identities are not historically fixed reinforces the idea that normative standards must be continually re-negotiated, and that authoritative status must ideally be 'earned' through various forms of demonstrated competence.

Modernist hermeneutics has challenged traditional understandings of religious truth and cultural meaning through what some individuals call a 'subjective revolution.' A strong proponent of a purely 'secular and subjective turn' for Arabs (in particular) is the well-known Arab poet, Adonis. In an article entitled 'An Arab Poet Who Dares,' in *The New York Times* by Adam Shatz, 13 July 2002, Adonis states,

> We live in a culture that doesn't leave space for questions ... It knows all the answers in advance. Even God has nothing left to say! ... What the Arab world needs, more than anything ... is a 'revolution of subjectivity' that would emancipate people from tradition. Until this inner revolution occurs ... Arabs would know only secondhand modernity, a dangerous brew of hollow consumerism, rigged elections and radical Islam ... There is no more culture in the Arab world. It's finished. Culturally speaking, we are a part of Western culture, but only as consumers, not as creators.

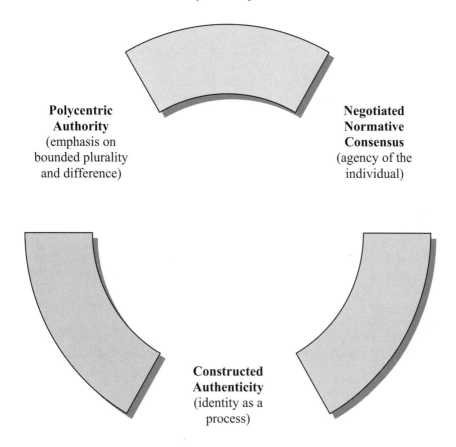

**Polycentric
Authority**
(emphasis on
bounded plurality
and difference)

**Negotiated
Normative
Consensus**
(agency of the
individual)

**Constructed
Authenticity**
(identity as a
process)

Figure 4.2 Identity, authority, and norms: the modernist paradigm

Because metaphysical questions are beyond the bounds of modern scientific epistemology, they become matters of individual agency and choice. Difference and plurality become primary modes of relating to the world. Instead of just focusing on the processes of the 'signified' (in religion, the ideals and realities described symbolically in religious texts), emphasis is placed on the 'signifier' itself – on *claims* as much as on that which is claimed. As Farid Esack pointed out at a conference on cultural diversity and Islam, modern (and, indeed, postmodern) discourse on Islam produces a change in the basic questions that are asked about religion and religious truths: 'From what Islam? To what Muslim?' (Esack, 2003, 165–85). Religion is no longer viewed as a monolithic reality with uncontestable truth claims. As my interviews (see below) suggest, many believers find this new openness – the idea of 'multiple Islams' – liberating, while others distrust the accompanying worldview, with its deep unease with metaphysics and polycentric lack of 'moral absolutes' and intellectual certainties.

The advent of modernity and of 'modernist' outlooks has introduced a number of new questions into discourse about Islamic identity and norms, and a great deal of tension. What follows is a brief list of some of these questions:

- Why has Muslim tradition (that is, *taqlid*) been historically perceived as permanent closure instead of as a continual disclosure? In other words, why cannot *taqlid* be understood as a process of sustained negotiation that is open-ended?
- Must modernity be conceptualized as a rational, non-transcendent Western age?
- Why has communication across the boundaries of Western/modern/secular vs. Islamic/traditional/religious dichotomy been so problematic?
- Why is it that the mere effort to sympathetically represent the views and concerns of a Muslim from a competing worldview is sometimes regarded as an act of disloyalty, or even as a form of treason?
- Must Muslim identity remain bounded to an 'us' vs. 'them,' 'traditionalist' vs. 'modernist' (or, as the case may be, 'reformist' or 'revivalist') contrast?

Though scholars and cultural commentators have proposed answers to such questions, the gap between 'modern' and 'traditional' paradigms is not easily bridged, and many Muslims continue to feel 'pulled' in opposite directions (see Figure 4.3), toward idealized recollections of the past and projections of a progressive but largely non-religious future.

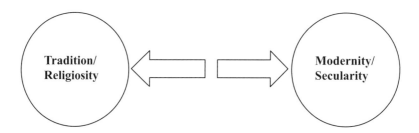

Figure 4.3 Competing normative systems

For many Muslims, meaning and identity formation are constructed through the experience of and negotiation between tradition and modernity. There is a politics of interpretation: How can a Muslim uphold his/her tradition which was given by his/her own familial hermeneutic circle while at the same time experiencing tradition as a living, modern reality? Are tradition and modernity truly irreconcilable? Can dialogue between Muslims who feel allegiance to differing paradigms produce more than threats to the very values upon which their respective social identities are founded?

These questions loomed large in the minds of many of the individuals whom I encountered. A surprising number, however, questioned the manner in which the 'traditionalist–modernist' dichotomy has ordinarily been framed. Rather than perceiving traditionalism and modernism as bounded camps or as mutually exclusive ideologies, many experienced the two paradigms as competing normative systems, each of which held out promise and problems – bases for allegiance and bases for independence. Some sought to problematize certain premises of each paradigm, particularly the exclusive identification of modernity with secularism, and of tradition with religiosity. After all, were there not exemplars of more secular visions in the past? And cannot there be some basis for religiosity in the modern world?

The world of hermeneutical negotiations and identity debates described during my encounters suggests the possibility of another, more differentiated schema for representing the normative systems that contemporary Muslim interpreters – especially those dealing with the status of women – must negotiate as they form their identities and worldviews. This schema is depicted in Figure 4.4.

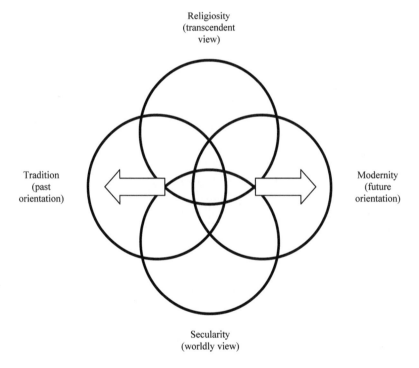

Figure 4.4 **'Transnational dialogue': negotiating contemporary Muslim identity**

Figure 4.4 suggests that Muslim interpreters are faced not only with choices between traditional and modern orders and orientations, but also between secular and religious visions that may be found within as well as between these two tendencies. While different Muslim thinkers tend to gravitate in one direction or another, the push and pull of competing tendencies is experienced by most as a constant. Most Muslims do not simply live 'in' tradition or 'in' modernity; rather, they dwell 'in between' these two poles, as well as 'in between' their secular and religious ideas. To a considerable extent, the norms of daily life in contemporary Muslim societies are forged through conversations among the exponents of these competing ideas. Constructive efforts to come to terms with the rival claims necessarily require dialogue.

Dialogue: Its Meaning for Muslim Identity

'Sharing of Logos': Understanding-With

My encounters with a wider range of activists and intellectuals revealed no definitive consensus on the meaning of dialogue or the practice of hermeneutics. The current cultural and intellectual divisions among Muslim thinkers were quite apparent. Despite disparities and tensions, however, I did discover a number of cross-cutting themes pertaining to the meaning of *dialogue* for Muslim identity.

Ever since Plato began recording his reflections on the teachings of Socrates, 'dialogue' has been a central fixture in academic life. All of Socrates and Plato's knowledge was conveyed through the form of dialogue. Through the act of dialoguing – of searching for knowledge and wisdom through direct, person-to-person encounters – Socrates set a precedent that, though often celebrated, has seldom been perceived as an epistemological or methodological model. Even in the fields of philosophy and social sciences, the 'Socratic method' is more often viewed as a teaching device (whereby the 'learned' professor tests the knowledge of students) than as an actual means of knowing. For Socrates, however, dialogue was a means of bringing the search for knowledge into everyday life through conversation and constantly being 'in relation' with others.[2] To be in relation was to be in dialogue. In other words, knowledge was not so much a commodity that can be accumulated as a pursuit of wisdom and transformation. The pursuit of meaning, or *logos*, was a constant process of construction and negotiation within the context of relationships.[3]

---

2   It is interesting to point out that Plato warned in the book of *Phaedrus* that the written can destroy 'the living soul,' implying that a written text is susceptible to being dead whereas the oral word through human dialogue is alive and open to further examination. In comparison, the significance of the 'oral' in the construction of early Muslim identity was also emphasized over the written. 'Living memory' of conversations was not to be lost to simple repetition. For more about dialogue in Plato's works and in Qur'anic experience, see Fischer and Abedi, 1990, 120–53.

3   Ultimately, Socrates was skeptical about the prospects for accumulating the variety of knowledge sought by social scientists, expressing more confidence in his ability to know love – that which dwells in-between the cognized and the cognizer. It is interesting to note that throughout the writings of Plato, Socrates only mentions one teacher: Diotima of Mantineia, 'a wise woman' who taught him 'the only subject in which [he] professed to have any knowledge,' that being 'love' (Plato, 1993, 6) According to Diotima, 'Love is the mean between wisdom and ignorance ... [it] is the power which interprets and conveys to the gods the prayers and sacrifices of men, and to men the commands and rewards of the gods; and this

Even though dialogue can be seen as the root of Western intellectual traditions (that is, for it is in the act of dialoguing that knowledge claims are to be questioned rather than blindly accepted), only recently are we beginning to see a 'hermeneutic (re)turn' to dialogical thinking. The word is now acquiring renewed meaning for increasingly diverse groups of people, from philosophers and peace educators to international relations theorists.[4] In contrast to the popular notion that 'knowledge is power,' a variety of Muslims whom I encountered perceived knowledge as something that must be created through dialogue. For them, knowledge for human agency is derivative of relationships – of dialogical ways of knowing, being, and doing.

It is arguable that the eagerness of many interviewees to respond to questions about dialogue reflects not only their training and intellectual outlooks as individuals, but also the many challenges of their social milieus. To be concerned with matters pertaining to Muslim women is to encounter profoundly anti-dialogical tendencies in society. Muslim activists and intellectuals – especially those engaged in conversations about the status of women as 'authorities' in Muslim societies – have long been marginalized from authoritative social discourse about values and norms. Their efforts to enter into discussions about these values and norms put them in contention with powerful forces – not only those of traditionalism, but also those of modernism and secularism, constructed along Western lines. In effect, the intellectual 'battle lines' between traditional and modernist paradigms have been quite rigidly drawn, and women enter the discourse primarily as objects of discussion – as symbols of tradition or modernity – rather than as subjects. Insofar as it can be actualized and achieved, dialogue affords more 'non-traditional' (but not necessarily anti-traditional) women and men with a means of transcending their marginalization and exclusion from authoritative social discourse. It also provides a means of generating new (or renewed) meanings that they somehow 'own' because they have participated in the processes of creation or discovery – meanings that are somehow 'sacred' even when they are not explicitly religious in content. It also provides them with a means of safely encountering and engaging with the many differences that divide Islamic societies.

As I engaged Muslim thinkers and activists in a dialogue about dialogue, three key themes became apparent:

- Open identity: dialogue provided a means of enhancing knowledge about self and others, in an atmosphere that suspended standard tropes of self-referential discourses about identity.
- Dynamism: dialogue created a quality of active engagement with a world 'in

---

power spans the chasm which divides them, and in this all is bound together...'(Plato, 1993, 26).

4   Given the contemporary volume of writing about dialogue, it would appear that the Greek word *dialogos* is experiencing a renaissance (however, the act of dialoguing is still under construction). See the works of such philosophers as: David Bohm, 1990; Hans Georg Gadamer, 1998; and M. Bakhtin, 1981. See the works of such peace educators as: Raimon Panikkar, 1996; and Fred Dallmayr, 2002. See also the work of the international relations theorist Xavier Guillaume, 2002a and 2002b.

motion'.

- Relationship: dialogue enabled shared meaning across diverse cultural texts and contexts.

Open Identity

> Dialogue depends on flexibility and creativity. The sense of dialogue is to lose a fixed positioning; rather dialogue enables one to move from functional fixedness to the openness of creativity.

> [Khamseh further elaborated that] the core personality of everyone is shaped in-relation to others. There is no single self. There is no monologue. The self is comprised of a variety of dialogues.

In the above quotation, Akram Khamseh, a Professor of Psychology and Women at al-Zahra University in Tehran, Iran (a women's school that can fairly be described as one of the more conservative institutions of higher learning for women in Iran), stressed both the intrinsic importance of dialogue and the value of embracing an open-ended approach to it.[5] To many interviewees, including Khamseh and many of her colleagues at al-Zahra University's Women's Research Center, dialogue meant assuming an attitude of 'principled openness' to others, and to the ways in which they perceive oneself and one's own canon of cultural texts and assumptions. Only through openness could dialogue provide new experiences and insights. A. Pakniam, a colleague of Khamseh at al-Zahra University, added that: 'I believe in the construction of the world and that human beings are one world. There is no difference between the United States, Iraq, and Iran. We live together … We need to make life for the good of all human beings. If you think peacefully, there will be peace … all problems come from attitude.' Additionally, Ali-Reza Ahmadi, the only male colleague at al-Zahra University's Women's Research Center, stressed the importance of thinking in terms of 'open-ended relations' when defining concepts such as dialogue.

Openness to dialoguing signifies a readiness to actively 'trans-act' with the other, the stranger. This idea was recollected quite clearly in the following encounter with Farida Shaheed, who currently helps to direct Shirkat Gah and Women Living Under Muslim Laws (WLUML):[6]

> Dialogue is the act of engaging with the other: to understand the other's point of view without necessarily coming to any definite end. It is different than negotiation and

---

5   Akram Khamseh, interview by author, 29 May 2004, at al-Zahra University's Women's Research Center in Tehran. This interview was part of a larger 'focus group' interview with the research professors at al-Zahra University's Women's Research Center. I was introduced to this group by Homeira Moshirzadeh, a Professor of International Relations at Tehran University in Iran, who helped me connect to a variety of Muslim woman scholars and activists working on women's issues both locally and globally. The key interviewees whom Homeira introduced me to and who will be mentioned throughout the next four chapters were Mahboubeh Abbas-Ghulizadeh, Saideh Lotfian, N. Mosaffar, Jaleh Shaditalab, and Seyed Kazem Sajjadpour.

6   For more on Shirkat Gah and WLUML, see Chapter 5.

mediation. [In] dialogue you do not know where you will go but you should be open to an exchange of ideas, feelings and whatever else.[7]

It is not an exaggeration to point out that Shaheed's statement – together with many other comments by interviewees – echoes the wisdom of Socrates and Plato: we may not always be able to agree with one another but, if we engage in open and honest conversation (that is, genuine dialogue), we may be able to empathize with one another and with the larger human predicament. We may discover issues of deeper significance at the core of our human lives – issues that transcend differences of society or culture.

To approach life through an attitude of open-ended dialogue is to experience encounters with an orientation of openness: open to the discovery of new meaning in self and other (whether conceived as an embodiment of traditional Muslim authenticity or of Western or modernist forces).[8] As many interviewees pointed out, through dialogue they are coming to perceive that identity and authority may be derived through including others as well as through exclusion. Hermeneutical experience does not have to insist on an ethnocentric contextuality that preserves or reinforces boundaries; rather, it can aspire toward innovative intercontextual understandings of *open identity* to new experiences of the self and the other.[9]

When a social identity is normatively wedded to practices of conservative, objectivity-seeking hermeneutics or to a belief system that is constructed as strictly

---

7   I first learned about Farida through Mahboubeh Abbas-Ghulizadeh, a convenor of a transnational Muslim women workshop entitled 'Forum for Dialogue: Learning from Each Other,' at Tehran's Institute for Women's Studies and Research. For more on Mahboubeh and Farida's transnational linkage, see Chapter 5. After interviewing women in Iran, I traveled to Pakistan and was able to meet and interview Farida Shaheed on 24 May 2004 at the Shirkat Gah office in Lahore, Pakistan. In response to my question, 'What kind of dialogues do you find between different approaches?' Shaheed shared the following:

I think we try to bring these different individuals [see Chapter 5 for details] together with very specific interests or themes … [She then gave an example]: We have worked for a long time, ten years, to make a book on the 'Women in Law' program which consists of 22 different societies. Some are from minority societies in non-Muslim majority states and some are from majority Muslim states, some have laws which are defined as secular, some have laws which are defined as Islamic, some multiple systems, etc. However, the convergence of these groups is 'women's rights and women.' What we do hope is that through bringing information and people face-to-face that people can be inspired by each other and learn from each other even if they do not share the same strategy for achieving what they believe. We work with people whom I would call 'progressive' whether they work within the framework of Islam or not.

For more on Shaheed's interview, see the following chapters.

8   This line of thought is also echoed in Recep Senturk's theory of 'open ontology.' See Chapter 3.

9   Such an attitude of openness reminds me of my encounter with Mohammed Arkoun at his home in Casablanca, Morocco. At the end of the interview, I shared my gratitude for his time and gracious hospitality and then stated to him, 'You are a true beacon to the world.' Arkoun then stared at me and said, '"Beacon," I like this word – "Be Can – Be Possibility."' His insight also reminded me of Hwa Yol Jung's seeing *in* the 'compossible' of the 'both/and' not the 'either/or' (Jung, 1999, 288).

'anti-traditional,' an opportunity to test received wisdom within a broader context of human experience is missed. The other is encountered not as a source of knowing or as a partner in dialogue, but rather as a text that cannot be assimilated without compromising received values. In contrast, when the other is greeted as a bearer of distinctive but not necessarily contradictory truths, dialogue becomes a basis for new discoveries. As one interviewee put it, '*Ana fi al-akhr wa al-akhr fi ana.*' (I am in the other and the other is in me.)[10]

In my interviews with women activists – many of which were conducted in Arabic and Farsi – I followed up questions about the meaning of dialogue with queries about the context of the word 'dialogue' in Arabic and Farsi. Arab interviewees pointed out that dialogue can be represented by two Arabic words, '*hewar*' and '*munaqasha*.' One interviewee, Halima Oulami, co-founder of Club du Livre et de Lecture Marrakech in Morocco,[11] pointed out that she prefers the Arabic word '*munaqasha*' over '*hewar*,' and then discussed how *munaqasha* implies a more intimate setting which involves a person's *nafs* (translated as 'soul' or 'self').

> In *munaqasha*, we share thoughts together: this closeness creates new synergies that then can be shared in new contexts ... Difference is needed for new thinking. Such thinking depends on the act of *munaqasha*: an intimate understanding of self and other as living shared meaning.

It is interesting to point out that the word *munaqasha* is derived from the Arabic trilateral verbal root, *naqasha*, which means 'to paint' or 'to carve out' and is connected to the third form of the root (*naaqasha*) which connotes the act of questioning, examining, as well as listening. In contrast, the Arabic word *hewar* comes from the root, *hara*, which means 'to diminish' or 'to be reduced.'[12]

Dynamism

The act of dialoguing is also connected to the understanding that life and the social construction of reality are dynamic in nature. As reflected by Zainah Anwar, the Executive Director of the Sisters in Islam organization based in Kuala Lumpur, Malaysia, 'Dialogue is an active engagement with the other – it is a dynamic process

---

10   Amina, interview by author, 9 April 2004, at the 8th Caravane Civique Conference, Hotel Idou Anfa in Casablanca, Morocco. This interview with Amina (an elderly woman whose profession is making woven baskets) was part of a larger 'focus group' interview with women activists representing the Zagora region of Morocco for the Caravane Civique (see Chapter 5 for more details).

11   Halima Oulami, interview by author, 12 April 2004, at Hassoune's Bookstore in Marrakech, Morocco. Oulami is also coordinator of 'des Projects Alphabetisation Juridique' and a member of the Caravane Civique (see Chapter 5). During the interview, Jamila Hassoune, manager of the bookstore and co-founder of Club du Livre et de Lecture Marrakech, would interject a thought here and there into the conversation. The Club du Livre et de Lecture Marrakech is a local effort to raise awareness about intercultural as well as civil issues (that is, women's roles) facing the society of Marrakech. Hassoune is also the former principal organizer of the Caravane Civique; for more about Hassoune and the Caravane, see Chapter 5.

12   See Cowan, 1980, 191 and 212.

rather than a static objective.'[13] The act of dialogue can be seen as moving from moments of appropriation and assimilation to moments of association, relation, integration, and transformation. Seyed Kazem Sajjadpour, the Director General of the Institute for Political and International Studies in Tehran, Iran, described the dynamism of dialogue in the following terms:

> Dialogue is a sense of being similar and different at the same time. [He then gave the example of being Iranian and going to Turkey] … People are like me but yet they are not … We should not construct our conceptions of the other for static purposes; rather dialogue can add to the *dynamism of discovery*.[14]

This notion of being 'in motion' with the other was also pointed out by Jamila Hassoune, the former principal organizer of the Caravane Civique in Morocco: 'to be in dialogue, one must travel to the other.' She then added that 'concepts need to travel in order for emerging knowledge to be understood.' For Hassoune, dialogue is a means of understanding how dynamism of life is to 'be engaged with,' and not avoided. When life is conceived dynamically, there is no past, 'pure' state of fossilized, changeless ideas; rather, ideals and ideas are constantly evolving through historical processes of interaction. Having based her own work with Morocco's 'caravane civique' on this notion, Hassoune stated that this 'sharing of knowledge with the other (*al-akhir*) is the caravan which is constantly moving.' From this perspective, dialogue is a journey. To be creative, one must be open to a more dynamic reading of self and of collective identity as well as sacred values. (For more about Hassoune and the Caravane Civique, see Chapter 5.)

For many interviewees, the concept of identity can be used as a vehicle of change. It is neither fixed nor entified. It is more complex: constantly in formation (however, it is not always being contested). Another scholar and activist for women's rights in Pakistan, Salima Hashmi, the daughter of Faiz Ahmed Faiz (who is known as the 'greatest Urdu poet after Iqbal') eloquently pointed out that life is about encountering the other and getting beyond moments of the static self:

> The embracing aspects of life are searching for the other in order to feel whole. The other or the stranger is the one who brings the ominous, the 'in-human' quality into conversation, into the processes of encountering. However, the other is made by an enforced border that

13 Zainah Anwar, interview by author, 6 October 2003, at the Marriott Hotel in Cairo, Egypt. I was initially introduced to Zainah and the Sisters in Islam by Amina Wadud, and was then able to spend time with her while attending a conference which I coordinated at the Library of Alexandria in Egypt. The conference was entitled 'Contemporary Islamic Synthesis,' and Zainah presented a paper entitled 'When Silence is Not Golden: Muslim Women Speak Out.' For more about the Sisters in Islam, see Chapter 5.

14 Seyed Kazem Sajjadpour, interview by author, 30 May 2004, at the Institute for Political and International Studies in Tehran, Iran. As mentioned previously, I was introduced to Sajjadpour through Homeira Moshirzadeh, a Professor of International Relations at Tehran University, who also introduced me to a variety of women's research centers in Tehran, Iran.

references the non-familiar within oneself. The self no longer is a mirrored image; rather it is a living moment.[15]

Additionally, when asked about dialogue, Hashmi automatically referred to her profession as a teacher and artist:

> In being a teacher it becomes second nature to be dialogical. One engages in a process of mutual learning. This to me is dialogue. To be an intellectual is to be in dialogue. Art itself is a continual dialogue.

Interviewees also suggested that the positive dynamism created by dialogue – that is, through full engagement of the self with the other – can be highly empowering, particularly when knowledge is shared or created jointly. For instance, Jamila Hassoune stated that: 'Knowledge is power only when it is shared, when there is a dialogue of exchange. Only when knowledge is static does it become an ideology.'

Hashmi's and Hassoune's insights also invite profound questions about human cognition: Why do humans so often construe identity categories in static, homogeneous, and mutually exclusive terms? Why are they so susceptible to perceiving the other in static terms? Why do we often think in terms that predispose us to avoid dialogical encounters with others?

In-Relation, Not Out of Relation

Narratives of dynamism and exchange within a context of dialogue often included commentary on the intrinsic value of forming relationships of understanding. This was pointed out by Homeira Moshirzadeh, Professor of International Relations at Tehran University in Iran, who stated that dialogue 'is an encounter of self and other with the purpose of understanding. Understanding is trying to see the world from the perspective of the other and then understand[ing] the notion of difference locally and transnationally.'[16]

As my encounters suggested, to be in dialogue is to be 'in relationship' with others rather than 'out of relationship.' Dialogue often entails deliberate effort to move from solipsism to relationality, from morbidity to creativity, from defensiveness to openness, from a competitive focus on the negative to a cooperative affirmation of positive possibilities, and even from the politics of fear and projection to the politics

---

15   Salima Hashmi, interview by author, 23 May 2004, at her residence in Lahore, Pakistan. Hashmi is also the Dean of Beaconhouse National University in Lahore, Pakistan, and is author of *Unveiling the Visible: Lives and Works of Women Artists of Pakistan* (Pakistan: ACT, ONAID, 2002).

16   Homeira Moshirzadeh, interview by author, 16 May 2004, during a conference entitled 'A Gathering of Women on Socio-Cultural Issues and Globalization' at Tehran University, Iran. Two other colleagues of Moshirzadeh, Saideh Lotfian and N. Mosaffar, both Professors of Political Science at Tehran University in Iran, added to Moshirzadeh's thought. Lotfian stated: 'Dialogue is more than a conversation. It is a continual conversation without any set goals. Therefore, it is more about the negotiation of identity than the assimilation of identity.' Mosaffar added: 'Dialogue is a way of relation. It allows us to respect ourselves and others. We can find something that we did not know before.'

of hope. Fatima Mernissi, who is co-founder of the Caravane Civique (which will be discussed in Chapter 5), in her booklet *The New Cheherazads: Women and Civil Society in Digital Islam* (2000), argues a similar thought that:

> Dialogue allows us to see new ways that you could not discover by yourself ... Regardless of sex, the winners of the 21st century are definitely the dialogue-nurturers ... Dialogue between the sexes in the public arena is the new feature of civic Islam ... The New Scheherazad dialogues non-stop with men, be they relatives or strangers. Male strangers in the public arena are fellow citizens for her. The New Schererazad speaks night and day, no king limits her speech. Worse, the New Scheherazad creates her own public space (Centers created by women's non-governmental organizations, NGOs) and invites male strangers (citizens) to dialogue with her (Mernissi, 2000, 5 and 7).

Like Mernissi, many interviewees produced commentary that resonates positively with the idea that the present world affords very little scope for authenticity in isolation or security through rigid boundaries: authenticity, security, and well-being must be sought through the forging of relationships, whether between the sexes, ethnicities, sectarian differences, as well as nations.

Hamid Bashiriyeh, Director of International Affairs at the International Center for Dialogue Among Civilizations (ICDAC) in Tehran, Iran, conceived of dialogue as a basis for comprehending reality, both ontologically and epistemologically, as relational:

> Dialogue is a constructive unbiased interaction between two or more parts (or sides). This interaction necessitates the recognition of the other side's rights. The acceptance of the other side's rights also creates an acceptance that one's own rights are not absolute. Difference then makes 'the other' both an opportunity and a limitation in understanding self. However, dialogue enables the self to understand the importance of difference ... [He then described how dialogue was practiced at the ICDAC and added:] in dialogue, there needs to be an understanding of relational systems.[17]

According to Bashiriyeh, because we are part of the systems we study, learning requires that we analyze our experiences, assess our conditioning and core beliefs, and explore our changing relationship with the world. In other words, dialogue affirms that knowledge is built relationally between us and our surroundings.

Therefore, to gain new insights into the values, identity, and foundational texts of the other, the practitioner of *dialogical hermeneutics* utilizes cultural empathy as a way of knowing. By regarding the other's texts as sources of knowing that must be interpreted in a dialogical manner, an opening is created for those moments of understanding that Gadamer described with the phrase 'fusion of horizons.'[18] When

---

17 Hamid Bashiriyeh, interview by author, 15 May 2004, at the International Center for Dialogue Among Civilizations in Tehran, Iran. This center was among the many institutes funded by the former reformist Iranian president, Khatami, to open discussion on a variety of issues from inter-civilizational dialogue to women's rights. For more information about this center, see <www.dialoguecentre.org>.

18 Bashiriyeh referred to Mujtahid Shabistari, who is also known for arguing a similar thought, as reflected in Ashk P. Dahlen's analysis of Shabistari:

arrived at through shared inquiry into common problems of human existence, such a hermeneutic process can develop a sense of common, inclusive identity across cultural boundaries. Self and other becomes a *nexus* rather than a dichotomy – a dynamic relationship that is not influenced but not fixed by past assumptions and understandings. The process of inquiry shifts from an insular and 'retrospective' justification of the self toward an open and 'prospective' attitude toward the self–other relationship. Knowledge of other and knowledge of self unfold together.[19]

In interviews with Muslim women, the importance of forming relationships across cultural divides was another common theme – not just relationships among women activists from different cultural contexts, but also relationships between Muslim and non-Muslim cultures. Many perceived dialogue as a means of transcending not only those differences which are inherently cultural, but also those which are fed by politics and nationalism. Jaleh Shaditalab, Director of the Center for Women's Studies at Tehran University, Iran, provided in-depth commentary on this subject. She began by expressing her frustration with the image of Iranian women in the international media:

> [The] international media has harmed Iranian women. They could have done good, but they have had too many political agendas. There are so many black, dark images. My main mission is to help the world see the bright picture also. And to let the international community know that with all the challenges we have survived and progressed.
>
> I am not denying that we do not have problems, but who doesn't? On the one hand, we need to engage with our problems more analytically – in more critical thinking, but on the other hand, we need to have dialogue with the world.
>
> The media has [written] about us the way they perceive us, not in the way that we experience it. Now is the time for 'the insiders' to write to 'the outsiders' ... [so that the 'outsiders' can] learn from what we have to say.

Significantly, Shaditalab emphasized that misunderstandings did not exhaust her relationships with non-Iranian and non-Muslim others. Although she believes that obsession with viscerally evocative symbols and slogans at the expense of disciplined analysis have led to a polarization of identities, the present impasse need not be understood as inevitable or final. When dialogue is preferred to coercive measures, areas of shared meaning can be found:

> Strangers become friends because they are giving us the opportunity to share. [She then shared an example that her Center was] receiving so much positive reactions from strangers

---

Since all interpretation is conditioned by its prior history and stands in a tradition of interpretation, the interpreter must similar to a translator serve the text through a dialogue during which the horizons of the text and the reader are fused (Dahlen, 2003, 179).

19   This 'retrospective/prospective' argument is articulated by Mohammed Arkoun in his paper, 'Islam, Europe, the West: Rethinking the Mediterranean Space,' for the international conference, *The Frontiers of the Mind in the 21st Century*, at the Library of Congress in June 1999.

(especially non-Iranian) that the Center never knew before. I believe what Khatami stated, 'People are friends, governments are strangers.' Strangeness comes from nationalism.

> Dialogue is an exchange of information on equal basis. None of the two parts should feel superior. The most important principle of dialogue is to respect and feel equal: to respect people on the same level and tolerate cultural differences. When people do not judge us with their own criteria. We should be judged by our own criteria.

> If any change happens because of the exchange in dialogue it is because of the free decision-making process – not the forced changes.[20]

For Shaditalab, dialogue creates a context of respectful, non-coercive relationship in which ideas can be exchanged without paternalism or imperialism. Employing a hermeneutics of dialogue as a tool for transforming conflict implies seeking *power with* the other rather than *power over* an alien culture. Ideally, such egalitarian cultural engagement should not merely be an elite endeavor, but rather a more broadly participatory process in which members of estranged cultures reread and rediscover their respective texts, traditions, and motivations. Rather than focus primarily on the negative task of debunking stereotypes (as manifest in tendencies of Orientalism and Occidentalism), dialogue seeks to develop new, mutual understandings on a collaborative basis.

Mahboubeh Abbas-Ghulizadeh, a convenor of the Muslim women workshop, 'Forum for Dialogue: Learning from Each Other' at Tehran's Institute for Women's Studies and Research, pointed out that it was a 'support network of dialogue' that helped her overcome feelings of marginalization and isolation:

> Dialogue is genetic. When you are lonely, you find other people who are lonely too. Dialogue helps you understand that there are many more individuals (men and women from other contexts) like yourself who are lonely and who are struggling and living in-between like you. You find [the] same questions and same problems but not in the same area and same atmosphere. From this support network, I made many friends and networks, both professionally and personally.[21]

Dialogue involves a vigorous counterpoint to the hubris and disdain associated with triumphalist conceptions of innate cultural superiority. Rather than pit one cultural context against another through self vs. other value dichotomies, it seeks points of convergence and complementarity: to live 'in-between.' In other words, it seeks to

---

20   Jaleh Shaditalab, interview by author, 29 May 2004, at the Center for Women's Studies, Tehran University, Iran. At the beginning of the interview, Shaditalab shared her personal story of having worked since 1968, over 35 years, on women's issues in which she has seen much change: from Iranian women's employment status to land reform and the women's right to vote. She pointed out that when she became a professor at the university, this appointment encouraged her to become more active. Ever since, she has been the main driving force in creating the first Center for Women's Studies at the university. For more about the Center's transnational activities, see Chapter 5.

21   Mahboubeh Abbas-Ghulizadeh, interview by author, 27 May 2004, at the Institute for Women's Studies and Research (IWSR) in Tehran, Iran. For more on my interview with Mahboubeh Abbas-Ghulizadeh, see Chapter 5.

counteract the distortion and devaluation of presumably 'alien' traits without seeking to stigmatize or deconstruct ideas of patterned cultural difference.

Another Iranian woman brought a strikingly different, yet complementary, set of experiences to the discussion with Abbas-Ghulizadeh. As a self-proclaimed Iranian feminist who had been living in exile in Denmark, Susan Rakhsh was in Tehran temporarily for a conference – her first time back in her home country for many years. For Rakhsh, dialogue held out the promise of bridging deep divides: 'Dialogue is a tool to heal the disconnection of exile Muslims to homeland … [Otherwise] the exile voice has no citizenship.'[22]

Whenever we slide into the consciousness of non-dialogical solipsistic tendencies, we find that it is remarkably easy to become fixated on 'either/or' value dichotomies that split the world into opposing camps – first by positing two 'pure,' abstract qualities, and then by elevating one quality above its presumed opposite. As a result, important aspects of human experience are denied or repressed, and regarded largely as distinguishing characteristics of the other. In the absence of effort to reclaim denigrated values, the putative virtues of each culture became vices. As Hamid Bashiriyeh recognized, such 'biased' tendencies negate any opportunity for dialogical encounters; rather 'constructive unbiased interaction between two or more parts/sides [which] … necessitates the recognition of the other side's rights' is the foundation for, what he calls, 'dialogical being-in-the-world.'

In a group interview with members from a recently established women's forum RAHM[23] in Karachi, Pakistan, Seyed Jaffar Ahmed, Acting Director of the Pakistan Study Centre at the University of Karachi, Pakistan, reflected that relationships formed in dialogue can also be sources of innovation:

> The culture of dialogue is a culture of innovation. When I negotiate with you, I do not only give you some information, I too affect myself. I improve myself. Dialogue is a reciprocal process. This process of dialogue is woven into life, it is not separate from life. We should not think of life as separate (distant) from dialogue. Life is dialogue.[24]

---

22 Susan Rakhsh, interview by author, 27 May 2004, at the Institute for Women's Studies and Research (IWSR) in Tehran, Iran. Susan, in her final presentation at the women's workshop, also stated: 'Perhaps there can be a compromise between tradition and modernity … We are going through a secular system. In such a postmodernist time, we have to find new strategies, new ways. Islam cannot answer all are questions.'

23 RAHM is a Muslim women's development organization based in Karachi, Pakistan. Their main projects focus on training in human rights and Muslim ethics, as well as multicultural and inter-religious dialogue. I was introduced to RAHM by its General Secretary, Farhat Naz Rahman, who then connected me to a variety of Muslim scholars and activists working on women's issues locally and globally. The individuals whom she introduced me to were Muslim women students pursuing their PhDs in Islamic Studies at the University of Karachi, members of the Centre for Women's Studies at the University of Karachi, members of the Pakistan Study Centre and Manzooruddin Ahmad.

24 Seyed Jaffar Ahmed, interview 20 May 2004, at the University of Karachi's Pakistan Study Centre, Pakistan. This interview was part of a larger conversation with Farhat Naz Rahman and Anwar Shaheen, the founding members of RAHM (see previous note).

Dialogue, for Ahmed, is the recognition of contextual and moral *complexity*. What follows is a sincere effort to counteract misperceptions and double standards. This means replacing moral self-images and immoral other-images with perceptions that are closer to reality. In addition, it requires putting brakes on habits of contrasting the self's cultural ideal (be it 'freedom' or 'faith') with the other's practice. One need not abandon particularism or preference for the value system of community; all that is necessary is recognition that developing a realistic and constructive relationship with the other is impossible without cultural empathy: the ability to see the other in the self. As reflected by Rachida ben Faida, a Professor of Humanities at the Université Cadi Ayyad in Marrakech, Morocco:

> Dialogue is seeking for truth in the sharing of otherness … There is a verse in the Qur'an [49:12]: 'We have made you peoples and tribes that you may come to know one another,' to me, this verse symbolizes dialogue and civic responsibility.

In the same conversation, Jamila Hassoune added: 'You are responsible for every moment. Dialogue depends on such responsibility.'[25]

The Epistemology and Hermeneutics of Dialogue: Three Views

Although my original objective was to focus my research efforts on Muslim women activists, my interviews with women made it clear that Muslim men are often important allies of Muslim women's organizations and networks, and are playing a particularly important role in intellectual debates about religious epistemology and hermeneutics.[26]

By following references provided by interviewees, my research led to discussions with male Muslim intellectuals and activists whose outlooks inclined, to varying degrees, toward all four of the orientations depicted above in Figure 4.4. Many, if not most, expressed a degree of sympathy or resonance with multiple normative systems. Among those interviewees whose intellectual bents had led to deep reflection on epistemological issues, three stood out for their views: Gholam Reza A'wani, Director of the Iranian Institute of Philosophy in Tehran, Iran; Mohammed Arkoun, Emeritus Professor of the History of Islamic Thought at the Sorbonne Nouvelle in Paris, France; and Manzooruddin Ahmad, former Professor of Political Science and

---

25 Rachida ben Faida, interview by author, 12 April 2004, at Hassoune's Bookshop in Marrakech, Morocco. During the interview, Jamila Hassoune, who introduced me to ben Faida (after helping the wandering customer), would contribute some of her own thoughts to our discussion.

26 Although women are also involved in Muslim debates about epistemology and hermeneutics, *academic* discussions about these topics are still somewhat 'male-dominated,' and philosophy appears to be a more male-centered area of discourse than the social sciences. Noting this, of course, is in no way equivalent to suggesting that women are absent from high-level academic discussions or that men are of one mind in their views. Male Muslim academicians hold diverse views, as my interviews indicate. Many members of Muslim women's networks regard 'progressive' thinkers in philosophy and hermeneutics – be they male or female – as important allies.

Philosophy as well as Vice Chancellor at the University of Karachi and currently the Chairman of the Executive Board for the Usman-Institute of Technology in Karachi, Pakistan.[27]

When questioned about epistemology, A'wani expressed his affinity for 'traditionalist' hermeneutics quite clearly and decisively, invoking a mystical paradigm with affinities for neo-Platonism and Islamic Sufism. 'Epistemology,' he stated, 'is hermeneutics, the art of *tawil*: naming and understanding.'

> Hermeneutics is the science of interpretation and understanding. What does it mean to understand? It connotes 'meaning.' What is the reality of things? What is the first principle of things? This seeking of one single principle is the reality of monism.

> *Logos* is the First Principle of things which has manifested itself in everything. Everything is the manifestation of *Logos*. For Heraclitus: *Logos* is the one reality of everything ...

In other words, the search for meaning is a search for first principles that provide a unitive vision of all reality, understood to encompass both the visible world addressed by the physical sciences and an unseen world of metaphysical essences.
With respect to dialogue, A'wani offered the following commentary:

> You have to go to the etymological root: 'dia-logos.' To listen ... to logos as it has manifested in everything is the task of the philosopher.

> Understanding is listening, as 'dia' is 'through': to be in dialogue with the logos, the nature of things. Logos is Reality and Reality is Al-Haqq [Arabic for 'the Truth'] which is constant in everything.

> In contrast, mythos comes from 'Mu' (to become silent) which is connected to 'Mystery and Mystic.' This brings us to the knowledge of the Symbol, *ar-Ramz* ... As Suhrawardi once stated, 'Symbols can never be refuted.'

> Therefore, Logos and Mythos did not understand the form as material but as symbol ... The form is a symbol representing a principle ...

A'wani's traditionalist cosmology is based on a metaphysics of mystical monism, in which every apparent phenomenon in the universe points back to a form in the world of ideas, and hence to a transcendental point of origin. Though expressed more philosophically than the ontological visions of traditionalists who operate

---

27 Gholam Reza A'wani, interview by author, 17 May 2004, at the Iranian Institute of Philosophy (IRIP), Tehran, Iran. I was introduced to Gholam by Homeira Moshirzadeh. For more information about the Institute, go to <www.irip.org>. Mohammed Arkoun, interview by author, 11 April 2004, at his residence in Casablanca, Morocco. Arkoun was often cited and highly regarded by many of the Muslim women activists, such as Jamila Hassoune and Zainah Anwar. For more information on Arkoun, please see <www.arkoun.org>. Manzooruddin Ahmad, interview by author, 20 May 2004, at the Usman-Institute of Technology in Karachi, Pakistan. I was introduced to Ahmad by Farhat Naz Rahman, General Secretary, RAHM Women's Research Organization in Karachi, Pakistan. For more information about the Usman-Institute, please see <www.uit.edu>.

within a more explicitly legalistic framework of thought, A'wani's worldview is in harmony with the Revelation-predicated orientation of traditional legal scholars – and quite distinct from modern worldviews in which metaphysical formulations are viewed with skepticism. Modern discursive philosophy, he stated, understands mythic symbols incorrectly. It 'demythologizes … [but] if one refutes a myth, one has not understood.'

An interview with Mohammed Arkoun provided a stark contrast to A'wani's approach to epistemology of metaphysical certitude:

> Epistemology is not *Adab al-Yaqin* [the discipline of learning or acquiring certitude by studying with a traditional master]. The process of knowing is not engaged with the process of certitude. Rather, epistemology is connected to the understanding of *logos*. Logos is connected to all discourses, which are dictated by reason and language.

Whereas A'wani framed *logos* as a transcendental, unitive, *a priori* reality to which human knowing must conform, Arkoun perceived *logos* as human reasoning – as linguistically contextualized discourse that is creative and relative, but not static or transcendental. Moreover, *logos* is obscured by *mythos*, not revealed by it:

> [An important question to ask] about *logos* is, 'Who is articulating the narrative?' This leads us to question the process of mythology.

> *Mythos* is defined by a storyteller: the knowledge of immersion [in *mythos*] creates ideological memories which are competing for power, not meaning.

> We need to go beyond *mythos* to *logos*. The core of *logos* is the critical use of imagination.

Arkoun also provided intriguing commentary on dialogue as an exchange of meaning, of *logos*:

> *Dia* is the living exercise of *logos*. 'Dialogue,' then, is the sharing of *logos* between two people: Sharing all the requirements, all the goals, all the rules, all the conditions, all the fruits related to the exercise of *logos*.

> Knowledge, itself, [consists of] moments of disclosure; however, most people are in the imprisonment of narratives. They are watching life through different singularities which are concretized in institutional ignorance …

> Epistemology [then] is the consciousness of the necessity of identifying at any level of work a point where what you do is not any more relevant. It is a discontinuity of the relevance of the tools you are using. Watch over every word, every point – watching over every action from reason and accepting the discontinuity of *logos*.

Far more than any traditional Islamic ideas about epistemology, Arkoun's vision of human knowledge reflects modern and, indeed, postmodern philosophical trends. His conception of meaning is immanent rather than transcendental, and does not project the possibility of creating a unified system of knowledge. Knowing is a moment-to-moment experience of awareness, reflexivity, and presence – not an ideological system or a closed narrative, be it traditional or modern.

Yet another view of epistemology emerged from an interview with Manzooruddin Ahmad, who happens to know both A'wani and Arkoun through mutual colleagues. In many respects his perspective on dialogue seeks to bridge – or perhaps to toggle between – their 'traditional' and 'postmodern' visions, by offering an attitude that seeks to live with 'complementary contradictions' from the perspective of dialogue. Evoking a theme that appeared in many of my less philosophical encounters with Muslim women activists, he spoke of the need to acknowledge internal contradictions in one's sense of identity and in one's intellectual outlook. Accepting the legitimacy of contradictions is the basis for dialogue:

> In religion, power is more absolutized: you consider yourself as right and the other as totally wrong. So, there is a question of basic contradiction and the emphasis on elimination of the other who contradicts. This contradiction makes civil society difficult.

> The difficulty with each and every religion, including Islam, is that there is such a sharp differentiation between right and wrong. If one exists, the other must be eliminated. This is the problem. This law of contradiction is a universal law and we will eventually realize that this law of contradiction only applies in the abstract world, and not in the real, concrete existential world. *I have so many contradictions within myself, but I am still one.* A part of myself goes on fighting with another part of myself and yet I am still one. When you are living a life and you are in an existential situation, you have to live with contradictions as realities existing in your life. Religions in the beginning were not such. What happened with every religion (especially the Abrahamic traditions) … that in the beginning the prophets were reformers, they came to reform. Later on there was a system, a construction. Difference emerges in different constructions of what was to be reformed.

> The moment the religion becomes a dogma and the moment the dogma acquires the methodology of Greek logic, then fractalization happens. A dogma becomes a construct. This is why there is so much emphasis on deconstructing these dogmas and mythologies. All of us have these mythologies. *Dialogue is only possible in the religion when and if we critically examine this law of contradiction which has become a self-evident ruse in explaining religions, like Islam* [Speaker's emphasis].

Accepting the existential reality of contradiction – and not forcing the complexities of life and of religion into a closed, exclusive system seeking dominance – is the key both to epistemological puzzles and to problems of dialogue and coexistence. When the inevitability of contradiction and diversity is embraced, new opportunities for learning and creativity emerge:

> I visualize the possibility of having a world consisting of veil-less entities – be those entities raised on ethnicity, language, territory, belief structure, ideology, whatever it is. But I would rather love to live in a world where all these things exist and they talk to each other; rather than they try to dominate each other. The problem of globalization or whatever arises, is not because of the existence of many cultures in the world, but because of this desire to dominate others. Not necessarily for cultural or altruistic reasons, but for

other reasons. I agree that the Western civilization is the best civilization now. But the moment the Western civilization tries to dominate, I will object to it.

Good qualities of one civilization should bring out the good qualities of other civilizations. It is the power of the idea and the power of the argument, power of living. Transnationalism is simply recognizing the rights of each and every nation, civilization, culture to live the way that each would like to live.

In Ahmad's view, eclecticism is an intellectual virtue rather than an intellectual vice. In many respects, Ahmad's approach indicated a desire to transcend conventional ways of framing dichotomies such as 'traditional vs. modern' as well as 'Islamic vs. Western,' in a search for ways of knowing and being and identifying oneself that are built upon sustained experiences of intercultural encounter – on conversations between thinkers and cultural elements from diverse origins:

I am a student of philosophy and I have been reading philosophy for some time. In the beginning, I read philosophy and started teaching it and what I knew was Plato said this, and Kant said this, and Hegel said this ... and I did not know what to do with that. But later on I learned that doing philosophy is not a theoretical work. It is basically like cooking. Unless you fry your own egg, you will not know how an egg can be fried, so you start doing your own philosophy. You start thinking.

As far as I am concerned, I have been much impressed by the twentieth-century multi-dimensional logic which showed me the possibility to answer many questions which I had in the beginning and for which I could not find answers. We have been working within the paradigm of two-dimensional logic of Aristotle – either right or wrong, either good or bad, either is or is not; later on I learned through a host of philosophers (including Hegel, Marx, Wittgenstein, Mulla Sadra, Ibn al-'Arabi), I came to realize that, no, this two-dimensional way is not the way to understand the world. If you have to understand the world, you have to let your mind not work in closed, watertight compartments of right or wrong. And try to see that there are combinations, that right and wrong are mixed together and sometimes you cannot differentiate the two, but it is one. This solved a lot of questions which I was facing, particularly about religion, systems, essentialism, capitalism, communism, globalization and things like that ...

For Ahmad, the encounter of deep thinkers from different civilizations produces new insights and dynamic, open-ended personal and cultural possibilities. The principal aim of the reflective person, he proposed, is to remain creative and committed to a life of growth:

I am [an] eclectic type of person, and this has probably helped me to have this type of perception. I never say to myself that I am right or will be right because it is quite possible that I might change tomorrow. This is in human nature: you go on changing and developing, growing. The moment you are static, you are dead.

This earnest effort to transcend boundaries and live *in relation* to diverse cultural and normative systems may be seen as an example of how dialogue is more than just a practice of skillful conversation. It can also become an attitude that reflects and embraces encounters with otherness. Significantly, there are bases for this attitude in Islamic tradition as well as in the philosophical reflections of more 'modern' or 'postmodern' Muslims. One 'premodern' thinker whose ideas resonate with Ahmad, as well as many 'traditional–reformist'-minded Muslims, is the thirteenth-century Muslim philosopher Muhyi' ad-Din Ibn al-'Arabi.[28] The following quote by William C. Chittick, a contemporary scholar of Ibn al-'Arabi, mirrors many of Ahmad's previous statements:

> [Ibn 'Arabi] acknowledges the validity of every mode of human knowing, and at the same time he recognizes the limitations of every mode. Thus he considers every perspective, every school of thought, and every religion as both true and false. He does not offer a single, overall system that would take everything or most things into account, but he does present us with a way of looking at things that allows us to understand why things must be the way they are (Chittick, 1994, 10).

The existence of such philosophical currents suggests that even 'postmodernity' is not entirely without precedent in Islamic thought. Given the internal pluralism of the Islamic intellectual tradition, dialogue can be approached from multiple paradigmatic standpoints, with the only prerequisite being an attitude of existential and intellectual openness to the other.

It is interesting that, when asked about the meaning of dialogue, all three thinkers discussed above (A'wani, Arkoun, and Ahmad) immediately noted that the word 'dialogue' comes from the root 'dia-logos.'[29] After observing that 'dia-' means 'through' and that 'dialogue' literally means 'through the logos,' they immediately connected the principle of dialogue to hermeneutics and epistemology. They differed, however, in their understandings of 'logos,' which they connected variously with 'the word' (the literal translation), 'reason,' *a priori* or transcendental meaning, and *a posteriori* or derived meaning.

---

28   Born in Andalusia, a cultural 'isthmus' where West met East, Muhyi'ad-Din Ibn al-'Arabi (1165–1240), also known as 'Ibn Flatun' (the son of Plato), became the synthesizer of theological and philosophical paradoxes: he sought to reconcile opposite positions by giving legitimacy to their contradiction. Being one of the most encyclopedic and eclectic Muslim thinkers (known for having written over 846 manuscripts), Ibn al-'Arabi constantly sought to reconcile apparent paradoxes within Islamic doctrine and philosophy, and to trace the outlines of a multi-faceted, monistic way of experiencing reality. For Ibn al-'Arabi, the traditional doctrines of Muslim thinkers, such as al-Ghazali, and the teachings of the rational philosophers, such as Ibn Rushd (known in the West as Averroes), were ultimately reconcilable, provided that one recognizes the manifest limitations of linear, symbolic cognition.

    For Ibn al-'Arabi, every thought, claim, and concept was interdependent. Such thinking begged the question, 'Can two parts which define each other ever be separated?' He regarded it as curious how humans have come to perceive oppositional qualities as separate modalities, effectively ignoring the relationship connecting the two opposites (each of which cannot be discerned without the other).

29   In common speech, we often use words such as dialogue, discussion, deliberation, and debate interchangeably, without considering the basic meanings of these terms. Also, in philosophy you find dialogue mixed in with the 'dialectic' and the 'discursive,' which both have a variety of connotations.

Despite their differences concerning the basic meaning of *logos* and, by extension, their differing assumptions with respect to ontology (be it metaphysical monism, discursive humanism, or discontinuous pluralism) A'wani, Arkoun, and Ahmad appeared to agree that the act of dialoguing involves both 'sharing' and 'understanding.' The common ground they shared on this matter was familiar terrain to Hans Georg Godamer, whose views are aptly summarized by Fred Dallmayr, a Professor of Political Philosophy at the University of Notre Dame:

> What is particularly important in Gadamer's view of dialogue is its radically non-instrumental sense: dialoguing here involves not only an act of questioning but also the experience of being questioned or being 'called into question' – often in unsettling and disorienting ways. The openness of dialoguing means precisely the readiness of participants to allow themselves to be 'addressed' and challenged by the other: particularly the stranger, the different, the exile … Hence … dialogical understanding as the 'true locus of hermeneutics' always hovers in the 'in-between': between self and other, familiarity and strangeness, presence and absence (Dallmayr, 2002, 27).

In particular, a similar line of thought about the hermeneutical and relationship-building significance of dialogue was expressed by Ahmad in the following terms:

> Hermeneutics is the process of understanding the other: the other, other self, other text, other story. Basically, trying to establish a relationship between you and the rest (whatever be the rest) …[30]

> Dialogue is a process of living in-between and finding a common language, a common meaning. A dialogue is when you are using similar language. This means when you know what the word means not in the dictionary but what it means as it is in you, as it is your own creation. Dialogue then is developing a deeper relationship of understanding between two persons … When difference opens our minds to the meaning of the other's otherness, this is dialogue.

As thinkers deeply engaged with both dialogue and hermeneutics, A'wani, Arkoun, and Ahmad – not to mention many other interviewees who were highly expressive on the subject of dialogue – are 'living in-between,' in the search for

---

30 Ahmad further elaborated on this idea:

In theology, hermeneutics is limited to the interpretation of the holy texts (Qur'an and Sunnah). How a word is used, how many meanings a word has, the process of understanding, is based on language and the meaning of words. [A] Word can only be known by seeing how the word is lived and developed (for example, [the] best way to view this is by seeing a child learn language).

I amness is an existential feeling that you have which sometimes needs words and other times not. But the moment this self, which is me, wants to be known to you, I will talk to you. I use words. So whether I am talking to a tree or you. This is basically knowing the other. The other is what is other than me, in the limited sense and also in the vastest possible sense. What happens, whenever I come to know the other, the other becomes a part of me. So, I return to me again. This becomes my knowledge. My knowledge comes back to the relationship between subject and object. The moment one starts to differentiate between the subject and object, from that point of othering and a creation of a border.

shared meaning. Somewhat surprisingly, interviewees were quite quick to point out that relationships with otherness (however defined) were sources of knowing – bases for a hermeneutic process that forges common meaning as well as enduring bonds.

Conclusions

My encounters with leading Muslim activists and intellectuals – especially those engaged in conversations about the status of women in Muslim societies – suggest the potential viability of dialogue as a means of grappling with the contending normative systems or paradigms that have hitherto polarized Muslim lives. Interviews in a variety of settings suggested a desire to move towards a more open identity, and to achieve dynamism through relatedness with others. Though modern and indeed 'secular' values were commonplace in much of the discourse, traditional values, symbols and identities were also very much in evidence, together with a strongly felt need among many to avoid becoming caught on one side of a cultural polarity. In particular, dialogue provided a means of 'opening up' discourse about Muslim identity, permitting discussion of ways to integrate different aspects of identity – Muslim, modern, religious, and professional – and values. In effect, it is a means to help them rethink standards for authority, authenticity, and normative consensus without exclusive reference to a modernist or traditionalist paradigm.

Significantly, few of my interviewees seemed to take dialogue for granted, in the sense of seeing it as something that comes naturally and without effort. Many noted that it is sometimes more difficult to establish rapport with 'others' who share the same nationality or locality than with 'others' whose ideological and cultural differences can be viewed as more 'legitimate' – those who are not part of one's own immediate context of relationships, politics, and experiences. As will be discussed in the following chapters, dialogical encounters facilitated by *transnational networking* are becoming a means of building bridges across interpretive chasms – of generating 'new languages' for talking about shared as well as divergent priorities and understandings.

By making it easier for Muslim women to accept and dynamically engage with their differences, transnational dialogue is creating new partnerships to address longstanding issues: the failure of nation-states to provide adequate frameworks to support women, the limitations accompanying traditional ethnic and religious identities, the challenges of finding coherence between secular and religious activist practices, the challenge of engaging Muslim public spheres to find roles in civil society, and the historical 'othering' of Muslim women within their own societies as well as in the 'women and Islam' literature produced by non-Muslim societies. I will deal with each of these issues in the subsequent chapters. Chapter 5 will address the role of the transnational in changing the character of Muslim women's identity, as well as emerging forms of mutual engagement and activism. Chapter 6 will discuss how transnational as well as local dialogues among Muslim women are generating new meanings pertaining to roles in the family and in society. Chapter 7 will discuss the problem of 'othering,' and efforts by Muslim women to reclaim 'selfhood' and agency.

Chapter 5

The Transnational and the Politics of Community

Throughout the course of my fieldwork, conversations with activists from throughout the Muslim world revealed a consistent engagement with 'the transnational.' Seldom were interviewees at a loss for words when asked to comment on the significance of transnational connectivity for their thinking and activism. Though definitions of the transnational sometimes differed, the word itself had remarkably positive resonance and was demonstrably part of a widely used activist vocabulary – a vocabulary that is affecting the way Muslim women see themselves, define their identities, and pursue social change.

By examining attitudes toward transnational dialogue and networking from localities throughout the Muslim world, this chapter seeks to comprehend how conversations that transcend the borders of national communities are shaping the conduct and nature of women's activism. I will provide commentary that illuminates ways in which experiences of transnational dialogue are not only helping many Muslim women to transcend their experiences of localized marginalization, but are also stimulating creative thought and creating a new 'hermeneutic field' – a conversational 'space' within which Islamic identity and intellectuality take on new meanings, beyond defensive rebuttals of 'foreign' ideas and reflexive imitation of the West. Facilitated in part by increasing access to the internet, these transnational conversations are stimulating new forms of critical discourse about gender relations and their attendant norms. They are also providing a basis for new forms of civic activism on issues pertaining to the agency and authority of women in Muslim societies.

Engaging the Transnational

Islam and Transnationalism

Studying transnational networking provides unique opportunities to understand how differing constructs of collective identity – be they national, ethnic, tribal, or religious – interact to yield new meanings. It becomes possible to glimpse the world 'in-process,' as peoples from hitherto supposedly 'distant' regions and cultures establish relations with one another and struggle to make sense of similarities and differences. (Re)Construction of meaning in the midst of transnational networking was a central theme that emerged from my interviews; many interviewees were in fact quite self-conscious about the relevance of their micro-level experiences to larger processes in which they are embedded – processes whose ultimate outcomes may not be predictable, but which are beyond the purview of traditional international relations theory. Put simply, my interviewees did not conceive of themselves merely as citizens of a single nation-state, with unproblematic identities. Rather, they imagined themselves as members of multiple communities, with plural heritages and loyalties that are significant but not static or closed to new meanings. They conceived of their identities relationally and in reference to their own subjective experiences and aspirations.

Hamid Bashiriyeh[1] articulated his experience of transnationalism in the following terms:

> Transnationalism is a highly concentrated relationship among nations due to the phenomenon of globalization. Every nation has an impact on other nations. This process is a highly intensified context. When we compare the present world situation we see that many social norms and values were distant from each other. Now they are tied to one another. Every nation is engaged in a national context and cultural relation. Culture was an absolute concept; however, [it] no longer remains so. Now, culture has developed into multiple contexts and multiple civilizations.

> This connects to how self-identity is formed: every human being makes an identity through the notion of separation. However, if identity was conceptualized through dialogue which emphasizes shared values of all human heritage, then identity can be formed through the notion of human relations. This also connects to the role of women. When conceptualizing the role of women and men, they should never be 'separate.' There are differences, but these differences should not limit social rights.

As will be illustrated in this chapter with the emergence of a more *transnational identity* among Muslim activists, a more pluralistic and dialogical understanding of identity can provide a basis for transcending deficiencies in traditional understandings of national identity. Although the concept of the nation-state is important to most interviewees, it is not their sole category of politically and socially significant identity. Seyed Jaffar Ahmed[2] proposed that contemporary activists are 'transcending borders in self, society, and nation …':

> [T]his is the emerging paradigm of being-in the transnational … Entities (like the nation-state) can never be permanent. They will always change. Globalization has already reduced the nation-state. We are already global citizens physically … like this [pointing to a] SONY tape recorder from Japan … but we have not caught up mentally, emotionally, or intellectually (to a certain extent). For what is a border? Borders will always be there. Globalization does not mean that all identities will vanish. National, cultural identities will be there, but not as significant.

---

1   Hamid Bashiriyeh, interview by author, 15 May 2004, at the International Center for Dialogue Among Civilizations in Tehran, Iran. See Chapter 4, note 17.

2   Seyed Jaffar Ahmed, interview 20 May 2004, at the University of Karachi's Pakistan Study Centre, Pakistan. See Chapter 4, note 24.

Like other interviewees, Ahmed sees the nation-state in historical context – as a contingent rather than fixed reality of human social and political life. He situates his national identity in relation to other identities, as an activist, an intellectual, a humanist, and a Muslim.

This point, in particular, was elaborated more thoroughly in an interview with Cassandra Balchin and Anissa Helie at Women Living Under Muslim Laws (WLUML) London Office.[3] At the beginning of the interview, Balchin stated:

> The nation-state is not so rigid anyway. It is having problems establishing itself. This makes the national boundaries not so rigid in some sense ... at the people to people level there is a recognition that some of these boundaries are constructs of colonialisms.

> There is not such a rigid adherence to the national boundaries in the women's movement ... Women have really challenged and worked against this rigidity. This is why the network exists in order to facilitate interaction and communication between women where boundaries do prevent direct communication. This is [also] why we have the WLUML office in London because it is difficult for women to directly communicate to each other. So you need a 'third point' as neutral ground. [She then gave the example that they facilitate telephone calls for people.][4]

In response to Balchin's statement, Anissa Helie added the following thought:

> Not all women want to challenge the nation-state. It is not always the boundary to challenge. If you take the example of Nigeria and its inter-community problems: BAOBAB's project of 'Reach-Building' where they organize women in the Muslim community in the North and women in the Christian community in the South. They try to bring together [these two communities]. So they are not working on the level of nation-state, but they are working on the level of breaking barriers between communities. Because that is the whole construction of identity and how you deconstruct the 'other.'[5]

As will be a recurrent theme in this chapter, Muslim women are, on the one hand, seeking to transcend as well as challenge national identity by engaging in transnational networking and yet (almost paradoxically), on the other hand, reaffirming that their identities are still significantly constituted by the national. This finding became

---

3   WLUML was founded in 1984 as a transnational network calling for women and women's groups within the Muslim world to link together in solidarity in order to support women whose lives are being subjugated to unfair Muslim laws. For more information about WLUML's historical development, see Shaheed, 1994 and Moghadam, 2005, 142–72. Additionally, to learn more about WLUML advocacy, go to: <www.wluml.org>.

4   Cassandra Balchin, interview by author, 8 July 2004, at WLUML London Office, England. Since 1991, Balchin has been working for Shirkat Gah, the Pakistani women's organization which is the Asia Regional Coordination Office of the WLUML network. Her first meeting for WLUML was in 1993. Since 2000, she has been working to help coordinate the WLUML network and establish its international coordination office in London. At the time of this interview she was the Deputy Office Coordinator of WLUML. This interview was part of a larger conversation with two other WLUML staff, Anissa Helie and Hoda Rouhana.

5   Anissa Helie, interview by author, 8 July 2004, at WLUML London Office, England.

apparent as I discussed matters of identity with my interviewees, and discovered that they were quite conversant with the idea of 'transnationalism,' and eager to discuss its relation to their own experiences. As will be discussed in my concluding chapter, there is a need for further research on the relationship between the transnational and other concepts that can be used to analyze contemporary manifestations of global change, such as the transcultural and the translocal.[6]

As Muslim scholars and activists often note, the 'transnational' is a relatively recent historical reality for the Muslim world; for centuries Muslim identity has been defined by an aspiration towards the consolidation of the transcultural, trans-ethnic and trans-tribal religious community of Islam. In contrast, the 'transnational' began its history with the establishment of secular nation-states – a project that can also be connected with efforts to 'nationalize' Islam in relation to local geographic, ethnic, and linguistic experiences. The counter-movement against the spread of transnational secularity manifested itself in the activism of transnational revivalism and a program to re-establish the preeminence of Islam by creating an 'Islamic state.'

It is rather ironic to note that nationalism often spread through the Islamic world by transnational means. It came not only with the arrival of occupying European powers, but also with organized efforts of Muslims to find new bases of solidarity for resistance and state-building. Transnational Arab nationalism, or pan-Arabism, for example, was a largely secular project. It was transnational in a functional sense, but 'national' in its objective to consolidate various Arab polities into a single political nation-state. The chief protagonists of this endeavor sought to compartmentalize the religious and secular/political spheres, effectively promoting a privatization of religion. This movement – which has declined in popularity relative to Islamic revivalism and statism – sought not only to nationalize religion but also to define it in culturally specific terms, in relation to Arab, Persian, or Turkish identity. In contrast, transnational Islamic revivalism was transnational in both character and objectives, but also reactive in relation to the secular state-building project. It was rejectionist in this sense.

Although women have participated in both movements, ethnic nationalist and Islamic revivalist projects within the Muslim world have been highly androcentric in their leadership and discourse. In response to a variety of factors – that is, the failure of Arab secular nationalism, as well as the elusiveness of Arab unity, the mainstreaming of Islamic revivalism, and the creation of Islamic states (Moghadam, 2002) – identities of Muslim women and men are reflexively being constituted more and more by transnational hermeneutics – self-conscious application of effort to the interpretation of texts and their social contexts – as influenced by transnational encounters. Many interviewees agreed that these encounters can produce solipsistic or dialogical tendencies (see Chapter 4).

---

6   Though quite relevant to contemporary analysis of global politics, terms such as 'transcultural' and 'translocal' did not appear to be part of my interviewees' active vocabularies.

Women, Islam and the Emergence of Transnational Identity

Though transnationalism is not new to the Islamic experience, the public engagement of Muslim women in transnational networking represents an apparent discontinuity with the Muslim past. In recent decades, Muslim women's activism has become increasingly transnational, and ever more preoccupied with religious issues. Whereas previous generations of Muslim women activists sought (and were often able) to bypass cultures of religious interpretation through participation in powerful secular nationalist and socialist movements, the resurgence of Islamic identities and cultures brought about by the revivalist counter-movement has placed women's activism in a new context. Faced with a transnational Islamic revival movement, more and more Muslim women are finding it necessary and beneficial to engage in transnational networking themselves, and in the process to enter the dialogue about Islamic identity and culture.

As will be illustrated in this chapter, for many interviewees, the transnational has become a form of 'public space' that enables women to transcend isolation and derive inspiration for actions in their own local realities. It is beyond the boundaries of the nation (not to mention family and tribe) and yet it is bounded in the same sense as the internet: it is an open network that is constituted by those who actively engage in dialogue and participate. In other words, it transcends the more limited statist national identity in order to explore, live, illustrate, and act upon such identity. Inherent in transnational identity is the desire for new frontiers and to dwell in the 'space between' – interstitial space where one's identity may be local and at the same time beyond any specific locality.[7] As stated by Cassandra Balchin:[8]

> In a globalized context, the transnational is where there is a greater flow of information (i.e., strategies and ideas) across boundaries which can be national boundaries as well as other boundaries. This is very important for constructing networks: breaking boundaries so that the 'trans-'basis is not just 'transnational' but also 'trans-' a lot of other boundaries.

Increasingly, women are living in social spaces that are 'transnational' in nature. This phenomenon was emphasized by many interviewees:

> Transnationalism is crossing the border and experiencing identity in more than one country.

(Saideh Lotfian)[9]

---

7   As analyzed by Peter Mandaville in *Transnational Muslim Politics* (2001):
The new Islam hence exists in spaces which institutionalized forms of politics cannot reach ... The new Islamist intellectual thus represents an interstitial political identity, one which inhabits the gaps between institutional forms (Mandaville, 2001, 177).

8   Cassandra Balchin, interview by author, 8 July 2004, at WLUML London Office, England. See note 4.

9   Saideh Lotfian, interview by author, 29 May 2004, at University of Tehran's Department of Law and Political Science, Iran.

Transnationalism is redefining human thought. National borders are also being reconceptualized. We are living in the most exciting moment wherein larger blocks of communities are extending identity. There is a shift of smaller groups (tribal and familial affiliations) into larger groups (transnational in nature). (Maryam Hussain)[10]

Transnationalism is not a new concept. It is age-old truths which continue to be truths. The pursuit of humanism and the right for every human being to work for these objectives. It is the meeting point for all ways of knowing. (Salima Hashmi)[11]

Context-transcending and identity-transforming experiences ultimately lead to new alliances and networks, but begin with an attitude that seeks dialogue as a means of encounter.

Tracing Tendencies of Transnational Attitude and Dialogue

To understand how contemporary Muslim women are *experiencing* the transnational, I not only wanted to derive an understanding of how contemporary activists perceive self/other and society, but also transnational engagement. In a nutshell, what is it that inspires Muslim women to engage one another across great distances?

In an interview at Tehran's Institute for Women's Studies and Research, Mahboubeh Abbas-Ghulizadeh, the editor of *Farzaneh* (an Iranian women's studies and research journal), began by sharing her personal experience of 'feeling alone' in Iran, as if she was 'in exile' in her own homeland.[12] It was in the space of the transnational where she felt a sense of belonging:

The transnational is not limited to geographical or cultural contexts. I meet individuals from different parts of the world and I instantly connect with them … For example, when I met with Farida Shaheed[13] I felt I had so much in common with her and that I can communicate with her very easily …

After these initial comments – which were offered immediately after the interviewee had completed her work as host to a transnational Muslim women's workshop, with participants from Turkey, Afghanistan, and Europe – Abbas-Ghulizadeh compared herself to Hans Christian Anderson's 'Ugly Duckling' and stated: 'The transnational is this: that all the ugly ducklings will come together from all over the world and that they will understand that they are not so ugly as everyone has said; rather, they are beautiful swans.'

As these words suggest, an attitude of feeling like a marginalized 'other' is common among those who seek or develop a sense of transnational identity. Similar

---

10   Maryam Hussain, interview by author, 24 May 2004, via phone in Lahore, Pakistan.

11   Salima Hashmi, interview by author, 23 May 2004, at her residence in Lahore, Pakistan. See Chapter 4, note 15.

12   Mahboubeh Abbas-Ghulizadeh, interview by author, 27 May 2004, at the Institute for Women's Studies and Research (IWSR) in Tehran, Iran.

13   Farida Shaheed currently helps to direct WLUML and Shirkat Gah, a Pakistani women's rights organization. For more information about Shirkat Gah, go to: <http://www.net-ngo.com/detailpage.cfm?ngoid=94>.

sentiments emerged in many other interviews throughout the Muslim world. This feeling of marginalization in one's homeland can lead to a search for other 'others' who are somehow like oneself. These others can then be encountered as sources of knowing or as partners in dialogue. In the process, each other is greeted as a bearer of distinctive but not necessarily contradictory truths, and dialogue becomes a basis for new discoveries.

In encountering others via transnational dialogue, Abbas-Ghulizadeh felt that there were many Muslim women like herself. These women were like her in the sense of feeling isolated or 'other' vis-à-vis their homelands, and yet the presence of shared experiences did not necessarily mean a sameness of insights or contexts. This shared attitude of feeling 'otherness,' then, did not in itself constitute 'sameness' among the women activists. An attitude of openness was still required for learning – learning about each other's similarities and differences:

> Transnational dialogue is like cooking. My friends [like Farida Shaheed] might tell me how I should make *tacchin* [a Persian dish]; however, it is my own imagination, my own experiment on how I am going to make *tacchin*. Having contact with [a] transnational network is like cooking. Someone tells me this or that, and then each one of us analyzes how to practice this or that in our society.

> Therefore, Farida [like other transnational participants] must be very honest and hear all of the recipe. Unfortunately, in the kitchen, we always have these problems. A good cook always has the last to say about how much salt, how much pepper ... When Farida makes *tacchin*, Mahboubeh must like it. When Mahboubeh makes it Farida needs to like it.

> Transnational dialogue then is like marinating together, there are roles, attitudes, morals, and emotions. The women's transnational movement is like the story *Like Water for Chocolate*: through this work, you form yourself and find yourself.

Additionally, in my interview with Abbas-Ghulizadeh, the questions about dialogue and the transnational brought us back to the beginning of our encounter and Abbas-Ghulizadeh's thoughts about self and other:

> In transnational dialogue, you do not have one identity; rather, when I talk to one individual [pointing to Suzanne from Norway] I have one identity, when I talk to another [pointing to Melhem from Turkey] when I talk to you [myself] I have another identity. Through these dialogues I come to understand my identity and my self.

As Abbas-Ghulizadeh's words suggest, Muslim women activists develop new understandings of their identity through dialogue: both their sense of local particularism and of transnational solidarity are heightened. They experience a new context for the thinking about their activism and their own place in the world.

Before interviewing Abbas-Ghulizadeh, I was able to participate in the last day of a workshop coordinated by her. The workshop was entitled, 'Forum for Dialogue: Learning from Each Other.' It was part of a series of annual workshops hosted by

Tehran's Institute for Women's Studies and Research.[14] During this last day, I was able to interview many of the participants, hear all of the participants' final presentations, their critiques about the workshop, and reflections about meeting one another. As reflected in the following comments, one of the main issues that participants stressed was the need for further transnational dialogue and networking. Jamila Afghani, Director of the Noor Educational Center in Kabul, Afghanistan, stated:

> Women are between division and cohesion which ultimately creates confusion. For me, the future is not clear. There is a need for facilitation and dialogical training (where Muslim women listen to one another) and for more encounters amongst Muslim women from diverse backgrounds/understandings. There also is a need to avoid stereotyping and the need for listening to the other in order to overcome the secular/Islamist divide.

> [As a participant from Afghanistan, Afghani also noted that] Iran and Pakistan have an effect on Afghanistan. Identity crosses borders and influences thought. This is why governments need to support 'freedom of thought' and participatory citizenry.

Meltam Agduk, Project Coordinator for the United Nations Population Fund (UNFPA) in Ankara, Turkey, also stated: 'Perceptual change is happening and dialogical nurturing and communication is the main tool for change.' She then stressed the need for more forums (like this workshop which she called a 'model for Muslim women throughout the world') in helping the processes of 'gender-mainstreaming across borders.' Also, as a response to Afghani's comment that 'Women are between division or cohesion which ultimately creates confusion,' Agduk ended by stating that 'Confusion can be a catalyst for dialogue which ushers in hope.'

Many of the participants, like Roja Fazaeli (an Iranian university student who has been actively involved with the transnational workshops through Tehran's Institute for Women's Studies and Research), also agreed that Muslim women are in-between feminisms: secularist and Islamist.[15] However, these divisions should never be understood as fixed. Dialogue, then, is a way of talking about their ideological as well as cultural and political differences. For Fazaeli, the purpose of the workshop was 'to dialogue and learn from each other and challenge our opposite viewpoints.'

Before the conference concluded, participants formulated a number of suggestions for future dialogue sessions. These suggestions included the following:

- Future events should be planned in ways that ensure effective translation of proceedings, and should not rely too much on participant comprehension of the English language as a 'neutral' medium of expression.
- Events should include more engagement with women working on domestic and international violence.

---

14   This workshop was the third of its kind bringing together Muslim women from different localities of the Muslim world 'to foster discussion for the region, create a quarterly publication, and form a "women in transition" network' (as stated in their brochure and on their website). For more information, see: <www.ngotc.org>.

15   Afghani added to this point by stating: 'Feminism is used for different benefits, both exclusive and inclusive; especially for political identity.' She then used the example of 'secular conservative' and 'Muslim conservative,' and how the 'political overrides all aspects.'

- Young men should be invited to participate, to facilitate greater cross-gender awareness of women's issues.
- Participants in conferences should be brought into contact with local knowledge and experience of social issues and everyday life – for example, a conference in Iran should help non-Iranian visitors to develop a more direct understanding of the Iranian context.
- There was a great deal of enthusiasm for enlarging the conference size and including more non-Iranian participants (despite potential visa issues).
- Many argued that there was a need to incorporate more inter-generational dialogue.

A key, overarching theme of the workshop was that experiences of transnational dialogue help local struggles. This, then, was the source of widespread references to and affirmations of the value of dialogue.

As enthusiastic as the women at this Iranian workshop were about dialogue, it was also evident that dialogue takes time to mature and flourish in ways that lead to sustained cooperation across contexts. There were real and significant cultural as well as ideological differences among the women who had gathered for the event. As Farida Shaheed pointed out in an interview at the Shirkat Gah office in Lahore, Pakistan, enabling people to 'transnationally cook' can be quite difficult:

> The greatest challenge is how do you raise people's consciousness and get them to think about the different options. In the network, the most terrible thing that happens [is] when women are isolated in the context in which we live and have no access to information … they no longer dream of a different world. So depriving women of the ability to dream – [to imagine] that life can be different to us – is critical and it is the attempt of the network, therefore, to help people dream. We see this as the first step to changing reality. You only change reality when you think that life can be different.[16]

This emphasis on overcoming isolation as the beginning of transnational network formation was reiterated by a WLUML colleague of Shaheed, Cassandra Balchin, who also emphasized Abbas-Ghulizadeh's point about the simultaneous need to work through the differences that emerge:

> The first step [in forming a network] was to know there are other ways of being in Muslim contexts. Before Muslim women were told there is only one way of being. This was important to identify other contexts that signified difference. So, the very first step was to establish this diversity and break the myth of homogeneity …

> WLUML has been around for 20 years. Our central purpose has been to strengthen women's purposes in Muslim communities. However, our strategies have changed in these 20 years. Initially, WLUML was to link people and have people feel less alone and break the isolation which was an immediate physical, geographical barrier. Now isolation can mean not only physical but political and ideological …

---

16 Farida Shaheed, interview by author, 24 May 2004, at the Shirkat Gah Office in Lahore, Pakistan.

The early work of WLUML was dialogue: a lot of exchange and people talking to each other. This act of talking to each other was a reaching out and discussing things. We [in WLUML's core group of activists] no longer do this so much because we have been swept away with activities and responsibilities. However, this dialogue is very important and rich because that is when you get to form analysis. The annual meetings of WLUML are very important because it is when we have the opportunity to sit down and reflect together, face to face.

However, in forming a network, there is paradox ... on the one hand you have to take a position which constitutes a common convergence and yet, on the other hand, a network is deliberately setting itself up to have diversity in opinion, wherein sometimes there is not one position to be taken. People in the network can agree to disagree.

Dialogue [in addition to being an exchange, also] depends on how open people are to change ... [She then gave an example:] I was involved in a case wherein a woman was given a fatwa against her and then the man changed and apologized to her. Is this dialogue?[17]

According to Shaheed, successful transnational networking requires being open to differences – being willing to reconceptualize areas of cultural divergence, in order to impose limits on conflicts and enhance the ability of Muslim women to respond constructively to adversaries:

Therefore, for Shirkat Gah and the WLUML network, our objective is to try and inform women about the differences that exist which all may be called 'Muslim.' In the network, the first collective work that we did was an exchange program which we would define as a success since it opened the minds of the participants to difference ... We deliberately had two plans of action: 1) we brought together very diverse resource persons (persons who spoke from within the framework of interpretations and theology as well as people from the opposite genre who were absolutely secular – there is no salvation in religion). We did this so that women could experience that all of these women are from the Muslim world and they could see the different strategies that are found in the Muslim world. Then from the exchange, these women could choose their own ... 2) We sent Muslim women from one Muslim context to live in a very different context: so we took women from Southeast Asia and South Asia and sent them to the Middle East. We took women from the Middle East and sent them to the Far East.

For Shaheed and Balchin, when diverse groups respond to provocations with unprocessed emotion and local cultural ideologies, they allow a narrow contradiction to define an entire relationship. To avoid such an outcome, both words and deeds must communicate cooperative and constructive intent to deal with shared problems on the basis of common standards. Where ethnocentrism and ideological inflexibility imply a closing off of the ability to listen to the other, the aspiration toward a larger

---

17 Cassandra Balchin, interview by author, 8 July 2004, at WLUML London Office, England. See note 4.

framework of cultural encounter and shared values can open up the space for contextual understanding.[18]

These thoughts were echoed by Zainah Anwar, Executive Director of Sisters in Islam (SIS) and a transnational colleague of Abbas-Ghulizadeh, Balchin, and Shaheed. According to Anwar: 'there is not a synthesis happening, rather there are like-minded individuals coming together.' In an interview,[19] Anwar pointed out that it was only in Spring 2004 that she and Asma Khader[20] (General Coordinator for the Arab Resource Center on Violence Against Women in Amman, Jordan) brought together for the first time Southeast Asian women with Middle Eastern women in Bologna, Italy. She then added that although SIS is a localized organization which primarily focuses its activism on the transformation of Malaysian Islamic society, through its activism it has gained transnational support and notoriety. Evidence of this support may be found in the list of eminent transnational scholars and activists who have helped shape and support this organization's growth and development (for example, Amina Wadud, Fathi Osman, Farid Esack, and Shahla Sherkat).[21] Through transnational dialogues, SIS has been able to share and learn diverse strategies for challenging traditional authority (for example, by using publications, the internet, and media).

In 2002–04, several US advocacy institutions, such as the National Endowment for Democracy (NED), the United States Institute for Peace (USIP), and the Center for the Study of Islam and Democracy (CSID), recognized SIS as an exemplary organization for the promotion of 'women, political participation and democracy in

---

18   For more about Shaheed's thoughts about Muslim women and identity formation, see also Shaheed, 2001.

19   Zainah Anwar, interview by author, 6 October 2003, at the Marriott Hotel in Cairo, Egypt. Anwar was attending a conference which I coordinated at the Library of Alexandria in Egypt. The conference was entitled 'Contemporary Islamic Synthesis.'

20   At the time of this interview, Asma Khader was also recognized as a Minister of State and Government Spokesperson for Jordan, and was the former general coordinator of the Sisterhood is Global Institute's Jordanian Office (SIGI/Jordan), a non-profit women's rights organization, and the founder of the Jordanian National Network for Poverty Alleviation. To see the Arab Resource Center on Violence Against Women, go to: <www.amanjordan.org>.

21   Amina Wadud, a Professor of Religious Studies at the Virginia Commonwealth University, is the author of the popular book, *Qur'an and Woman: Rereading the Sacred Text from a Woman's Perspective* (1999). For more about Wadud, see Chapter 3, section 'Critique of Patriarchal Authoritative Hermeneutics.' Fathi Osman, a scholar of Muslim intellectual development and the contemporary Muslim world, has taught at prominent universities in the Middle East, Asia, and the West. Recently, he has been a scholar in residence to study the role of Islam in the contemporary world at the Omar Ibn Khattab Foundation in Los Angeles, CA. Farid Esack (for 2007–08) is the Prince al-Waleed bin Talal Visiting Professor at Harvard University and he occupied the Besl Family Chair for Ethics, Religion and Society at Xavier University, Ohio. Esack is also the author of many books, including *Qur'an Liberation and Pluralism: An Islamic Perspective of Interreligious Solidarity Against Oppression* (1997). Shahla Sherkat is the license holder and editorial director of *Zanan*, a Persian journal which contains articles and reports related to women's issues. All of these scholars/activists have influenced the formation of SIS in one way or another (that is, strategies for reinterpreting the Qur'an).

the Muslim World' (NED event, 26 June 2002). Such popularity has enabled SIS to participate in, as well as be supported by, transnational Muslim women networks, activism, and alliances. For instance, due to critical reformists' local successes in raising public awareness (for example, SIS in Malaysia, Mernissi's civil society project in Morocco, Sisterhood is Global Institute/Jordan's microfinance project), many of these activists, scholars, and organizations have established reciprocal working relationships: women's groups are participating in joint advocacy, such as the co-signing of letters to editors in different Muslim countries. Such organizations include, but are not limited to: Sisters in Islam, Women's Learning Partnership, BAOBAB for Women's Human Rights, Sisterhood is Global Institute, Women Living Under Muslim Laws, National Council of Women's Organizations, All Women's Action Society, Association of Women Lawyers, Amnesty International Malaysia, Women's Development Collective, Wijadi Labor Resource Center, and Movement Opposing the Unethical Suppression of Expression (SIS letters, 25 February 2002, 9 May 2002).[22] From these formal engagements, conversation and dialogue emerge and a 'language of familiarity' becomes established. Anwar adds that 'a sharing of different strategies' becomes the process for initiating a transnational discourse which, if nurtured, eventually supports transnational alliances.

After interviewing Anwar at a conference in Egypt, I interviewed Heba Rauf Ezzat, a Professor of Political Science at Cairo University and co-founder of IslamOnLine.com (one of the largest cyberspace Muslim networks). I also was able to bring together in a rare meeting Anwar with Rauf Ezzat. It is important to note that even though both Rauf Ezzat and Anwar knew of each other, this was the first time that they had met. In the conversation between the two, Rauf Ezzat added to Anwar's insight that the transnational is not only a coming together of 'like-minded individuals,' but it is also paradoxically a coming together of diverse personalities:

> Transnational discourses are emerging out of the need for them. For instance, the coming together of secularist and Islamist discourses is an emerging new Islamic discourse. This transnational dialogue is on the horizon ... It will depend on future generations to take these debates to the next level ...[23]

For Rauf Ezzat and Anwar, before the resurgence of Islamic social movements, several generations of Muslim women intellectuals were trained in the framework provided by a secular revolution, in which epistemology was separated from traditional religious ontologies. With the emergence of postmodern thought as well as new popular ideologies, more Muslim women intellectuals have felt inclined to reclaim Islamic identities and ontologies. They have sought to reform premodern religious epistemology through reflection on modern critical epistemologies. In the process, they are beginning to think that which was unthinkable – or not permissible – for previous generations, which sought to avoid asking questions about Islam

---

22   More information about these letters and/or organizations is available on SIS's website: <www.sistersinislam.org>.

23   Heba Rauf Ezzat, interview by author, 7 October 2003, at the Marriott Hotel in Cairo, Egypt.

through a 'secular bypass' of religious reasoning or a traditionalist aloofness to modernity.

Transnational Alliances and Networks: Some Illustrations

While it nurtures new relations with 'opposing' interpretive communities (that is, reformist vs. traditionalist, secularist vs. Islamist) and intensified dialogue with like-minded activists, transnational interaction also produces networks of local and global support for religious as well as cultural transformation. Through sharing of experiences, local organizations provide models for other local as well as transnational organizations in the Muslim world. These interactions, in turn, create transnational alliances and support networks.

Many informal alliances start in local contexts and, after gaining recognition or notoriety, become capable of producing alliances transnationally. A good example of informal alliances may be seen in the activism of the University of Tehran's Center for Women's Studies,[24] directed by Jaleh Shaditalab. Like SIS, which sought an alliance between Southeast Asian and Middle Eastern women, the Center for Women's Studies is working to create alliances amongst Iranian, Central Asian, and South Asian Muslims. In an interview, Shaditalab strongly affirmed the value of transnational activism:

> Transnationalism is the work of networking: transaction and transfer of knowledge brings about more understanding. Transnationalism, ultimately, is a network of understanding. We can learn from each other, rather than 'reinventing the wheel.'

> Exchange through transnationalism is the most important part of transnationalism. Through transnationalism we also keep our culture, it is not invasion like globalization. It is acculturation that happens. We exchange cultures and information, rather than ideologies.

> Ultimately, transnationalism is like islands of lights that are forming an archipelago. It shows that we are all interconnected.[25]

Another example of informal transnational alliances may be found in Morocco, where women activists have created an annual event called the 'Caravane Civique.' The idea for the Caravane came out of a conversation between Jamila Hassoune, the manager of Hassoune's Bookshop' in Marrakech as well as a traveling bookseller, and Fatima Mernissi, a Professor of Sociology at the University of Mohamed V in Rabat, Morocco. On her website, Mernissi describes the initial stages of the Caravane:

> In 1999, with the help of their teachers [Jamila Hassoune] conducted a survey of 1000 rural youth reading needs. 'They dream of a 10 DH (1 dollar) paperback' Jamila explained

---

24   See the Center for Women's Studies website: <http://cws.ut.ac.ir>.

25   Jaleh Shaditalab, interview by author, 29 May 2004, at the Center for Women's Studies, Tehran University. See Chapter 4, note 20 for more information about Shaditalab.

to me, weaving her statistics like a magic talisman. 'They also dream of meeting writers, artists, and mostly lawyers and doctors outside of courtrooms and hospitals.' Then after a long silence. 'Fatima, do you think lawyers and doctors from Casablanca would want to come to meet my youth up on the mountain?' This is how the 'Caravane Civique' started.[26]

In an interview with Hassoune, she stated that: 'The Caravane [then] was initially created to establish a forum for community and civic activism amongst a diverse group of Moroccan individuals who would be committed to breaking down the barriers between the rich and the poor as well as artists and professionals.'[27] For Hassoune, the Caravane then became a way to bring together Moroccans as well as transnational guests from all walks of life to discuss civil society as well as women's issues. Therefore, although the Caravane began as an intra-Moroccan dialogue, it soon spread across Morocco's borders into the realm of the transnational, linking activists from the Middle East, Europe, and South Asia.[28] Though now an independent project, many interviewees regarded the Caravane as a project that is closely allied with Fatima Mernissi's civic Islamic empowerment project (see <www.mernissi.net>). This belief is strongly supported by the fact that the Caravane's presence in cyberspace is channeled through Mernissi's popular website.

Interviews[29] with participants yielded a number of strong statements underscoring the usefulness of dialogue as local and as transnational. One participant called the project a 'transnational bandwagon'; another simply stated that: 'There is need for information to be shared across borders ... [as a basis for] success in alliances.' A European participant stressed the importance of the project being an 'intra-Moroccan' discourse where the transnational dimension was only there for 'outside support.' However, most of the participants stressed the growing importance of digital/virtual empowerment. (that is, cyberspace partnerships and support networks). One participant shared the timeliness of digital alliances and how, on the one hand, they nurture the 'individual's contact to the world of diversity [that is, information]' and, on the other hand, they provide a way for 'individuals to become resources to one another.'

Additionally, Hassoune eloquently pointed out that 'to share knowledge with the other is the caravan which is constantly moving. If you want to dialogue you have to travel.' To Hassoune, whose family has nomadic roots, such dialogue is both local and transnational, and from such dialogue comes a crucial exchange in ideas, projects, and strategies. For Hassoune, the nature of any caravan is never to be limited to 'a border'; rather, the only limitation upon a participant of any caravan is his/her responsibility to be a fellow traveler. She then shared a local expression:

26 To learn more about Jamila Hassoune and the Caravane's history, see: <http://www.mernissi.net/civil_society/caravane_civique/index.html>.

27 Jamila Hassoune, interview by author, 12 April 2004, at her residence in Marrakech, Morocco.

28 Hassoune also described how the nature of the transnational can be understood as 'mobile space.'

29 I interviewed several participants of the Caravane Civique at their annual conference which was hosted from 9 to 11 April 2004 at the Hotel Idou Anfa in Casablanca, Morocco.

'Haraka ka Baraka' which literally means 'Movement/Motion is a Blessing' and described it as 'to be in a caravan you have to move together and connect with new individuals who then too move together with you. This is the process of the journey wherein no person is greater than the other.' In asking Hassoune where she fits into the Caravane, she replied that she sees herself as 'a guide for this new nomadic caravan.' She then elaborated: 'A guide is the one who goes ahead of the caravan and makes sure that the path is safe. A guide is one who helps people travel and guarantees their arrival without any problems.'

In addition to informal women's transnational alliances, there are many other types of transnational networks that provide 'virtual' support to groups which advocate gender equality. These networks include, but are not limited to, an informal network of scholars (a 'reformist' group composed of such thinkers as Mohammed Shahrour of Syria and Abdul Karim Soroush of Iran); Progressive Muslims.com (some members are Farid Esack, Amina Wadud, Omid Safi, and Khaled Abou El Fadl); the Wisdom Circle for Thinkers and Researchers (based in Morocco, but members are located throughout all of North Africa); human rights groups (for example, BAOBAB for Women's Human Rights in Nigeria, Women's Alliance for Peace and Human Rights in Afghanistan); and democracy groups (for example, Center for the Study of Islam and Democracy in America, the International Movement for a Just World in Malaysia, and the International Center for Dialogue Among Civilizations in Iran). Some observers perceive these transnational organizations, alliances, and virtual communities as a 'Muslim global civil society' in the making – a virtual space where diverse individuals and organizations come to negotiate the differences in Muslim identities (an-Naim, 2002, 66).

The most well-known formal network of transnational activism for women in the Muslim world is Women Living Under Muslim Laws (WLUML). Cassandra Balchin placed particular emphasis on the virtues of forming active transnational networks:

As a network, one of the constant challenges is its structure and defining who does what … The theory of the network for WLUML is that all of the groups which are linked are autonomous (in terms of policy, strategy, financing); however, they link with us in terms that they find the network interesting. This interest depends on what we are doing. Therefore, we cannot force anyone to link with us or force anyone to not link with us. Instead of organization, where you 'sign-up,' a network is about writing to us and staying in touch where you engage in two-way flows. You send information, we send information … and a variety of relations emerge: those individuals/groups who engage actively with us (which we call 'active networkers'), those individuals/groups who occasionally check-in (an undefinable group), smaller group who gets involved in two-way activities (working on specific activities). The network, ultimately, requires a commitment to international solidarity and reaching out. In our work, we have noticed a shift in women who were not so willing to engage internationally or engage beyond their immediate boundaries; however, now they are recognizing the value in reaching out to other women in [a] transnational network. We have a smaller group of program implementation council (core group) which chooses the collective projects (overriding published documents – i.e., Qur'anic interpretation, building civil societies) [rather than representatives in different regions]. We do not pursue this idea of having representation.

Women involved in the local situation, know what is the best solution. We do not enforce/suggest any outside solution. This is where we are different from an international organization (like Amnesty International). First level is giving priority to the person who is at risk and the second level is giving priority to the strategy of the local group. This is the network principle: local people know the most appropriate local strategies. This recognizes that your strategy is not necessarily my strategy; however, we are interlinked: what happens in your locality does connect to my locality. Network then connotes both 'insider and outsider' perspectives all at the same time.[30]

These points were developed further by another WLUML woman activist, Anissa Helie:

I would add that within the networks, we also conceptualize transnational links by taking into account two-way relationships: breaking barriers of class, communities, nations in order to work together on a common project or common good. Making sure people involved gain from each other's interaction … I think also it is not just between different ethnicities, religious or national identities but also ideological estrangements. Because we work with secular and religious [groups and individuals] …[31]

Muslim women like WLUML are using networks to share information, create exchanges, pursue common projects, and develop solidarity. Their example has provided inspiration for other experiments that link local groups, experiencing transnational contact as a form of bridge-building.

One specific example of transnational networking and bridge-building is Sisters in Islam's (SIS) relationship with WLUML. Historically, WLUML has been recognized as a more secular, Western-oriented network that emphasizes human rights without specific reference to Islamic knowledge claims or methodologies. Anwar commented that, at first, WLUML had a hard time accepting SIS's methodological framework of participatory Islamic hermeneutics. As a result, SIS saw WLUML's tactics as more concerned with the abolishment of discriminatory laws and the abandonment of

---

30   Cassandra Balchin, interview by author, 8 July 2004, at WLUML London Office, England. For more about Balchin's thoughts on WLUML's network, see Cassandra Balchin's interview with Yoginder Sikand on the WLUML website (14 February 2005): <http://www.wluml.org/english/newsfulltxt.shtml?cmd%5B157%5D=x-157-119983>. Also see Balchin, 2003, 40–47. This article is also available on the WLUML website: <http://www.wluml.org/english/newsfulltxt.shtml?cmd%5B157%5D=x-157-20149>.

31   Anissa Helie, interview by author, 8 July 2004, at WLUML London Office, England. Helie also stated:

The world has changed and there is more complexity. Twenty years ago, the religious extremes were strong but now they are much more so. There is a shift between a time when secular initiatives were seen as valued options and now when there are more and more religious options … The religious right has gained a lot of 'know-how' (especially in political discourse and technological savviness) and powerful alliances. Because of this there has been a cooptation of human rights language by the religious right … [She then gave the example that very well-organized campaigns by Fundamentalist Islamic Groups in Nigeria are gaining more lobbying power and legitimacy at the UN and the European Council].

For Helie, one of WLUML's main concerns is to shed light on the cooptation of secular human rights as well as women's rights discourse by rigid fundamentalist groups.

Muslim ways, whereas SIS was not concerned with imitating the secular interpretive practices of Western feminists. Instead they sought to develop interpretive practices that reflected their own cultural realities and local needs. However, due to SIS's successes in Malaysia, WLUML has come to recognize SIS's 'reconciliatory' approach as dynamic, appropriate, and contextually relevant. This shift toward greater solidarity among activists with different philosophical outlooks is reflected in a speech by the founder of WLUML, Marie-Aimee Helie-Lucas:

> We must create such solidarity so that we will be able to retain control over our protest ... women and women's groups from seventeen countries or communities now communicate with each other through the Network, ask for documentation, compare so-called Muslim laws in different countries, send appeals for solidarity, inform each other about their strategies in very practical terms ... internationalism must prevail over nationalism.[32]

Unfortunately, as pointed out by Anwar, progressive Muslim voices in the West often compete in order to establish names for themselves. Basically, instead of Muslim reformist intellectuals coming together on issues, they are more likely to emphasize their differences (for example, Western-oriented, secularist Muslims vs. critical, reformist Muslims) than to seek common positions. In the final analysis, this competitive attitude has not served the causes they support or advanced the issues that need to be addressed.

A recent initiative that tries to address this attitude, of which SIS and Anwar have been a part, is the formation of the Women's Islamic Initiative in Spirituality and Equality (aka WISE), a group of over 100 diverse 'Muslim feminists,' including: Baroness Uddin, the first Muslim woman to enter the British House of Lords; Ingrid Mattison, the first Muslim woman to be elected Executive Director of the Islamic Society of North America; Massouda Jalal, Afghani presidential candidate; Asra Nomani, a popular Muslim woman writer and journalist who wrote *Standing Alone in Mecca*; and Daisy Khan, the Executive Director of the American Society for Muslim Advancement (ASMA). One of their first projects, spoken about at their first meeting (17–19 November 2006 in New York City), was to assemble an International Shura Council of Muslim Women in order to 'provide a much needed platform for diverse Muslim women to discuss global Muslim women's issues, assert [Muslim women's] rights through use of and in accordance with Islamic law, and build a coherent movement that empowers and connects Muslim women everywhere' (ASMA website, 2006). It is interesting to note that this initiative is heavily funded by prominent institutions such as the Ford Foundation, the Henry Luce Foundation, the Rockefellers Brothers Fund, and the Marshall Family Fund. Since it is in its embryonic stage of development, there will be need for further research on how WISE influences the variety of regions represented by its transnational members, especially in reform of Islamic law and the advancement of Muslim women's rights.

---

32   Marie-Aimee Helie-Lucas, in Cooke, 2001, 115.

Cyber-Islam

A new sense of public is emerging throughout Muslim-majority states and Muslim communities elsewhere. It is shaped by increasingly open contests over the authoritative use of the symbolic language of Islam ...

Situated outside formal state control, this distinctly Muslim public sphere exists at the intersections of religious, political, and social life. Facilitated by the proliferation of media in the modern world, the Muslim public can challenge or limit state and conventional religious authorities and contribute to the creation of civil society. With access to contemporary forms of communication that range from the press and broadcast media to fax machines and audio- and videocassettes and from the telephone to the Internet, Muslims ... have more rapid and flexible ways of building and sustaining contact and constituencies than was available in earlier decades (Eickelman and Anderson, 1999, 1–2).

As pointed out by Dale F. Eickelman and Jon W. Anderson, in the last and present century, due to the nature of contemporary communication, Muslims have been able to engage, interact, and influence each other in unprecedented ways. In particular, the forum of the internet not only opens access to information, knowledge, and contacts, but also fosters new identities in an increasingly multifaceted world. As a result, cyberspace empowerment (for example, cyberspace partnerships and support networks) has significantly strengthened transnational solidarity. As Azam Khatam, a prominent urban sociologist who specializes in gender, socio/spatial inequalities, and life politics in Tehran, Iran, stated: 'Virtual societies are forming through the internet and satellite. Censorship is very limited through these societies making room for more access and security for emerging trends of thinking and acting in Muslim societies.'[33] Khatam's remarks were further elaborated by her colleague, another urban sociologist from Iran, Masserat Amir-Ebrahimi:

In Iran, where the public sphere is closely monitored and regulated by traditional and state forces, the internet has become a means to resist the restrictions imposed on these spaces. For people living in these countries, especially marginalized groups such as youth and women, the internet can be a space more 'real' than everyday life ...

---

33   Azam Khatam, interview by author, 29 May 2004, at her residence in Tehran, Iran. I was introduced to Khatam by Mahboubeh Abbas-Ghulizadeh. Azam Khatam currently works as Urban Sociologist for the UARC, Urban Planning and Architecture Research Center in Tehran, Iran. She is also director of the Urban Committee for the Association of Iranian Sociologists. Khatam has also recently received a Social Science Research Council (SSRC) 2001–02 International Collaborative Research Grant in Reconceptualizing Public Spheres in the Middle East and North Africa. The grant's title was 'Authority and Public Space in Iran.' Through this grant, Khatam is currently working with the other awardees (for example, Masserat Amir-Ebrahimi and Ugur Komecoglu) to bring together Turkish and Iranian women into dialogue about civil society initiatives. For more information about this project, see <http://www.urban-ity.com>.

In Iran, the internet has become a key space for the rediscovery of self, socialization, dialogue, and the creation of social life that for various social, cultural, and political reasons does not often exist in real public spaces. The lack of freedom in real public spaces has rendered virtual spaces an important site for new encounters, the formation of communities, finding friends (especially of the opposite sex) and, finally, the possibility of redefining the self according to one's own narrative/liking.[34]

Both Khatam and Amir-Ebrahimi's thoughts are also mirrored in the works of Jon W. Anderson, and his remarks about how the internet especially attracts Muslim women:

> The anonymity of the Internet, and its reach, are important for enhancing the ability to 'browse' opinion-givers prior to interacting with them, as is – as one woman put it to me – the ability to get access to a shaykh without regard to physical as well as social distance.[35]

Time and space seem to be compressed in the experience of e-activism, wherein the political as well as hermeneutical engagement is no longer restricted to geography and the need for the protection of borders (whether familial, tribal, communal, or national). Such a forum opens alternative worldviews:

> The social dynamics of the emerging public sphere of Islam intersect these Internet dynamics that foster creolized discourses and identities that in turn expand the space between elite and folk, esoteric and exoteric, linking text and tafsir, interpretation and interpreters in extended continua, along which people can move and meet, rather than some vague mixing or merged 'hybridization.'[36]

By providing an open forum in cyberspace, the internet has become a highly pluralistic arena for Islamic thinking, networking, and campaigning. As a medium, however, the internet is neutral, providing scope for progressive and traditionalist as well as radical discourses. Websites arguing for dialogue and 'rethinking' exist in juxtaposition with those that embrace illicit violence as a means of implementing anti-pluralistic Islamic interpretations and identities. By providing a forum for such diverse voices – voices that have often been repressed or driven underground in specific national contexts – the internet simultaneously *undermines* traditional authority and provides amplification for a variety of different voices that are *competing* for authority. At the same time, the internet democratizes and provides a forum for voices that are not necessarily democratic. It pluralizes and even fragments identity while allowing space for totalizing, revisionist political projects.

---

34 Masserat Amir-Ebrahimi is also the coordinator of the 'Atlas of Tehran Metropolis,' in which her research interests are urban studies, sociology of cyberspace, and gender studies. For more on Amir-Ebrahimi's thoughts, see 'Performance in Everyday Life and the Rediscovery of the "Self" in Iranian Weblogs,' in Bad Jens: Iranian Feminist Newsletter, Seventh Edition (September 2004): <http://www.badjens.com/rediscovery.html>.

35 See Jon W. Anderson, 2001.

36 Ibid. For further critique of the internet's influence on Muslim identity, see also Bunt, 2000.

Even though it is extremely difficult to measure precisely the role of the internet in the creation of new transnational Muslim identities, it is possible to recognize that it is a method and medium of transforming Muslim individual and communal identities. In *Muslim Networks: From Hajj to Hip Hop* (2005), Miriam Cooke and Bruce Lawrence describe the impact of the internet on Muslim women in the following terms:

> The Internet reveals a paradoxical aspect of the metaphorical function of networks: they are de-territorialized and gender inclusive even while remaining socially restricted in other ways. Unlike in the time of Ibn Khaldun, Muslim women today can travel, physically and imaginatively, forming their own networks. The network linking a Saudi woman in her country's capital with an Afghan refugee woman and an American Muslim woman becomes a forum of virtual connections in which three women can imagine themselves together for various purposes – friendship, solidarity, security, and commercial exchange. At the same time, however, this network links three physical beings in real places: Riyadh, Peshawar, and Chicago. The cyber network is powerful precisely because it allows these two ways of connecting that are at once free of space and bound to place. It allows individuals – in this case, individual Muslim women – to think themselves elsewhere while remaining in situ; it opens up the possibility for actual movement that serves to reinforce virtual connections (Cooke and Lawrence, 2005, 11).

In most Muslim countries, the internet is still a novelty. Fascination with the novelty of the internet, together with an attitude that might be described as 'cyber-optimism,' was highly evident in my interviews. In Morocco, for example, I encountered an emphasis on the enormous potential for what Fatima Mernissi describes as 'innovative sexual strategies in emerging cyber-Islam':

> Many see Islam and technology as opposed, the first being equated with tradition and the second with modernity. They might be wrong. Information technology might allow Islam for the first time in history to reach its full cyber-democratic potential by insuring free expression to all members of the Umma (the Moslem community), including many of the half billion women who have gained access to education and computers. If politicians are still allergic to women in parliaments, the ladies have organized their silent revenge by invading the worlds of sciences and technical professions …

> Educated women armed with computers have defeated extremists by denying them monopoly to define cultural identity and interpret religious texts. Armed with information technology, women have engineered a pluralist reading of both religion and culture, highlighting humanist verses of the Koran which deny sacredness to violence. 'There is no violence in religion.'[37]

Although such arguments do not place much emphasis on potentially reactionary uses of the internet, they do make a good case for the relevance of the medium to activist purposes. The internet seems to have a 'leveling effect' on Islamic discourse, providing access to diverse opinions and a means by which they can be expressed.

---

37 Fatima Mernissi, 'The New Cheherazads: Women and Civil Society in Digital Islam,' a text for her word–image exhibition and workshop project at the American University, 15–16 April 2000. See also Mernissi, 2005.

The result is a challenge to traditional forms of authority, a diversification of Islamic knowledge claims, and a consolidation of new activist networks.

Conclusions

> The women I network with, they inspire me. The people I have daily encounters with, they inspire me. You meet new people and find different inspiration from people.

> (Cassandra Balchin)

As the voices of these women testify, transnational dialogue and networking is providing inspiration for activism as well as a new framework for thinking about identity. When women from diverse contexts are able to make contact with one another through conferences, as well as through modern communications technology, they experience empowerment to approach their localized work with greater confidence and creativity. Simultaneously, they become co-creators of an emergent, transnational discourse that projects a pluralistic attitude toward Islamic identity politics. This discourse respects local and national identities that are not specifically Islamic, while also embracing wider Islamic and humanistic identities which it seeks to integrate on the basis of new intertextualities – new, dialogical approaches to Islamic hermeneutics. Dialogue becomes both a means of engagement and a norm that embodies what they are working for: more horizontal and mutualistic social and gender relations.

As women enter into dialogue with one another as well as with their diverse cultural contexts and the schools of thought that shape them, they begin to see themselves not merely as individual Muslim women activists or as members of a particular national community, but also as voluntary participants in a new interpretive project predicated on dialogical relations between self and other. Self-consciousness about being involved in transnational dialogue changes their sense of identity as well as their sense of possibility, opening new horizons for creativity. Activists begin to see themselves as interpreters – a role that was previously reserved for others – who are capable of engaging their cultural contexts on the basis of new 'interpretive identities,' or 'identities as interpreters.' Transnationalism becomes not only a means of empowerment, but also a doorway to redefinition of society, of self-identity and of roles within the Islamic community and an emergent global community.

Chapter 6

Muslim Society and State: The Politics of Public Space

A striking theme of my conversations with scholars and activists was the conviction that something 'new' is emerging – an approach to Islamic interpretation and activism that is at once transnational and dialogical, that enables women as well as men to imagine new roles for themselves in the public sphere. As the comments cited in Chapter 5 suggest, many interviewees were quite conversant with the idea of transnationalism. In the present chapter, I will discuss ways in which participation in transnational networks has affected the ways in which Muslim women perceive their agency in local social milieus. Quite uniformly, my interviewees argued that, far from distracting them from immediate public concerns, transnational dialogue was changing the ways they think about their identities as engaged citizens within the frameworks of nation-state and Islamic community (*Ummah*). Their testimony suggests the possible emergence of what might be called a 'transnational civic Islam' – a new interpretive community that embraces both the ideal of a transnational Muslim community and a cosmopolitan ethos of citizenship and social responsibility.

As we noted in Chapter 5, transnationalism is not new to Islamic contexts. Participants in the social networks explored by this book, however, are creating a qualitatively distinct variety of transnationalism. Traditional Islamic culture was distinguished by the transnational religious culture transmitted by the *'ulema*. Modern Islamic revivalism has been similarly transnational in character, taking advantage of modern printing, expanded literacy, and new forms of social organization and mobilization to transmit an arguably revisionist account of Islamic history in defense of Muslim values – especially, but not exclusively, 'family values' – and the concept of a justly administered Islamic *shari'ah* state. In contrast, the transnational Islam described by my interviewees could be characterized as a civic Islam – an Islamic identity that underscores pluralism and makes room for cultural diversity as well as individual expression. It is an Islam of women as well as of men, an Islam that seeks empowerment for peaceful change rather than for maintenance of traditional institutions or the capture of political power.

Reimagining National Identity and the Muslim Public

The State in Classical Western International Relations Theory and the Return of Religion

Since the Treaty of Westphalia in 1648, for classical Western international relations theorists, identity has been (and still is) predominantly configured in relation to secular, self-interested nation-states. Theoretical preoccupation with nation-state relationships in world politics has led to what some critics call a 'substantialist' understanding of identity wherein constructions of self and society are regarded as 'given': they are fixed, homogeneous across time and space, and non-negotiable.[1] When understood in such terms, the nation-state and its self-interest tend to be regarded as ends in themselves. The traditional literature on nation-states is conspicuously silent with respect to the possible existence of cross-cutting identities that might make relational cooperation among states and peoples more enduring.[2] For practical intents and purposes, each state is an island to itself.

In the search for parsimony or for an intellectual narrative that would be appealing to policymakers, traditional theorists of international relations largely sought to bypass or neutralize issues of religion, culture, gender, and communal identity. Rather than treat identity as intrinsically dynamic or multi-layered, theorists reduced identity to a normative constant that is congruent with the boundaries of the nation-state. In the historically dominant and still influential *realpolitik* school of thought ('political realism'), religion, culture, gender, and ethnicity have been regarded as largely irrelevant, because the causes of international conflict are, presumably, over-determined by an aggressive human nature and an international structure of competition among states. Politics, theorists proposed, has far more to do with material interests than with presumably 'soft' ideas, ideologies, and identities. States – whether Muslim, Christian, or secular – behave in similar ways and have the same basic motivations to compete for power and security.

Insistence on homogeneous and static notions of national identity (delineated by state boundaries) has led to serious conceptual limitations within international relations theory. Despite the emergence of competing theoretical frameworks such as neo-liberalism[3] (which emphasizes economic gain more than security competition, while largely retaining most aspects of the realist ontology), the teaching of international relations continues to begin with explorations of 'realist' assumptions that are not conducive to the study of transnationalism. These assumptions include:

---

1   These critics come from a variety of disciplines and analytical positionings; however, one could argue that each critic is mainly concerned about the problems of essentializing the processes of social reality. Some of these critics and their influential works are: Peter L. Berger and Thomas Luckmann, 1966; David Blaney and Naeem Inayatullah, 2003; Mustafa Emirbayer, 1997, 281–317; Charles Tilly, 2002; and Iver B. Neumann, 1999.

2   Gleaning from classical political theorists (for example, Hobbes, Machiavelli), some dominant contemporary international relations theorists of the nation-state and their influential writings are: Hans J. Morgenthau, 1973; Kenneth N. Waltz, 1956; Ernest Gellner, 1983; Eric Hobsbawm, 1990; John Hutchinson and Anthony D. Smith, 1994.

3   See Keohane, 1984.

1. Human beings are naturally and inevitably aggressive and acquisitive, particularly in their collective behavior;[4]
2. Religious, cultural, gender, and psychological dimensions of human conflict and difference are largely disregarded, with an emphasis placed on presumably universal processes of coercion, incentive, and contractual negotiation;[5]
3. Power is equivalent to capabilities for coercion and deterrence; military superiority and credible threats can deter many if not most armed conflicts;[6]
4. Because the international system is an anarchic 'jungle,' powerful nations can and should formulate and dictate the 'rules of the game' for weaker nations;[7]
5. Non-state actors only play a role in international affairs insofar as states allow them to participate – states influence non-state actors, but non-state actors have, at

---

4   This limitation has often been formally stated by theorists of the power politics, realist paradigm in the West (for example, Thucydides, Hobbes, Machiavelli, Hans Morgenthau, Kenneth Waltz, E.H. Carr,and so on). This assumption can also be traced in the thought of historical Muslim thinkers (for example, al-Farabi, al-Ghazali, and Ibn Khaldun).

5   Basically, if not simply overlooked in the course of Western military, political, and institutional analysis, religious, cultural, gender, and psychological dimensions of conflict are implicitly reduced to 'innate aggression' (Hobbes, 1985) or 'men are selfish' (Machiavelli, 1950, 61) or a drive for power (Morgenthau, 1973). Furthermore, in the Western perspective, overt consideration of religion, gender, and culture are sometimes ruled out not only because they are not parsimonious, but also because they are deemed superfluous. As reflected in a statement by Morgenthau: 'personality, prejudice, and subjective preference, and all the weaknesses of intellect and will which flesh is heir to, are bound to deflect foreign policy from their rational course …' (Morgenthau, 1973, 7). This preservation of 'rationality'/ 'irrationality' dichotomy obscures the fact that the world is driven by *plural rationalities*. Because of profound differences in value orientations and operating assumptions, there is no single, a priori universal standard according to which 'rationality' can be evaluated from a distance. The use of rationality as a simplifying assumption in power-political analysis may well be useful for the creation of generic models and systematic theories, but it does little to encourage serious, fair-minded inquiry into the different motivations and values of real human participants.

6   This third limitation, that military capability is the primary index of power and basis for peace, is upheld in classical sayings: *Flavius Renatus Vegetius* ('If you want peace, prepare for war'). In power-political theory, the threat of 'force' is a diplomatic trump card that can and should be played when other inducements are not producing results. Armaments and threats to use them enhance security; threats to attack can deter aggressive opponents. According to Waltz: 'The constant possibility that force will be used limits manipulations, moderates demands, and serves as an incentive for the settlement of disputes' (Waltz, 1956, 112).

7   The tendency to focus narrowly on the national interest without consideration of its connection to other interests can easily lead to highly idiosyncratic and even imperialistic definitions of national interest. From a power-political standpoint, it is natural that powerful nations formulate and dictate the 'rules of the game' for weaker nations, thereby creating an 'order' which need not or cannot be predicated upon justice. This theme recurs in many classic tracts and statements of power politics, from Thucydides' Melian Dialogue to Kenneth Waltz's structural realism.

best, a minimal impact on states and are therefore of little intrinsic importance.[8]

The implication of these assumptions is that, as experts familiar with competitive
rules of the international system, official diplomats and decisionmakers have nothing
substantial to learn or gain from collaboration with non-state actors. International
politics is viewed largely as power competition; the meaning and substance of
'politics' is regarded as fixed rather than as socially constructed and negotiated.

Despite the predominance of the nation-state in traditional international relations
thinking, newer theoretical trends have begun to place a stronger emphasis on culture,[9]
religion,[10] and gender[11] in world politics. In response to the *realpolitik* paradigm,
critical and constructivist voices in international relations are now arguing that their
discipline should avoid ethnocentrism and recognize the limitations of the 'power
politics' experience. National identity needs to be reconceptualized in relation to
dynamic, context-specific, and indeterminate historical processes of interaction and
negotiation. National identity, like self-identity, emerges within social processes
of 'imagining community' and is not a predetermined political fact or a natural
consequence of territorial boundaries.[12] The process of *imagining* community is an
ongoing dialogue of social networking experienced through the participants who
negotiate and re-negotiate boundaries of self and other at different levels of social
organization: societal, national, and transnational.

---

8   The danger of this power-political assumption is the entanglement of self-esteem/
pride and triumphal nationalism. As former Senator William Fulbright no doubt realized, self-
serving rhetoric is a part and parcel of power-political life:

[The arrogance of power is] a psychological need that nations seem to have in order to
prove that they are bigger, better, or stronger than other nations. Implicit in this drive is the
assumption, even on the part of normally peaceful nations, that force is the ultimate proof
of superiority – that when a nation shows that it has a stronger army, it is also proving that
it has better people, better institutions, better principles, and in general, a better civilization
(Fulbright, 1966, 8).

Though often intended for public consumption, repeated self-congratulatory talk defining
a country as 'the world's only superpower,' or 'the greatest democracy' easily becomes
part of elite common sense and shapes the psychological as well as hermeneutical context
of decisionmaking as seen in the works by Samuel Huntington and Francis Fukuyama. The
triumphalist spirit can be seen in the notion that international relationships can and should be
managed by 'official' experts; this idea results in a 'top-down' game of politics negating any
alternative vantage point(s).

9   See Lapid and Kratochwil, 1996.

10   See Petito and Hatzopoulos, 2003.

11   See Tickner, 2001; and Sylvester, 2002.

12   This idea of 'imagining community' is in response to Benedict Anderson's idea of
'imagined community' wherein social reality as seen through the lenses of the nation is reduced
to an already constituted manifestation. See Benedict Anderson, 1991. It is interesting to note
that many Muslim women scholars have found Anderson's way of conceptualizing helpful
(for example, Kandiyoti, 1991; Karam, 1998).

The rise of postmodernism and then constructivism in international relations theory,[13] together with post-Cold War and post-9/11 interest phenomena of ethnic and cultural politics, has led to new efforts to rethink identity in international affairs – to conceive of identity as dynamic, and as derivative of complex processes of interaction. Whereas earlier literatures on interdependence and transnationalism (for example, in the 1970s and 1980s) focused more on material interests and posited a *homo economicus* model of human behavior, the emergent literature is creating space for more open-ended inquiry into identity and politics.[14] Much less is taken for granted, including the preeminence and homogeneity of the nation-state. There is a new openness to writings from the human sciences on the dialogical construction of self-identity and other-identity, and of the relevance of this literature (with its tendency to focus on micro-level interactions) to relations among human collectivities (Neumann, 1999).

Islam and the Nation-State

It is a truism that the nation-state is weakly rooted in the Muslim world; some would go so far as to describe the nation-state as a forcibly transplanted European construct that arrived in Islamic lands through colonialism, and that was later accepted by Muslim elites who reconstructed local histories, often by placing greater emphasis on ethnic and linguistic (that is, secular) solidarities such as those presupposed by Western international relations theory. As constructivists and specialists on Islam have recognized, however, nation-states have not been able to maintain legitimacy through appeals to ethnic, regional, and linguistic solidarities alone. Political legitimacy throughout the Islamic world has also depended – at least in part – on symbolic invocation of a larger Muslim community to which the leaders and citizens of nation-states are accountable. Discourse about Islam and the authoritative interpretation of Islamic norms remains a potent factor in the politics of Islamic societies.[15]

Political identity and the very nature of public space in Muslim lands are contested subjects, with some individuals and social groups (especially those connected with the state) tending to define themselves in secular, nationalistic terms, and others defining their identity and agency in relation to the Muslim *Ummah*. Still others influenced by Western liberalism – typically a small minority – define their identities in more individualistic terms. Although the politics of identity vary in different

---

13   In addition to the critics of 'substantialist' social theory (see note 1 in this chapter), some other thinkers are James Der Derian and Michael J. Shapiro, 1989; R.B.J. Walker, 1992; and Patrick Thaddeus Jackson, 2002, 439–68.

14   This was particularly evident in IR literature emphasizing the impact of transnationalism on world politics, as seen in the emergence of transnational corporations and international organizations. See Risse-Kappen, 1995; and Rosenau, 1990. Later this literature would be followed by the emerging arguments about transnational social movements: see Smith, Chatfield and Pagnucco, 1997.

15   See works by Lapidus, 1983, 1988; Eisenstadt, 2002; Sohail Hashmi, 2002; Brown, 2000; Eickelman and Piscatori, 1996.

Muslim states, the basic dynamics of identity contestation are often quite similar even when outcomes differ (see Figure 6.1). Competition between secular nationalists and advocates of Islamic collective identities has produced quite different results in such states as Turkey and Iran. While some states have constitutions that designate Islam as the official religion (Saudi Arabia goes so far as to claim that the Qur'an is the constitution), others do not. Scope for individual freedoms of expression and association also varies.

Despite the apparent precariousness of nation-states in predominantly Muslim lands – especially in the Middle East, where pan-Arabism and pan-Islamic ideas have both been invoked to challenge the status quo – the nation-state has had a marked impact on the social and political development of Muslim communities. With few exceptions (for example, Yemen and Pakistan/Bangladesh), the boundaries delineated by departing Western colonial powers have held. Similarly, there is a marked (but not universal) tendency for elite social strata to uphold more secular forms of nationalism and identity than those who are not directly associated with the state. Social movements seeking to integrate or balance competing identities – national, Islamic, and individual/humanistic – are a relatively new phenomenon that appears to be linked to experiences of transnational dialogue. While it is too early to predict the outcome of these social movements, my investigation of women's activist networks suggests that there is a growing interest in transcending 'secular vs. religious' dichotomies, while providing greater scope for the individual in the face of assertive religious and nationalistic collectivisms. It is for this reason that the space at which national, religious, and individual-centered identities overlap in Figure 6.1 is labeled 'Transnational Civic Islam': the activists and thinkers who I interviewed are committed to reimagining public space and their roles as citizens within that space. They are seeking to transcend what they experience as restrictions imposed by the nation-state, traditional/revivalist Islamic identities, and secular individualistic outlooks. Participation in transnational networks appears essential to their process of envisioning integrative alternatives.

Significantly, religion tends to play a more influential role in Muslim polities than in the West. While this contrast can be overstated (a non-Christian, after all, would have difficulty becoming president of the United States and religious organizations are quite effective at mobilizing American voters), it is difficult to understand the politics of most predominantly Muslim states without analysis of the role of authoritative religious interpreters in the 'public sphere.' Stated simply, state officials in predominantly Muslim states routinely rely upon a state-supported (some would say 'co-opted') corps of religious leaders (the *'ulama*) to justify and legitimize government policies. Those who challenge the authority of the state also rely on religious discourse – often the discourse of anti-establishment Islamic revivalism. Advocates of incremental social reform also seek to advance religious arguments for their proposed changes in social norms and government policy. Religious legitimation of policy options is vital in Muslim public discourse, with 'authoritative' religious interpreters playing a mediating role between state and society. Figure 6.2 depicts the prominent role of religious authorities in Muslim politics by locating religious interpreters in between the state and the larger Muslim public.

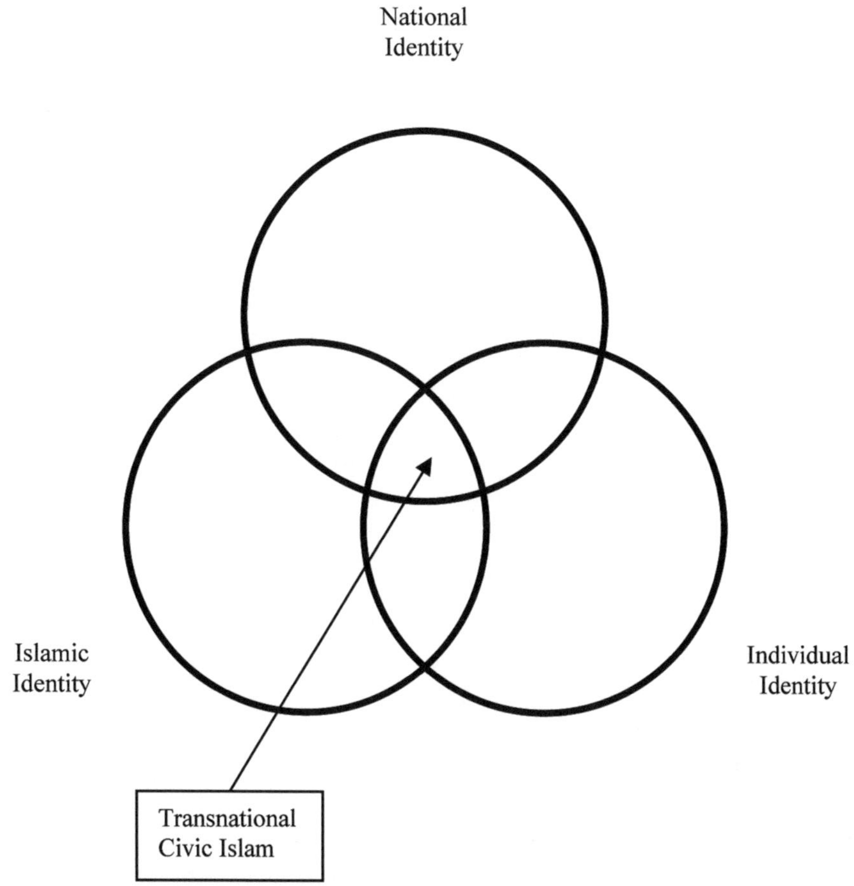

National
Identity

Islamic
Identity

Individual
Identity

Transnational
Civic Islam

Figures 6.1 Dimentions of identity contestation and integration

Differing from secular states in the West, Muslim regimes gain their legitimacy with the Muslim populace through the agency of religious leaders – typically the *'ulama.* Religious leaders, in turn, are dependent upon both the state and their popular followings for status in society (Kelsay, 2002, 17). As empowered representatives of Islamic authenticity, the *'ulama* mediate between state and society, pronouncing norms for relations of authority and submission – between state and society as well as between men and women in the so-called 'private sphere.' As some more 'reformist' voices have suggested, the perpetuation of an authoritarian state requires that traditionalist authoritative voices of Islam be co-opted and reconstructed to create a discourse that in turn results in the compliance of the Muslim populace to Islam as understood by traditional authorities (Abou El-Fadl, 2001, 34).[16]

---

16 Khaled Abou El-Fadl analyzes this vicious cycle of consent and coercion in his first book, *And God Knows His Soldiers: The Authoritative and Authoritarian in Islamic Discourses* (2001a) and then further argues his points in another book, *Speaking in God's*

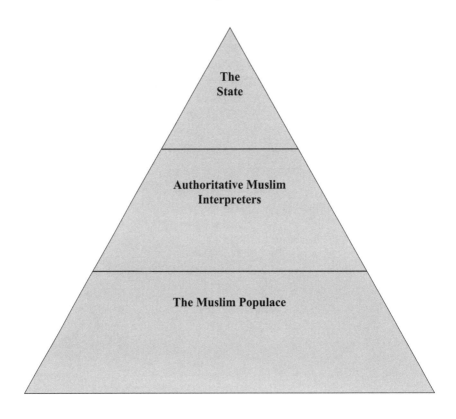

Figure 6.2 Religion and political legitimacy

Although the most influential religious interpreters tend to be ranking members of the *'ulama*, leaders of Sufi orders, populist preachers, and social reformers can also play – or compete for – influence in the Muslim public sphere. Particularly in the wake of resurgent Islamic revivalism, actors who are unable to invoke an Islamic normative basis for proposed policies may face significant barriers to effective political participation. Many of my interviewees argued that it is vitally important to

---

Name: Islamic Law, Authority, and Women (2001b) by alluding to the fact that the forming of a new Islamic public sphere would enable both men and women to hold the hegemonic state and its substructures accountable for their actions. According to Abou El-Fadl, although hegemony implies staying power and disproportionate (but not absolute) influence on the conditions that frame the actions of others, 'the state' cannot completely stand aloof from the society that it circumscribes, for government functionaries are, ipso facto, members of society. Therefore, Abou El-Fadl and like-minded reformist Muslims argue that it is in the interests of predominantly Muslim states not to suppress independent civil society groups because, in the end, progress comes from the dialectical as well as dialogical interaction amongst the Muslim state and Islamic civil society groups.

understand the Islamic bases of legitimacy in order to achieve authoritative agency in Muslim societies.

A key and oft-repeated point made by interviewees was that Islamic discourse is not an inevitably conservative factor in the politics of their societies. By seeking to 'rediscover' Islamic texts and contexts, would-be reformers can establish social and political legitimacy through utilization of culturally appropriate vocabulary and values. Using an Islamic idiom reduces the likelihood of political backlash, while also providing a basis for effecting desired changes in popular social and cultural practices as well as in the more authoritative norms, beliefs, and rules defined by religious specialists. By engaging rather than bypassing the authoritative Islamic discourse, they can participate more actively and effectively in local and transnational Muslim public spheres.

Utilization of Islamic interpretation in the pursuit of 'progressive' social change is not a completely new or unprecedented phenomenon (it arguably dates to the nineteenth century), but it remains true that for most of the twentieth century, advocacy on behalf of women relied more heavily on nationalist and socialist discourses. When nationalist and socialist ideological frameworks were preeminent, there was a tendency to dichotomize Islam and secularism. The perceived choice was between two diametrically opposed categories of legitimacy: 1) traditionalist Islam – in which the relationship between public and personal is *religiously* predetermined; or 2) complete secularism – in which the relationship between public and personal is *non-religiously* coercive. Most of the activists I interviewed framed matters differently, arguing that it is possible to gain legitimacy through engaging public discourse on its own terms, without avoiding religious bases of argumentation *or* bowing to established, 'authoritative' interpretations. They perceived 'civil society' – a term that surfaced with surprising frequency – as a public space that is intrinsically pluralistic and open to dialogue and multiple frameworks of interpretation.

Women, Islam and Civil Society

If traditional Muslim society generated and legitimated social norms through the agency of the *'ulama* and their relationship with the Muslim state, contemporary Muslim societies are increasingly debating the legitimacy of social norms and political institutions within the context of an expanded 'civil society' (in Arabic, *mujtama al-madani*). Although there are a variety of Western definitions of this concept, from Hobbes to Hegel to Gramsci, most of my interviewees had no knowledge of these definitions; rather, they only knew of the concept through their activist networks. 'Civil society' has become an element of the popular lexicon – a term that is used to denote a sphere of social activism. Seyed Jafar Ahmed discussed the subject at length:

> Civil society has been thought about differently in different times. The connotation of civil society changes with the contextualization of time. What was Marx's civil society might not be today's civil society in Pakistan. Presently, the term civil society is seen in a larger context of all institutions which are not governed by the operations of the state directly but, nonetheless, have relations. There are relational domains between state and society,

each influencing the other in a symbiotic relationship of legitimacy. The levels of maturity of the civil society and the state depend on the level of maturity in both realms. When the society is suppressed by the state, then the state inevitably is limited. Construction of the state is determined by the character of civil society.

According to Ahmed, the concept of civil society is relevant because it provides a context for thinking about action for social and political change. Like many Western theorists, he was generally positive about the innovative potential within civil society, but conditioned his comments by acknowledging that civil society activists are not always socially responsive and effective.

> Unfortunately, like history, society has been defined by the elites. However, not all good ideas have started from the lower class level, rather there is innovative thinking from all levels. The more innovation from any level is important. Also, energy should not be focused on who originated the idea … but on the idea itself. We need more ideas. I have worked with many NGOs throughout Pakistan, and I feel that many of them have reached their saturation point, meaning they lack ideas. This is not a negative comment but critical … They have become more as functionaries who follow donors' voices rather than vehicles of social change. They become static lacking dynamism. They also become disconnected. Their relationship with the donors becomes greater than the relationship with those who they are assisting (e.g., women in Pakistan).[17]

Many of my interviewees spoke of inherent challenges and tensions within their civic activism. Most, for example, were obliged to maintain active relations with the state to achieve legitimacy and security as social actors, while at the same time seeking to maintain autonomy in their efforts to affect legal and social norms. Relations with the state were both enabling and constraining – enabling because they were essential for legitimate social action in imperfectly democratic states, and yet constraining insofar as relations with the state can result in co-optation, loss of legitimacy vis-à-vis society, and loss of dynamism and independence.[18] In reaction to these limitations Muslim women have engaged in transnational activism, as discussed in Chapter 5, and in civil society projects.[19]

Significantly, some individuals did not care for the term 'civil society,' finding it either too restrictive or too specifically Western in origin. Farida Shaheed was among them:

---

17 Seyed Jaffar Ahmed, interview 20 May 2004, at the University of Karachi's Pakistan Study Centre, Pakistan. See Chapter 4, note 24.

18 For many interviewees, like Heba Rauf Ezzat, the state was more 'a barrier' than a catalyst for women's activism. As a result, according to Rauf Ezzat, women should focus more on the 'society' (which represented to her a forum of dynamism and potential change) instead of the 'state' (which connoted to her a static entity beyond hope).

19 For many interviewees, these two spheres are mutually inclusive of one another, as stated by Seyed Jaffar Ahmed: 'The extension of civil society and how globally imagined it is dynamically constitutes being in a transnational space. Transformation of societal space imagined engages and negotiates different collectivities which emerge as new conversations, new ways of understanding self and other.'

[Civil society] is a term that I have had enormous problems with. When I first heard this term and the context it was being used in, I was outraged. Someone was using it to state that 'Saudi Arabia had no civil society.' To me that was a peculiar statement. I do not believe that any society is devoid of civil society, meaning there is no society that is devoid of individuals who want to be engaged in changing their society.

I think the <u>term</u> has come to <u>mean</u> something very narrow. It means institutions of civil society which excludes all non-formal organizational means that people make to engage with their decisionmakers, and yet this happens. It is considered very positive.

I do not use any of these labels ... The network is trying to bring about some feminist consciousness in order to change the structures of power ... The main issue is to address the balance of power whether it is at the household, local village level, national level, or international level.[20]

Seyed Kazem Sajjadpour shared Shaheed's perception that misuse of the term 'civil society' could amount to imposing a loaded concept reflecting another society's experiences:

There are different layers of civil society. But the essence of civil society is a space for people to actively participate in the public sphere but are connected to the state. But the notion of civil society is very Western where you have the separation between private and public spheres. However, in the Middle East, these differentiations are more difficult to define. Cultural and political phenomena make this impossible.[21]

Many interviewees did engage in conversations about civil society when invited to do so through questioning. While some did challenge conventional usages, most would disagree with Cassandra Balchin at WLUML, who stated that 'Civil society is a sweet word for "non-governmental organizations."' Rather, as was conveyed in a conversation with Rachida ben Faida in Morocco:

Civic Islam or civil society in Islam reconceptualizes the individual as active in a public sphere that has flexible borders. In such a sphere there is equal citizenship in participatory volunteerism.

When there is no censorship and there is freedom of expression wherein one can be critical about the monarchy of Morocco.

Women's energy is manifesting differently. More younger Arab women are putting their nurturing instincts into civil society. Becoming mothers of society wherein society is becoming their children. This process is deconstructing the family and the role of man in order to reconstruct new possibilities.[22]

---

20   Farida Shaheed, interview by author, 24 May 2004, at the Shirkat Gah office in Lahore, Pakistan.

21   Seyed Kazem Sajjadpour, interview by author, 30 May 2004, at the Institute for Political and International Studies in Tehran, Iran. See Chapter 4, note 14.

22   Rachida ben Faida, interview by author, 12 April 2004, at Hassoune's Bookshop in Marrakech, Morocco. See Chapter 4, note 25.

Other interviewees were even more affirmative when speaking of civil society. Hamid Bashiriyeh (Tehran) offered what amounted to a counterpoint to skeptical views, cautioning against what he saw as excessive concern with cultural contextualization of the concept. Rather than a specifically 'Islamic' or local definition of 'civil society,' he argued for a more universal approach:

> Civil society must not be 'conditioned' by a label. Labels are exclusive to a special group
> of people ... We need to get away from [the] ideological weight of conditional labeling ...
> Therefore Islam can be an obstacle to civil society.[23]

Civil society, as suggested by Ahmed and ben Faida above, can convey a diversity of meanings. In my interviews, three convergent connotations of civil society received strong emphasis: 1) space for critical distancing; 2) space for pluralistic dialogue and debate; and 3) space for cultivating individual as well as collective rights.

A 'Buffer': Civil Society as a Space for Critical Distance

In Western political theory, civil society is often conceived as a buffer between the individual and the state – a counterweight to or constraint upon the exercise of state power.[24] Manzooruddin Ahmad echoed this theme: 'Civil society is a "buffer" between the directing and the directed, between the government and the public. This buffer tries to bring the two together, to relate the two.'[25] Many other interviewees invoked similar ideas, while adding an additional conceptual dimension to the 'buffer' notion, in relation to powerful social institutions such as the *'ulama*. They argued that civil society helps to satisfy the need to acquire 'critical distance' not only from the state, but also from the Muslim *'ulama* (the learned, religious male leaders), whose opinions and pronouncements on the authoritative interpretation of religious texts play a central role in definition of social norms within the Muslim public sphere. The creation of civil society organizations, networks, and forums, they argued, generated a space for autonomous and critical reflection.

Mahboubeh Abbas-Ghulizadeh discussed civil society's role in Iran in the following terms:

> I do not know anything about how other societies define this term.

> Civil society is a 'neo-liberalist movement' in Iran and it started when the government
> could not help people at the grassroots. So, people started to take on the responsibility for
> their society on themselves.

---

23 Hamid Bashiriyeh, interview by author, 15 May 2004, at the International Center for Dialogue Among Civilizations in Tehran, Iran. See Chapter 4, note 17.

24 This is especially seen in the works of Yoshikazu Sakamoto; see his 1997 article. In this, he defines civil society as 'an alternative *public* space which is autonomous *vis-à-vis* the authoritarian state' (211).

25 Manzooruddin Ahmad, interview by author, 20 May 2004, at the Usman-Institute of Technology in Karachi, Pakistan. See Chapter 4, note 27.

When people understand that the government has problems and cannot work with them, then the charismatic relation between the people and the government (especially leaders) was lost. Then you [the people] start thinking [for] themselves and civil society begins to form.

The society's cooperation is not based on charisma but on logical relationships. For example, at the beginning of the revolution, many Iranians had a charismatic relationship with their leaders – they were ideal and all-powerful. However, people realized that these leaders were not perfect and did not know all the answers, so they started to form civil society for themselves.

However, the GOs [governmental organizations] are so tired now; whereas NGOs are bringing new life to GOs. They have fought for so long. Some of my friends who are in high positions feel that they have failed and they envy Mahboubeh for my own freedom from the GO system. At the beginning of the reformist movement, the GOs believed reform would come about from the top down; now, they have come to the conclusion that civil society from the bottom up is the only fortress that can protect the society.[26]

Other interviewees echoed this idea that civil society creates space for critical reflection and bottom-up change. When asked about what are the everyday activities of civil society, Abbas-Ghulizadeh stated: 'Civil society is like a girl or boy under the parents control, yet in reality it is the girl or boy in control of the parents.'

Like Abbas-Ghulizadeh, many interviewees made the case that the forming of a new public sphere within Muslim society would enable both men and women to hold the hegemonic state and its authoritative substructures (religious and governmental leaders and institutions) accountable for their actions. Such accountability, in turn, would weaken the hegemony of state authorities, as well as the disproportionate power of elite religious leaders. As a result, the state as well as the *'ulama* would have to become less aloof in their relations with the society over which they exercise influence.

Dale F. Eickelman and Jon W. Anderson discuss this 'buffering' function of civil society in relation to a 'new sense of the public' and the emergence of a distinct 'Muslim public sphere':

A new sense of public is emerging throughout Muslim-majority states and Muslim communities elsewhere. It is shaped by increasingly open contests over the authoritative use of symbolic language of Islam ... Situated outside formal state control, this distinctly Muslim public sphere exists at the intersections of religious, political, and social life. Facilitated by the proliferation of media in the modern world, the Muslim public can challenge or limit state and conventional religious authorities and contribute to the creation of civil society (Eickelman and Anderson, 1999, 1).

The development of civil society, then, is associated with the emergence of new, critical interpretive practices that provide means of holding traditional authorities accountable. Engagement in social criticism that advances new social priorities,

---

26   Mahboubeh Abbas-Ghulizadeh, interview by author, 27 May 2004, at the Institute for Women's Studies and Research (IWSR) in Tehran, Iran.

interests, and values follows the formation of new networks and forums.[27] As mentioned in Chapter 5, civil society networks may start within national borders, but become stronger and more dynamic when linked to other groups in ways that transcend national boundaries.

One civil society network that has successfully distanced itself from the traditional Islamic *'ulama* and discovered the potential range of interpretations that can be derived from core religious sources is the Sisters in Islam of Malaysia (SIS). In their discovery process, SIS challenges the *'ulama's* claim that any status group possesses exclusive rights to interpretation or administration. Instead, they beseech the traditionalists to surrender their exclusive claims and come into dialogue. This is reflected in their mission statement on their website:

> We as a society must debate and discuss in a rational and informed manner which interpretation will serve the best interest of our multi-ethnic, multi-religious, industrializing and modernizing society ... We believe that Islam does not endorse the oppression of women and denial of their basic rights of equality and human dignity. We are saddened that religion has been used to justify cultural practices and values that regard women as inferior and subordinate to men and we believe that this has been made possible because men have had exclusive control over the interpretation of the text of the Qur'an.

> We believe that for the Ummah to grow and flourish, everyone must have the opportunity to fully participate in all spheres of life. The participation of Muslim women as full and equal partners in the Ummah's socio-economic development and progress is the need of the day ...[28]

Feminist advocacy in the Islamic world moves dialectically back and forth from engagement with the culturally mainstream institutions and critical distancing that allows the formation of a distinct network and discourse of dissent and reconstruction. According to Norani Othman, a Professor of Sociology at the Universiti Kebangsaan Malaysia, the latter process has helped to produce the stable group identity that has empowered women to effect changes in the role and status of Muslim women, as well as to build links with other non-Muslim Malay women (Othman, 1997, 189).

Another prominent intellectual who is supporting the development of civil society is Fatima Mernissi. Quite recently, Mernissi was appointed by King Mohammed VI of Morocco to assist in efforts to enhance public discourse on human rights and civil society in Morocco.[29] Mernissi views the development of a discourse on human

---

27   This thinking is consistent with Alberto Melucci's observation that culturally counter-hegemonic activity arises from latent sub-structures or 'sub-merged networks.' (Melucci, 1985, 800). These social networks cohere on the basis of alternative meanings, identities, and lifestyles and are not dependent on actors such as NGOs. Therefore, as argued by Melucci, it is not oppressive structures per se that determine oppressive outcomes; rather, any structure provides opportunities and constraints for purposive action, and coordinated strategies for change can slowly transform the structure.

28   See the Sisters in Islam website, <www.sistersinislam.org.my>.

29   For more about Mernissi's activism in promoting civil society in Morocco, see her website: <www.mernissi.net>. Also, for more about King Mohammed VI's support for reform and women's rights, see Hoagland, 2003; and Sabra, 2004.

rights and civil society as crucial for social change through empowerment of women to engage in public sphere dialogue. In her booklet, *The New Cheherazads: Women and Civil Society in Digital Islam*, Mernissi argues that:

[The] unprecedented dialogue between the sexes gives a huge impetus to civil society, by intensifying collaboration on key issues such as freedom of expression.

[D]ialogue via digital communication brings those who see Islam and technology as opposed, the first being equated with tradition and the second with modernity, to re-assess their views. Information technology might allow Islam to reach, for the first time in history, its full cyber-democratic potential by insuring free expression to all, including women and minorities.

[Mernissi then shared many statistics which demonstrate how women are 'infiltrating culture and media'] ...

When I shared these statistics with a Casablanca Qadi (*Shari'a* judge), he lamented: 'Papa's harem is shifting to mama's civil society!' Asked to clarify what he meant by civil society, the Qadi said, 'Civil society is the opposite of a harem. In harems, women obey without uttering a word. Civil society is chaos itself because the ladies talk loud. It is the end of the "hudud," the sacred boundaries of authority which condemns them to silence in public. As a judge, I call this chaos; in the West, they call it civil society.'

For Mernissi, dialogue in the public arena is an indicator for modern civic Islam. She calls these new public spaces for women, the 'new harems.' Her thoughts were shared by Halima Oulami, another member of the Caravane Civique from Marrakech:

Civil society has not one definition. The notion of the civic must be conceptualized in 'constantly new language'. The civic is always changing and being created: it is a constant gathering of the public in dialogue.[30]

Jamila Hassoune added to Oulami's insights with her own comment: 'Society is open and government is closed. Society allows government to open.'[31]

In any efforts to rediscover, reinterpret, reappropriate, or reform, there must be a process of distancing. In this process of distancing and creating stable spaces for dialogue, interviewees called for the creation of a 'separate' but 'integrated' public sphere in which they could critically reflect, both through collective processes of

---

30 Halima Oulami, interview by author, 12 April 2004, at Hassoune's Bookstore in Marrakech, Morocco. See Chapter 4, note 11. In asking Oulami about Islam's role in civil society, she responded: '*Islam al-Hayy, Laysa Mujamad*,' which, translated into English, means 'Islam is Living. It is never fixed.' Therefore to Oulami, Islam and civil society have a reciprocal relationship: 'each feeding the other.'

31 Such thoughts on civil society were also echoed in an NGO Roundtable with the former First Lady Hilary Rodham Clinton on 17 June 1999 in Fes, Morocco. Some of the participants at this roundtable are also members of the Caravane Civique (for example, Rachida Ben Massaoud).

deliberation and through a growing sense of intellectual autonomy and individual agency.[32]

For many interviewees (for example, Sajjadpour, Khatam, Lotfian), such 'separate' spheres did not necessarily have to be in the forum of an NGO or organization; rather they also shared the notion that within Islam there have always been cultural traditions that reinforce the contemporary civil society framework. Socio-religious events such as *Ashura* and *Nu Rooz*, according to Sajjadpour, are civil society events because they bring women together in ways that provide opportunities to discuss a range of interests and concerns. These events 'bring back the sacred and the subjectivity into the public.' Also, other events like *Doreh*, *Sofreh*, and *Roseh*[33] invoke what Lotfian calls the 'privatization of the public and vice versa ... [wherein] there is a change in attitude in being in the public places.' Another interviewee, Khatam, pointed out that in Arab cultures there are similar civil events, like the informal forum of *Divani*, which creates a sense of connectivity amongst a diverse group of peoples from officials to non-officials. She also stated that 'peoples no matter where they are located will use every opportunity to be with each other.' She then gave the example of the recent earthquake that occurred in Iran (June 2004): 'People will use any excuse to be with each other, being in the public is an essential trait of any Muslim.' Lotfian, at Tehran University, added to Khatam's remarks:

> Civil Society is any assembly or association in which the government has no control or limited control (NGO association) and it facilitates people-to-people contact. It is very important and crucial for those countries in particular who are developing the process of political development.

> In Iran, there are informal groups, like 'Doreh' or 'Mehmani', 'Sofreh' or 'Roseh' ... These informal associations can inspire more formal gatherings, like the creation of NGOs.

For Lotfian, Islam can play a role in legitimizing civil society activities. It can also provide the means of getting conservative families involved in social discussions. However, she recognized that civil society is a 'new concept in our society' and that the 'last seven years after Khatami [was] elected, the term [civil society] became used everywhere ... but it is new and needs stability, continuation, and patience.'[34]

---

32   This intellectual distancing instigates and allows for what Western thinkers, like Gramsci and Melucci, framed as a process of differentiation and ideological transformation (Gramsci, 1971; Melucci, 1985). In addition, as reflected in Anthony Cohen's *The Symbolic Construction of Community*, it is this distance that allows both women and men to reach the conceptual boundaries of their interpretive communities:
   ... people become aware of their culture when they stand at its boundaries: when they encounter other cultures, or when they become aware of other ways of doing things, or merely of contradictions to their own culture (Cohen, 1985, 69).
33   These are traditional Persian informal gatherings which are usually used for spiritual gatherings (and Qur'anic recitation), women's groups, weddings/celebrations and/or family occasions.
34   Saideh Lotfian, interview by author, 29 May 2004, at Tehran University's Department of Law and Political Science. A colleague of Lotfian at Tehran University, N. Mosaffar, also

A Forum: Civil Society as a Space for Pluralistic Views

Although many interviewees shared the opinion that civil society is a 'buffer' or 'separate' sphere for critically distancing the self and society from the state and the traditional Muslim authority, many also underscored that it is a forum for pluralistic engagement and the pursuit of understanding. Manzooruddin Ahmad offered the following commentary:

> This society requires a good amount of understanding, common bonds of humanity. In this society, dialogue is possible. Civil society is a society wherein individuals can talk to one another without harm: a space where a *plurality of views exists together* and entering into a relationship together.

Hence, as mentioned in Chapter 4, interviewees like Ahmad understand that it is in their interest to infiltrate processes of legitimacy formed by religious and governmental authority. They see pluralistic dialogue and debate as a means of contesting established assumptions and creating space for new ideas and social practices. From this perspective, reconciliation of diverse social as well as interpretive communities is not simply 'made' by one-time interactions; rather, it is constantly in the making, with multiple actors and networks participating.

For Khatam, civil society is supposed to facilitate a 'pluralizing mentality for any society.' It is through the socialization of plurality and participatory consciousness that monolithic, homogenous narrations of ethics and moral values are broken. It is also through civil society that being different and tolerating difference is upheld. She then gave an example that in 'everyday life you can see signs of resistance as represented in one of the most popular musical group[s] in which the lead singer is a woman in *hijab* who plays electric guitar ... You can be a Muslim woman and a guitarist and it is acceptable.' She continued by stating that civil society also upholds the 'principles of living together in the public space':

> When the government is enforcing certain rules of behavior as principles, then the public life of the city becomes a way for certain protest or resistance. It is not only a certain group's interests, there is something more: the majority of people want to be active (as seen in the earthquake). People want to come together, and leave the isolation that has been imposed on them by the government.
>
> Civil society initiates dialogue and it is a space in-between society and the state ... The process of negotiating common issues in the society. If we pay more attention to these negotiations, we can go further as humans. We can see different public spheres.[35]

As pointed out by Fatima Mernissi, the true test for Muslim states is to see if they will support and nurture pluralistic public debate and dialogue:

---

stated: 'Civil society is related to the people. This is a way for them to articulate their demands. The process of articulation is crucial for women and their role in civil society.'

35 Azam Khatam, interview by author, 29 May 2004, at her residence in Tehran, Iran. See Chapter 5, note 33.

Regardless of sex, the winners of the 21ˢᵗ century are definitely the dialogue-nurturers. Educated women armed with computers have defeated extremists by denying them monopoly to define cultural identity and interpret religious texts. Armed with information technology, women have engineered a pluralist reading of both religion and culture, highlighting humanist verses of the Koran which deny sacredness to violence.[36]

Like many interviewees mentioned in Chapter 4, Mernissi also argues that such public dialogues are vital for the well-being of any civilized society because they provide a secure, distinctive space for confronting and eliminating discriminatory as well as violent religious and cultural traditions rooted in tribalism. Ultimately, for Mernissi, these public dialogues support the empowerment of *all* individuals to fully participate in processes of social reconstruction.[37] This theme of defending pluralism was underscored by Jaleh Shaditalab:

> Unfortunately, after [the] Revolution, when we talk about civil society we are talking about the rights for ourselves, whereas Khatami said: 'In a civil society you defend the rights of your opposition' which I agreed with. But we do not have a common understanding of what civil society means in our political parties, in our groups in power. This is why we have so many problems (conservative vs. reformist power struggles). Each group is talking about the freedom, the rights for the self as a collective and not for the other as a collective.[38]

A Catalyst: A Space for Cultivating Individual and Collective Rights and Freedom

When asking interviewees about the role of Islam in civil society, many asserted that they saw no necessary contradiction between Islam and a civil society that affirms individual rights. Jaleh Shaditalab offered the following comments:

> Religion is related to one's individual life. I understand and feel it not the way someone tells me to understand or feel. The way that I define it, there is no contradiction between my religion and civil society. To my understanding, in Islam there is nothing that states that people are not equal. Men and women are judged according to their piety, their sincerity.
>
> Equality has no gender discrimination; rather, women have the same right that the man does in social, political, and economic participation.
>
> In such a perspective, morals are more important than rules … If there is anything in religion which is against civil society then I am not interested in those points …
>
> Civil society [then] has its own principles. If we want to be a civilized society, we must live by and act upon these principles. The major principles are democracy, freedom, the

---

36 Fatima Mernissi, 'The New Cheherazads: Women and Civil Society in Digital Islam,' booklet, 2000, 5.

37 Another Muslim 'reformist' scholar, Abdulaziz Sachedina, calls for 'dia-action,' or what I like to call 'dialogical interaction' (Sachedina, CSID's keynote address, 2003).

38 Jaleh Shaditalab, interview by author, 29 May 2004 at the Center for Women's Studies, Tehran University. See Chapter 4, note 20.

right to choose (collective and individual), equality and not any type of discrimination (because of race, religion, or gender). These are all inter-related.[39]

Shaditalab's understanding is closely aligned with the thought of Amina Wadud and Asma Barlas (see Chapter 3), who underscore the importance of individual conscience and interpretive effort in Islamic faith and practice.

In a conversation with activists from the women's organization RAHM (see Chapters 4 and 5), Seyed Jaffar Ahmed offered ideas similar to Shaditalab's, but with an added emphasis on the importance of conjoining individual interpretive effort with a spirit of dialogue:

Civil society needs to be conceptualized by Muslims (or any other religious group) who then have taken civil society as a means of constituting their own identity. So, I would re-phrase your question by asking: 'What is the role of Muslims in civil society, versus that of Islam?' Since Islam can be interpreted in different ways – there is not one Islam, there are so many Islams.

As collectivities, Muslim societies have lived under conditions in which civil societies have not developed. For the major part of Muslim history, Muslim societies have gone through long centuries of feudalism (dark ages I would say) in which there were monarchies and orthodoxy. Religion was defined and limited to a particular set of people who had the monopoly of explaining the religion. Just the fact that there are only four legalistic schools of thought in Islam tells one that there has not been that much liberal interpretation. And since the majority of Muslims subscribe to one of the four institutions of law [this] tells us that there is not much innovation or critical (as well as independent) thinking. If there is not much critical thinking or if people are not allowed to interpret their own religion – for example, if I do not have the right to interpret my religion – there cannot be a civil society in such surroundings. *Ijtihad* is a static notion. Every Muslim will applaud the idea of *ijtihad*, but no Muslim will attempt any *ijtihad* for him or herself. Even individuals like Iqbal was not courageous enough to attempt any *ijtihad* for himself. However, I feel that Sir Seyyed Ahmad Khan did and was rejected by the traditional ulema (yet was supported by the British). It was his modernist education system which gave life to the emerging middle class. He lived in between and still does today ... He was very outspoken. The environment at that time was so polarized, enabling him to say things that would not be appropriate for today's contexts. In other words, that was a time when it was easier to make a claim than to get into dialogue with people. Now is different, we do not need claims but more dialogue.[40]

---

39 When I asked Shaditalab to describe some everyday examples of civil society, she stated: 'The choice to work or gather in NGOs.' She then elaborated that 'when a state demands NGOs to register, this means that some institute wants to supervise: this means that it is not free-decision where the government has to supervise and demands answers.' She then gave the example of Uzbekistan where 'people are not free to speak Farsi but are forced to speak Uzbek.' For Shaditalab, such action ultimately signifies that 'the government is taking away their culture' and 'right as responsible citizens.'

40 Seyed Jaffar Ahmed, interview, 20 May 2004, at the University of Karachi's Pakistan Study Centre, Pakistan. SSA Khan influenced Fazlur Rahman, who influenced a whole movement in American study of Islam (see literature review, Chapter 3). According to Ahmed: 'Rahman and Iqbal were in a process of discourse that was not as strong as Khan.

For Ahmed and other interviewees, the fact that Islam has no central authority (in contrast to the Catholic Church) supports the notion that every Muslim is individually responsible for promoting public discourse and dialogue. This theme of individual responsibility for public activism was emphasized by another interviewee, Bine Bine Touria in Morocco:

> When change is filtered through government and not the people, this is not constructive especially if you are trying to change a mentality. Every change used to come from the state, now Moroccan society is becoming aware and a process of engagement is emerging from the work of non-governmental organizations.[41]

This recurrent theme of individual rights and responsibilities relates closely to what Abdul Aziz Said describes as the 'flowering of the individual.' For Said, the development of the individual person is the foundation for reconceptualizing the public sphere and its relation to the state in ways that broaden participation in political processes, enhance the accountability of governments to the governed, and promote respect for both the dignity of individuals and the integrity of communities (both Muslim and non-Muslim). Ultimately, while catalyzing and manifesting through the 'flowering of the individual,' the development of civil society is also a function of the development of social dialogue.[42] Such 'dialogical interaction' consists of raising public awareness (both locally and globally) and creating, as well as upholding, transnational alliances.

One of the most decisive components of civil society efforts for many interviewees is raising public awareness and, in turn, heightening public and individual critical thinking. Through continued advocacy in different public arenas, civil society advocates are gradually reshaping the Muslim public sphere – from scholars (who are writing publications, traveling and giving lectures, and creating formal conferences and informal gatherings which bring together like minds) to grassroots activists who utilize the media (for example, letters to editors and video conferences) to make their messages heard.

In reimagining the Muslim public sphere, new roles (both local and transnational) begin to emerge for Muslim women. These roles contribute to the consolidation of new Islamic public communities (again, on both a local and a transnational basis) that

---

They cultivated their arguments on the premises that were already acceptable.' Ahmed also stated that:

Khan also called for a 'Re-emergence of inductive reasoning in Islam.' Such a movement would establish Islam [as] a religion with universal values ... Islam's idiom is the same as all religions: to fulfill the psychological needs of a society ... There is that in religion which is relevant and irrelevant. The universal is always relevant (e.g., the spirit of religion), it is the particular that changes and becomes irrelevant (e.g., Arabian norms). Unfortunately, the (so-called) fundamentalists rely on the apparent features of Islam and the contextual versus the universal aspects of Islam.

41   Bine Bine Touria, interview by author, 12 April 2004, at Hassoune's Bookshop in Marrakech, Morocco.

42   Abdul Aziz Said, 'Islam and the West Today: "Blessed Are the Strangers,"' paper presented at the United States Institute of Peace's Workshop on *The Role of Faith in Peacemaking: An Islamic Perspective*, on 7 November 2001, 4.

enable both men and women to participate in organizational life. Such communities (whether virtual or physical) build on, yet transcend, family and tribal spheres, while simultaneously maintaining independence from state control.

Inevitably, the concept of a public space or public sphere connotes that there is a 'private sphere.' For civil society advocates, the opening of public sphere is intertwined with the opening of the private sphere (a development that is especially important in the work of women). In this process, new Islamic public communities, or new civil society enclaves, are seen as a mediating factor between public and private (Kelsay, 2002, 3). By raising public awareness in both public and private spheres, civil society networks seek to reconceptualize basic social concepts and norms. For example, women, formerly confined to the 'private sphere,' find new bases for entering the public sphere. Simultaneously, the structure of the private sphere becomes disentangled from normative constructions – products of the 'traditional' public sphere – that are no longer viewed as appropriate. This process ultimately creates new public sphere realities. As related by Seteney Shami, reconceptualization of the private as connected to the public, in turn, transforms not only the perceptions of the public sphere, but also of the state and of the Muslim *Ummah*:

> There can be no total separation of space into female/male, private/public and family/non-family. Rather, the use of space is characterized by fluidity and adaptability, both inside the dwelling and outside. From this perspective … the boundaries between private and public domains in an 'essentially' Middle Eastern, Arab or Muslim fashion … could be seen as emerging and re-emerging out of the articulation of the socially and culturally constructed strategies of various actors in a specific setting, including states, families, individuals, collectivities and communities (Shami, 1997, 88).

Overall, my interviews suggested growing commitment to the idea of a distinctively Muslim, yet also genuinely cosmopolitan, understanding of civil society, conceived as a means of injecting new dynamism and creativity into the public discourse of Muslim societies that have long been shaped by conservative religious thinking and restrictive state structures.

Conclusions

> Women can renegotiate the traditional patriarchal bargain to their advantage and seek empowerment and expanded opportunities within the more socially accepted sphere of religious activism that affirms their domestic roles. While historical and contemporary religio-political movements can offer women avenues of independence and initiative and in some cases help bring about progressive social reform … they usually involve major concessions and accommodations to a larger male-dominant, patriarchal order. Re-imagining other alternatives for women's agency and activism in society, and more particularly in politics, is perhaps the next step (Keddie, 1999, 6).[43]

---

43   See also Keddie's 1999 article, 'Women and Twentieth Century Religious Politics,' in Nikki R. Keddie and Jasamin Rostam-Kolayi (eds), *The Journal of Women's History*, vol. 10 (Winter).

As articulated by Nikki R. Keddie, through the efforts to engage in civil politics, civil society or civic Islam, Muslim women seek to give voice to change in all levels of the public space. In particular, a variety of Muslim women are reconceptualizing their role, not only in the secular or Islamic state system, but also in the Islamic authoritative sphere.[44] Significantly, a number of interviewees and prominent activists have been or are working with their governments in different capacities (for example, Anwar, Mernissi, Shaaban).[45] This development prompts a variety of questions: Is the barrier between civil society and government/state becoming less formidable, or are these women being co-opted by accepting the invitation to serve as spokespersons for the state? Is collaboration with the state a means of improving the state's image internationally, or is it a genuinely positive development that will bring about substantive change? Does it increase the effectiveness of advocacy, or decrease its potential popular legitimacy?

Although there are many Muslim women entering the state apparatus, women who are trying to enter the authoritative realm of Islamic interpretation and leadership face greater obstacles. Some have encountered greater receptiveness than others. On the one hand, women have been successful as advisors to imams in Turkey (Schleifer, 2005) and have made progress within a specifically female sphere as 'muftias' and women's prayer leaders in India (Lancaster, 2003; and Aljazeera.net, 2003). On the other hand, women who seek to offer religious interpretations that would apply to men as well as to women, or who have sought to lead prayers for mixed groups of Muslims, have found that their actions are met with intense opposition and even outrage.[46] In 2005, Muslim women in North America and Europe who led prayers and gave Friday *khutbahs* (Amina Wadud and Asra Nomani) were denounced by male religious leaders around the world as 'deranged women' who are 'corrupting the Muslim community' and 'violating God's law.'[47]

Clearly, the future of transnational civic Islam and its impact on the status of women in society cannot yet be predicted. Nonetheless, it is evident that women's transnational and local women's networks have in many cases increased the

---

44 In the last century, women's political participation in most 'secular' nation-states which are predominantly Muslim has substantially increased as seen in the percentage of women in higher political offices (that is, prime ministers, parliamentary members, presidential advisors, and delegated commissioners). For more about the recent trends and statistics, see the following articles: Gauch, 2005; and Bonino, 2005.

45 Muslim women are entering high-level political positions and more of these positions specifically address gender issues. Zainah Anwar was appointed as a Commissioner for the Human Rights Commission of Malaysia (SUHAKAM) which was ratified by the Malaysian Parliament in 2000. Fatima Mernissi was designated by King Mohammed VI to help develop civil society projects throughout Morocco. Bouthana Shaaban became an official Syrian Foreign Ministry spokesperson and was considered to be the Syrian Ambassador to the United States.

46 Many of these Muslims are associated with a new interpretive movement called 'Progressive Muslims'; for more about this movement, see Chapter 3, note 7.

47 For more information about Amina Wadud's thoughts and Muslim reaction, see Chapter 3, note 30. For more information about Asra Nomani's activism, see her website (<http://www.asranomani.com>); and Teotonio, 2005, A20.

confidence of women to articulate their own ideas about Muslim public space, and have amplified their voices. As Zainah Anwar has stated: 'I am not a scholar of Islam, but I am a Muslim and I have the right to speak about Islam ...'[48] By embracing civil society as a context for activism, women leaders and men who support their efforts are questioning established interpretations, claiming their own capacity to engage in hermeneutic agency, affirming pluralism, and aspiring to create spaces that can catalyze basic changes in understandings of gender norms.

My encounters with Muslim women from throughout the Islamic world suggest that there is a growing community of thinkers and activists who, like Zainah Anwar, refuse to be silenced or pigeon-holed by polarizing discourse. Familiar with the traditional status of women as 'others' in male-centered Islamic discourse, they have embraced dialogue and networking as a means of engaging in the major ideational and normative debates of our times. In the process, they have also sought to transcend the dichotomies that have long fragmented discourse about women and Islam into competing camps: traditional vs. modern, secular vs. religious, and 'Eastern' vs. 'Western.' They have sought to define their own identities as integrated and self-confident agents of civic activism and social change. As they enter the public space of national and transnational civil society, they are also redefining the cultural and normative bases of social agency.

---

48   In an interview with Zainah Anwar, current Executive Director of Sisters in Islam (a Malaysian women's rights organization), she shared an experience of being asked: 'Who are you to speak on Islam?' She then described how she came to the conclusion that authoritative authenticity must be connected to accountability and responsibility, especially in the context of Malaysia, a nation-state based on democratic principles:

I am not a scholar of Islam, but I am a Muslim and I have the right to speak about Islam ... I also am a citizen of a democratic country and I have the right to hold my country accountable to its democratic values and ideals ... If people are not empowered by authentic modes of knowing as well as by the established systems of authority, then there is no accountability or responsibility. There is no enabling framework ... (These thoughts would be reflected also in a speech by Anwar, see Chapter 7, footnote 28.)

Chapter 7

Muslim Woman as Self/Other: The Politics of Identity

Self and Other. It could be argued that there is no pair of concepts that is more laden with multilayered meanings. When we speak of 'self' and 'other,' we evoke not only a primal sense of differentiated existence as a human being, but also a deep set of existential and political questions. What is it that gives us our uniqueness and authenticity as individuals and as members of cultural groups? And what characteristics and values (or lack thereof) distinguish those whom we have come to regard as fundamentally different from ourselves – that is, as Other (and not merely 'other')?

Only a few of the individuals I interviewed regarded themselves as philosophers, but a surprising number were eager to discuss the political and existential ramifications of self/other distinctions when the subject was raised at the beginning of interviews. To evoke both the spirit of 'encountering' and elicit the experiences of similarity and difference that inevitably accompany transnational networking, I opened each interview with an invitation to dialogue. My first question was: 'How would you define the stranger?' As a newcomer from a foreign land, I followed this question up by asking for definitions of self and other. My rationale for asking these questions was not only to gather data about self-identity and identity politics – the 'women and Islam' issue, after all, is *saturated* with identity politics – but also to be up-front in addressing possible discomfort with myself as a stranger asking questions on sensitive topics. Beginning with 'self' and 'other' created a bridge to rich discussions of social activism and its cultural meanings.

There are competing definitions of what it means to be a Muslim woman, and of the significance of secularized national identities as intermediaries between these two terms. There are questions of what is emphasized and what is stressed, and of how valued self-definitions relate to the images and expectations of others. One striking theme that arose in interviews with ideologically and culturally diverse women was the experience of being somehow 'out of sync' with the identity categories created by others. As will be illustrated in this chapter, there was a common sense of being somehow on the defensive in a highly contentious, transnational debate about identities, images, and values – a sense of not fitting into the boxes created by the other – whoever that other might be … traditionalist, secular nationalist, Islamist, or Westerner. It is impossible for Muslim women to escape the politicized landscape of identity politics.

Muslim Woman as 'Other': Challenging Constructed Oppositions

Degrees of Separation: Struggles with Stereotypes

My encounters with a diversity of Muslim women living in different localities throughout the Muslim world generated fascinating commentary on the dynamics of contemporary identity politics. To be a socially engaged Muslim woman is be at the center of national as well as transnational debates about what it means to be an authentically modern or Muslim person. In my interviews, interviewees repeatedly testified to experiences of being essentialized as someone else's 'other': they were constantly finding that their own efforts to achieve a clear identity went against the grain of popular preconceptions and stereotypes. These preconceptions and stereotypes were linked to a number of dichotomies: secular vs. Islamic, traditional vs. modern, Oriental vs. Occidental. Whatever ideological, professional, or activist choice a woman might make (or in some cases, seek to avoid), there was no escape from the ongoing debates associated with these categories – debates about the veil, religious norms, nationalism, imperialism, globalization, and economic ideology (especially between socialism and capitalism).

Many interviewees pointed out that, historically, Muslim women have not been free to define their own identities, or to be agents of social change. As one interviewee stated: 'Historically, Muslim woman has been and is Other.'[1] This 'subject without agency' is echoed in the thought of Amina Wadud in *Qur'an and Woman*:

> Because women were nearly completely excluded from the foundational discourse that established the paradigmatic basis for what it means to be Muslim, they are often relegated to the role of subject without agency … In modern and postmodern discourses about Islam, extensive attention has been given to how women have been reduced from full humanity and moral agency, or *khalifahs*, to subjects (Wadud, 1999, xi).

In traditional Islamic culture, as in the West before feminism, women were not viewed as agents within the public sphere, and were seldom the referents in discussions of political matters. Muslim women who have asserted their right to fulfill new roles in the public sphere face the prospect of being categorized in ways that imply transgression of social norms.

Given this reality – most of my interviewees either attested to it or would not dispute it – some might expect that Muslim women would welcome Western discourse about Muslim women, but this was not the case. Rather than an open embrace of

---

1   This statement was made by Jamila Hassoune during an interview by the author, 12 April 2004, at her residence in Marrakech, Morocco. In addition, Hassoune stated: 'Woman forgets her "self" in the other through her overlapping activities and responsibilities.' Therefore, the notion of 'self' as an isolated phenomenon is what Hassoune would call a strange concept. For more information about Jamila, see Chapter 5. Another interviewee, Shehnaz Ismail, Director of the Indus Valley School of Art and Architecture in Karachi, Pakistan, expressed the same thought: 'From urban to rural life, constant struggle as a woman: a woman's self is defined by extended responsibilities. She is a mother to children, husband, father, mother-in-law …'

the West, and of Western views about Muslim women, Muslim women activists
– including those who presented themselves in secular terms – often underscored
strong discomfort with Western images of Muslim women. This discomfort was
often expressed just as emphatically as unease with the discourse of political Islam.

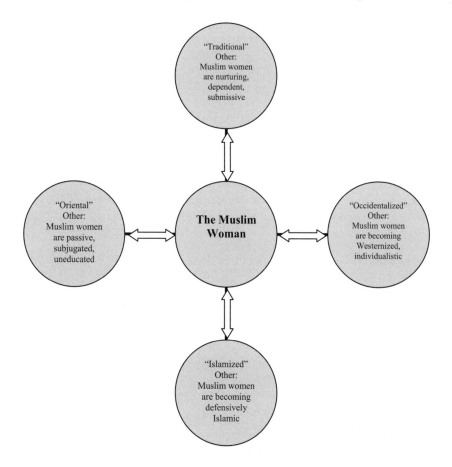

Figure 7.1 The 'othering' of the Muslim woman: a struggle with stereotypes

My interviews suggested that many Muslim women are seeking to form their
identities in the midst of various processes of 'othering,' or in other words, in cultural
environments in which the possibilities for self-definition are sharply constrained
by stereotypical categories. Whatever the way in which a Muslim woman activist
attempts to define and project her identity, she faces the prospect of having this
identity rejected in favor of a collective label that corresponds with expectations
derived from a preexisting cultural or ideological tendency. Whatever choices she
makes in life, she comes up against the alienating reality of existing as someone
else's 'Other.'

Ideological tendencies such as traditionalism, secularism, Islamic revivalism, Orientalism, and Occidentalism confront Muslim women with strong preconceptions about who they are and how they should (or should not) understand themselves. All of these worldviews have 'imagined' Muslim women in ways that many women experience as static and profoundly limiting. Taken together, they produce a number of 'us vs. them' mentalities that challenge Muslim women to live as someone else's 'Other' (see Figure 7.1). These 'Others' – the 'Traditional' Other, the 'Oriental' Other, the 'Occidentalized' Other, and the 'Islamized' Other – are described below.

The Traditional Other

The 'traditionalist' school of Islamic interpretation is strongly patriarchal and contains an inherent (and arguably romanticized) preference for patriarchal authority. From this traditionalist perspective, authority is a distinctly male prerogative, and interpretive authority is limited to specialized (male) scholars of Islam. For contemporary traditionalists, male domination of the Islamic public and private spheres requires that Muslim women delegate religious and worldly authority to men who – regardless of their level of religious learning – are responsible for creating order and transmitting meaning from one generation to the next:

> The Muslim family is the miniature of the whole of Muslim society and its firm basis. In it the man or father functions as the imam in accordance with the patriarchal nature of Islam. The religious responsibility of the family rests upon his shoulders. He is in a sense the priest in that he can perform rites which in other religions are reserved for the priestly class. In the family the father upholds the tenets of the religion and his authority symbolizes that of God in the world ... The rebellion of Muslim women in certain quarters of Islamic society came when men themselves ceased to fulfill their religious function and lost their virile and patriarchal character. By becoming themselves effeminate they caused the ensuing reaction of revolt among certain women who no longer felt the authority of religion upon themselves.
>
> The traditional family is also the unit of stability in society ... There is no doubt that in a small but significant segment of Muslim society today there is a revolt of women against traditional Islamic society ... In Islam also the very patriarchal and masculine nature of the tradition makes the revolt of those women who have become aggressively modernized more violent and virulent ...(Nasr, 1966, 110–11).

From this point of view, the problem with 'rebellious' Muslim women is their habit of 'thirsting for all things Western' (Nasr, 1966, 112).

What is unfortunate about this analysis is that it simultaneously romanticizes traditional institutions and misrepresents the motivations of women and men who critique the traditional paradigm. Romanticization is evident in the avoidance of difficult topics pertaining to the abuse of male authority – for example, domestic violence and 'honor killings.' While physical abuse of women is by no means a specifically traditional or non-Western problem, the traditional paradigm affords few avenues by means of which such practices can be challenged. Indeed, labeling women who are concerned about such issues as 'violent' seems rather inappropriate.

By forbidding questions about the medieval consensus on Islamic social norms, the traditional paradigm puts women in a vulnerable position, and prevents intellectual challenges concerning the extent to which traditional Muslim family law (with its provisions for unequal inheritance, polygamy, gender-biased divorce procedures, sanctioned domestic violence,and so on) truly satisfies the needs of women.

Contrary to traditionalist logic, there are many reasons other than 'intoxification with the West' that might drive a Muslim woman to challenge her status as the 'other' over whom authority is exercised. Muslim women who desire to participate in intellectual, religious, and political institutions need not be labeled as 'outsiders,' nor is it intellectually necessary to represent the desire for engagement in social, moral, economic, political, and educational activities as a movement that is contrary to the 'essential' character of Muslim cultures and societies. Rather, Muslim women who seek equal rights and participation in all societal spheres (for example, education, development of intellectualism, employment, political processes) are often quite affirmative when asked about their identity as Muslims, resenting only the fact that traditional Islamic authority has silenced their voices and treated them as 'others.'

Significantly, the traditionalist view of women is not monolithic, and many self-avowed traditionalists do selectively acknowledge the legitimacy of issues raised by activists. Usually the discourse of such traditionalists (or 'neo-traditionalists') affirms the intelligence and capability of women while simultaneously emphasizing that the most important social role for women is motherhood. These themes were prominent at a conference entitled 'General Gathering of Women on Socio-Cultural Issues and Globalization' that I attended at Tehran University in Iran (16–17 May 2003). At the beginning of this conference (which was held in a large auditorium accommodating over 500 individuals), Muslim men who were scattered here and there amongst the Muslim women (who were brought in from different Islamic seminaries throughout Iran) were asked to sit all together in the front rows while all the women were asked to sit behind them. After this time of reconfiguration, the keynote speech was given by Ayatollah Amid Zanjani, a Professor of Law at the University of Tehran. His statements from his speech illustrate the more 'neo-traditionalist' position:

> Woman is essentially cultural. She can play any role provided that it does not damage her main role as a mother. This is her most important role. The women's movement began when the late Imam Khomeini took the lead. He was the pioneer in this movement and the archetype for this movement was and still is Hazrat Fatemeh [the daughter of the Prophet Muhammad]. She is the woman who could play various socio-political roles without her motherhood being overshadowed.

> There are three groups of women:

> 1) When we speak of great women these are those who can promote the position of women. When your sisters in remote villages are so restricted you cannot talk about the promotion of women, their situation should be changed. Only women themselves can bring about such change. The women's movement should be spread into villages and small towns.

2) Women with special expertise. They can be the best advisors in planning and administrating affairs. The issue is not tokenism. Women should be there as participants in decision-making, especially when women's lives are affected. Here women are seen not just as a human being but as a high-level human being.

3) Women as a teacher for society not in the formal sense of the word but as the bearer of insight and knowledge. Woman has a special position as a mother. She can nurture better generations.

An Islamic women's movement does not seek just the promotion of women per se but is looking for the interest of the whole society …

Such discourse may well have progressive potential in highly conservative Muslim contexts, especially in the small villages from which many women attending this event came. The idea that all social participation be conditional on excellence in the domain of motherhood, however, imposes very real limits on the empowerment of women as agents of social change. It offers few if any opportunities to renegotiate household responsibilities, and presupposes knowledge systems and political ideologies that are still predominantly constructed, interpreted, and applied by men. As many of my interviews revealed, the current legal structures leave those Muslim women who venture into the public sphere extremely vulnerable, particularly if their husbands deem them to have neglected one or more household duties. As pointed out by Farida Shaheed, in general Muslim men (but not Muslim women) can divorce quite easily, taking children and family financial assets with them. The notion that women have a preeminent responsibility to be nurturing and dependent can severely restrict women's options.

Despite the rise of secular nationalism, patriarchy still persists as a strong social and cultural institution in the Muslim world. In most of the world's predominantly Muslim societies, the cultural norms defining female roles and status are strongly supported by 'traditional' androcentric readings of sacred texts. Muslim women argue that dominant norms and practices – far from being essential to the religion itself – are actually functions of traditional cultural contexts and styles of interpretation that privilege male authority.

As reflected in the voices of Muslim women scholars who are questioning the effects of the patriarchal monopolization of traditional and secular authority – whether in the public sphere (by Islamic jurists and political leaders) or private sphere (by the male provider and disciplinarian) – many women activists have shared experiences of being marginalized by patriarchal discourse and practice (Mernissi, 1991; Ahmed, 1992; Wadud, 1999; Afkhami, 1995; Mir-Hosseini, 1999). To be marginalized and hindered from active participation in normative discourse – that is, to be an object rather than a subject of such conversations – is to become the silenced other of traditional religious culture.

Mahboubeh Abbas-Ghulizadeh, an Iranian activist introduced in Chapters 4 and 5,[2] shared a particularly poignant story of what it means to be the traditional other:

---

2   See Chapter 5, section 'Tracing Tendencies of Transnational Attitude and Dialogue.'

The last 25 years I have had to struggle against so many boundaries. Sometimes, certain boundaries would encompass my being for more than two years. When I reviewed my own values and norms, I would get a new understanding of my values and norms. This process of self-introspection affected my social life, especially my family and friends. One of the most difficult and influential experiences for contrasting self and other was when I divorced my husband. The other – my husband – this time, was from a traditional patriarchal system.

Abbas-Ghulizadeh went on to describe how she overcame this period of her life:

At this time I met 'another other' who was so tolerant and understanding of my struggle.[3] This other made me see another context. Many women like me who have similar struggles are in such patriarchal systems and so the 'other' becomes also someone who brings 'new' values that contrast the patriarchal values. These new values help you to question everything. However, when you engage with this strange, new, other, you too paradoxically are not yourself, you become other as well. Such a process one constantly meets with one boundary after another (*Hudud ala hudud* in Farsi).

This 'new' self becomes one who learns to live in-between boundaries: in meeting boundaries one constantly seeks to live in frontiers. However, when one chooses to live a life in-between boundaries: one also leaves friends and family who are unable to transcend such boundaries.

She then further elaborated on the 'boundaries' which helped construct and constrict her own identity.

One example of a boundary was Imam Khomeini. At the beginning of the Revolution, I was one of the followers of Khomeini and his socio-political system. However, after some time, I had to leave this boundary too. At the same time, I also left God. But in doing so, I was able to create a new 'God' for myself.

However, this time of struggle was very difficult [she went on to explain a time of depression and emotional collapse]. I started to ask myself: How can we find ourselves outside of this patriarchal tradition? I came to the conclusion that my values needed to be based in the values for humanity as a whole. My values needed to be founded on *being human*.

Then I started to envision life in reform.

After sharing this account, Abbas-Ghulizadeh provided definitions of 'self' and 'other.' She offered the following:

To know others is a base for knowing self. When there is more distance between the other and self, there is more opportunity to learn about the self.

3   See Chapter 5 for more about Abbas-Ghulizadeh's story about the other being from the 'transnational.'

The time of ideological judgment is over and I try to not judge about the other. The 'other' should be defined in their social context (and society) not [his/her] personal life.

These encounters with the other can help me understand my own social context better and how ... networks [can] be made and worked with. The more I work and understand others, the more I want to explore myself.[4]

Abbas-Ghulizadeh responded to marginalization by seeking others who shared aspects of her own experience, and encouraged her to organize and participate in transnational workshops (see Chapter 5). Because such activities have put her at odds with many patriarchal traditionalists, her path has involved hardships: in July 2004, upon her return from a conference for women in Beijing, she was arrested, interrogated, and imprisoned, and in March 2007 she was arrested with 30 other Muslim women activists while protesting for International Women's Day (Feminist Daily News Wire, 2007). The mere act of engaging in transnational civil society projects that sometimes represented the Iranian regime in an unfavorable light was enough to bring her several months of confinement.[5] Several interviewees had been through comparable experiences, and Abbas-Ghulizadeh's personal journey parallels that of a variety of other individuals I encountered – activists who are reconceptualizing 'Muslim woman' as self rather than as other, and regarding this self as a complex, constructed composite rather than as a symbol of traditional cultural authenticity (see the last section of this chapter).

Before I go onto the next section, I want to point out that unfortunately in many cases there is a high price that comes with the rise of the alternative voice and public recognition of this voice. Such high prices manifest in the forms of 'official' and 'unofficial' exile (for example, Fazlur Rahman and Asma Barlas, both of whom became estranged ex-patriots from their homeland of Pakistan); imprisonment (for example, Fatna el-Bouih from Morocco);[6] marginalization (one excellent example of marginalization is accounted by Zainah Anwar in a Sisters in Islam's editor's letter, 19 April 2002, in which the Malaysian Department of Religious Affairs announced its intention to ban Muslims with 'no in-depth knowledge on Islam' from publicly expressing themselves on any matters related to Islam); as well as personal consequences (for example, Amina Wadud's teaching contract with the Department of Islamic Revealed Knowledge at the International Islamic University was not renewed as a result of her activism with Sisters in Islam in Malaysia, and

---

4   The question of the transnational brought us back to the beginning of our encounter where we were talking about the self. The interview then ended with Abbas-Ghulizadeh stating: 'This movement is unknown. You do not know where to put your next step. But you know that you can put your foot some place. I am waiting where to put my foot. I am always waiting on where to put my next step.'

5   Abbas-Ghulizadeh is not alone in her endeavors; there have been many other Iranian women activists treated similarly. The most well-known case is that of Haleh Esfandiari, an Iranian-American scholar at the Woodrow Wilson Center in Washington, DC, who was arrested in March 2007 on charges of conspiring 'to foster a velvet revolution' in Iran (Azimi, 2007, 50–55; Macfarquhar, 2007, A01 and A09; Wright, 2007, A10).

6   Fatna el-Bouih was one of the main coordinators of the 8th Caravane Civique conference. For more on Fatna el- Bouih's activism, see Brown, 2001.

more recently there are Muslims who want to sue her for leading Friday prayers
to a mixed-gender congregation).[7] Obviously, such abusive thought and action
is directed to delegitimize one's sense of Muslimness. Fortunately, most of these
individuals have been persistently undaunted by these actions; rather, more resistance
seemingly strengthens their efforts to continue to speak out publicly and act locally
and transnationally.

The Oriental Other

Though the impact of traditional patriarchal orthodoxy is more direct and immediate,
most of the Muslim women with whom I met were also deeply concerned about what
they perceived as an imperialistic, 'Orientalist' discourse emanating from the West.
Interviewees from contexts as diverse as monarchical Morocco and revolutionary
Iran expressed acute anxieties about how Orientalist images of 'oppressed' and
'exotic' Muslim women may be serving a larger colonial project. They worried
that their own work on behalf of Muslim women could easily be misrepresented
by Western scholars whose work provides ideological legitimation for American
hegemony over Muslim lands.

For my interviewees, the current meaning of the term 'Orientalism' argues that
Western scholars specializing in 'oriental' languages and cultures have historically
acted – consciously or unconsciously – as handmaidens to empire, by producing
knowledge claims based on sweeping generalizations and harmful stereotypes.[8]
These Orientalist patterns of representation have provided Western political leaders
with habits of thought that make a master–servant relationship with non-Western
societies appear justified and even morally desirable.

Instead of remaining just academic discourse, Orientalism became a political
process of homogenizing thought about Eastern 'others,' particularly but not
exclusively in the Middle East and the Islamic world. Such homogenization in turn
was predicated upon condescending and politically self-serving attitudes toward
those who became the 'objects' of investigation. Orientalism then becomes a 'system
of knowledge' premised on an idealized set of Western cultural norms. By projecting
these norms as hegemonic, Orientalist scholars and politicians reinforced the colonial
conquest of the Orient by promoting the idea that Europeans have a right to *own* (and
thereby *civilize*) the Orient. Orientalism allowed Westerners to confidently *know*
how inferior Orientals were to themselves. Muslim women, for example, were seen
as illiterate, passive objects of subjugation by traditional Muslim men – objects that
might possibly be 'liberated' or at least aided by a colonial project. At the same time,
they embodied repressed Western emotions such as sensuality, as epitomized by the

---

7   These Muslims who want to sue Wadud posted the following statement on <www.alt.
muslim.com>:

We American Muslims in New York should sue in court for libel and slander, to force them
[Wadud and the fellow mixed-gender congregation] to stop calling themselves 'Muslims' ...

For more on Amina Wadud, see Chapter 3.

8   It is interesting to note that many interviewees were familiar with Edward W. Said's
work, *Orientalism* (1978).

exotic and mysterious tales of 'A Thousand and One Nights' (Mernissi, 2000 and 2001).

Many of these themes emerged in an interview with Neelam Hussain, founder of Simorgh Women's Resource and Publication Centre in Lahore, Pakistan.[9] Hussain, being heavily influenced by Fatima Mernissi and her analysis of Orientalism,[10] talked about the importance of images, and that by controlling knowledge of the 'other' and even shaping the self-image of non-Westerners, Orientalists had created not only a system of knowledge but also a system of power – a closed discourse about the 'Oriental Other' that was not merely academic and scholarly, but also cultural and ideological. For Hussain, such Orientalist tropes have not yet been abolished; the Western media, as well as the policy elite and much of academia, continue to generate 'neo-Orientalist' images of 'passive,' subjugated Muslim women in need of liberation by external forces (Hussain and Malik, 1985). As many of my interviewees, including Hussain, emphasized, the implications for Western and specifically US foreign policy are quite clear, providing a basis for the deepening humiliation of foreign domination as well as for the intensification of reactionary forces in their own societies. As stated by Hussain's daughter, Mariam Hussain, an artist from Lahore, Pakistan: 'US foreign policy and Islamic fundamentalism are ideological products of "othering." They continue to reinforce a definition of self as bound by dichotomies.' She would then later state: 'there is need to transcend binary oppositions which shape Muslim women's lives … and reimagine the self as a collage of habitation.' She would add that each Muslim woman needs to learn how to 'co-habit within oneself' in order to transform dichotomies of self/other into dialogues.[11]

A consistent theme of my interviewees was that they did not want to be seen as agents of an Orientalist agenda. To avoid being seen as purveyors of Orientalism, some scholars and activists who are engaged with women's issues prefer to express themselves in secular, socialist terms – both to avoid 'essentializing' Islamic culture and to underscore their opposition to Western political and economic domination. Most of my interviewees, however, underscored the complexity of their identities and commitments – they were both *religious* and *secular*, and their extent of

---

9   Neelam Hussain, interview by author, 24 May 2004, at the office of Simorgh Women's Resource and Publication Centre in Lahore, Pakistan. I was introduced to Hussain by members of the Caravane Civique in Morocco.

10   In the interview, Neelam Hussain mentioned how she had read from Fatima Mernissi and was inspired by her to establish the Simorgh Women's Resource and Publication Centre in 1985. In fact, the name of 'Simorgh' was inspired by Mernissi and her writings on the mythical bird. See Fatima Mernissi, 'Conclusion: The Simorgh Is Us!,' in *Islam and Democracy: Fear of the Modern World* (1992), 172–4.

The Simorgh Centre has hosted transnational conferences for Muslim women and lecture series on prominent Muslim feminists such as Fatima Mernissi. As stated in their literature, this centre is a non-profit, feminist/activist organization which focuses on 'research and dissemination of information that will enable women and men to challenge the dominance of ideas that support social and economic divisions on the basis of gender, class, religion, race and nationality.'

11   Mariam Hussain, interview by author, 24 May 2004, via phone in Lahore, Pakistan.

identification with secularity and religiosity depended a great deal on contextual nuances of our conversations. Quite consistently, they were in favor of enhancing the lives of Muslim women, but adamantly opposed to foreign military and political intervention.

The Occidentalized Other

One of the chief concerns of interviewees, like Hussain, Abbas-Ghulizadeh, and Hassoune, who objected to Orientalism (or neo-orientalism) was that they themselves were wary of being rejected by members of their own societies – denounced as agents of a foreign agenda, as purveyors of an alien way of life and of a distorting, colonialist mindset. Simply put, Muslim woman activists are often represented as having abandoned Islam for the West, collectivism for individualism, and Muslim needs for an 'empty' or inauthentic human as well as women's rights discourse. Being perceived in these terms tends to have quite negative ramifications for the legitimacy and impact of social activism, and discomfort with this image is as pervasive as unease with images of women derived from Islamic traditionalism and Western Orientalism.

One woman who had felt pressure from her own society's 'Occidentalists' – that is, by thinkers who purvey the stereotypical image of a decadent, individualistic West, and use this image to deprive secular thinkers of legitimacy – was Mona Zulficar, a key activist in the Personal Status Law coalition and a founding member of the National Council for Women (a known 'secular' group of women).[12] In an interview, Zulficar noted that her general strategy as a Muslim woman lawyer is 'to change the laws that subjugate women, and by changing the laws, ultimately change will come to the culture.' She also stressed the importance of changing the law and then educating the public about the reform of the law. Such education is expedited by the media and NGOs.

Zulficar related that one of the most significant barriers to her efforts to change Egyptian laws was the perception that she was pushing a 'Western' – and therefore un-Islamic – agenda. Her focus on the changing of the law as a means of achieving social change ran up against an apparent incompatibility of the means she was using – secular legalistic discourse – with the ends of improving the status of Muslim women in a society with strong religious values. She expressed her realization of this tension in the following terms:

> Law is not just a mechanism for codification. It is a *means* not an end for codifying objectives. However, the means when focused too much become ends to themselves ... We start to question the means when progress seems not obvious. We also started to realize that we are embedded in a religious community.

---

12   Mona Zulficar, interview by author, 7 October 2003, at her law office in Cairo, Egypt.

For Zulficar, the law *could* be the means for change and for reconciling competitive trends in Egyptian society, but only through efforts to engage with religious discourse. Without renouncing the secular trends that had influenced her thinking (CEDAW/ UN Declaration/legal reform which did not speak to the ordinary man on the street), she came to understand that you 'cannot ignore the Islamic context of law.'

Hoda el-Sadda, another key activist in the coalition of legal reform advocates and a Professor of English Literature at Cairo University, pointed out that social change efforts must engage their cultural context if they are to achieve legitimacy. Speaking somewhat indirectly, she alluded to the fact that previous efforts to change social norms had failed to engage the societal mainstream with the language of expression that they found most meaningful and authoritative: Islam. She argued that activists must speak to – not past – this mainstream:

> [T]here is a 'big middle' of practicing Muslims in Egypt who are the majority. These women and men are ordinary faithful people who want freedom, but they get lost between two radical poles.

The 'two radical poles,' in el-Sadda's view, are secularists and Muslim fundamentalists.

When reflecting on ten years of experience in the legal reform coalition, Zulficar shared her perception that early efforts had failed due to ineffectiveness vis-à-vis popular Islamic culture. Helping to reform the Personal Status Law, she related, only became possible when the roots of these failures were analyzed:

> The first attempt at changing the Personal Status Law was reforming the marriage contract law which would ultimately help in amending divorce law. We wanted to allow couples to freely choose their own terms within their own agreement [that is, the original marriage contract], especially in regards to the possibility of divorce. This approach would be beneficial to the courts … Even though this first attempt appeared to be not successful [she then mentioned how there were various reasons, but the main one was the influence and impact of Islamist opposition], it [nonetheless] was one of our first victories because it taught us what we needed to stand for and prepared us for future opportunities.

The next 'victory,' according to Zulficar, came when Aziza Hussein, another activist and colleague (as well as relative) of Zulficar, was delegated to direct the United Nation's National Preparatory Committee for NGOs. Using this UN project as a platform and diversifying the coalition by including a variety of women's networks (activists from NGOs, scholars, and the National Council for Women[13]), government supporters (for example, Fathi Naguib, the Head of the Supreme Constitutional Court), media, and Islamic religious leaders (that is, the Grand Imam of Al-Azhar,

---

13   This council was/is supported by presidential decree and is headed by Suzanne Mubarak, wife of President Hosni Mubarak. For more information about Suzanne Mubarak's influence on women's rights in Egypt, see Dina Ezzat's interview with Mubarak entitled 'Women Can Make Peace a Reality,' in al-Ahram Weekly, <www.weekly.ahram.org.eg/ print/2004/680/intrvw.htm>.

Shaykh Mohammed Sayed El-Tantawi), they rewrote the Personal Status Law.[14] In our interview,[15] Zulficar stressed the importance of the manner in which diverse local organizations successfully created an interactive network that was simultaneously local and transnational. Muslim women, she stated, are beginning 'to be connected in unprecedented ways both locally (as seen in the example of the coalition) and transnationally (as seen in sharing of strategies across national borders)' and in their experience they are learning new ways to 'live in-between the secular and religious.' Living 'in-between' the secular and the religious is one of the ways in which Muslim women activists are avoiding the category of 'Occidentalized other.'[16]

Diane Singerman, Professor of Government at the American University in Washington, DC, who is currently writing about divorce law in Egypt, articulated the significance of this undertaking in the following terms:

> [A]lthough much of the international and national direction of the women's movement has been to promote female education, political rights, and equality for women, the Egyptian women's movement and others across the Muslim world recognize the importance of changing the balance of power within marriage, particularly its legal dimension, if they are truly to benefit and take advantage of these other changes. Women could become ambassadors, deans of Islamic philosophy, international corporate lawyers, wealthy businesswomen, leaders of organizations, scholars, and politicians, yet they still feared divorce, financial ruin, and losing the custody of their children if they worked, wanted to further their education, or traveled without permission of their husband ...

> The women and male supporters in the PSL [Personal Status Law] coalition not only tried to overcome the contradictions of their daily and professional lives through this campaign, but in the process they became part of a transnational movement of new Muslim intellectuals and activists that are reimagining the past and the Islamic canon, contesting

---

14   Although the coalition had to compromise (by not passing all changes suggested), Zulficar still feels that 'there is a revolution emerging.' See Zulficar's statements in Schneider, 2000, A16 and A17.

15   During my conversation with Zulficar, I was accompanied by Zainah Anwar who compared Zulficar's experience to Sisters in Islam's advocacy (SIS). Anwar agreed with Zulficar's analysis of ends and means and added:

Legal reform if not accompanied by the mindset just remains a right on paper but doesn't bring change on the ground ... Engagement with the traditional other is a process not an objective. Creation of law is done in the name of Islam, so the reform of law must also be done in the name of religion; however, we must remember that legal framework doesn't bring about a change of attitude.

Anwar also agreed that because the Islamist movement was such a threat to their governments, SIS had to become responsive and try 'to bridge gap between secular and religious voices.'

16   Zulficar also mentioned other successes in legal reform that she had helped to bring to fruition: 1) in 1999, the divorce law was amended; and 2) in 2002, the first woman judge (Tahani Al Gebali) was appointed. She also stated that in the near future there would be a new family law which she hoped would be in the spirit of the unified draft family law approved by the Arab League.

dominant frames legitimated by religious authorities who often have indirect or direct ties with the more conservative Islamist groups ... (Singerman, forthcoming, 4–5).[17]

According to Singerman, women are becoming more skilled in promoting legal change within a context of Islamic discourse, and are finding their cause strengthened when they embrace rather than avoid aspects of Islamic identity:

> Importantly, while the Islamic nature of personal status laws was seen until this point as a liability, this coalition of women turned it into an asset.

> The dual need to base a strategy for change on legal and religious grounds, that incorporates a subtle critique of Western colonial or imperial Ottoman influences on national traditions, places this coalition within a much broader international movement of activists 'reclaiming Islam.' Like many of their counterparts in Morocco, Iran, Palestine, Bangladesh, India, Pakistan, or Malaysia, this coalition continued to promote a 'rights discourse' but veered away from the liberal, individualistic, secular framework of feminism associated with the West and women's 'liberation' (Singerman, forthcoming, 10).

The emergence of such trends is highly significant and represents a discontinuity from the past. Previous generations of Muslim women activists more openly adopted Eurocentric models, assuming that secularism – in combination with nationalism or socialism – would provide the model for women's emancipation within Muslim societies. They used what some might call a 'secular bypass': an effort to avoid religious discourse altogether, perhaps with the assumption that religious concepts are fixed and inhospitable to new interpretations. Separation of mosque and state, therefore, was a primary goal. For many women living under Muslim laws, 'religion' in general was a problem rather than a potential solution or a means of promoting women's agency. Zulficar, in a paper presented at the International Conference on the Islamic Marriage Contract at Harvard Law School, succinctly expressed the complexity of competitive paradigms and how women are becoming mediators of religiosity and secularity:

> The New Marriage Contract [Initiative] adopted a strategy of engagement in the religious discourse, based on the women's reading of their rights under the principles of Sharia. We reclaimed for the first time our right to redefine our cultural heritage, as Muslim women under principles of Sharia. We could not afford to shy away from the challenge and continue using solely a strategy based on constitutional and human rights. We had to prove that the religious discourse could also be used by women to defend their cause. The religious extremist groups consistently place the women's issues at the forefront of their published agenda to implement Sharia principles or 'codify' Sharia and assert their cultural identity. Thus, any secular feminist opposition is immediately accused of being anti-Islamic, an agent of the then 'non-religious' Eastern block or 'the corrupt' Western

---

17 Singerman connected me to a variety of Egyptian women, like Zulficar, El-Sadda, Umaima Abu-Bakr, and Heba Rauf Ezzat. If interested in further detailed information about the PSL coalition, see Singerman's forthcoming book and her article, 'Women and Strategies for Change: An Egyptian Model,' in *Arab Reform Bulletin*, vol. 2, issue 7 (July 2004): available on the Carnegie Endowment for International Peace website: <http://www.ceip.org/files/Publications/ARB-7-19-04.asp?p=1&from=pubdate#fate>.

block. It was therefore essential for the women's movement to diversify its strategies and adopt a credible strategy which could reach out and win the support of simple, ordinary religious men and women (Zulficar, in Singerman, forthcoming, 1).

Efforts to reengage with religious discourse are also causing Muslim activists to rethink their identities. Rather than choosing between the two poles of a rigid, 'secular vs. religious' dichotomy, they are beginning to see themselves as existing in ways that are both secular and religious, and forming composite identities. They are seeking to embrace their history more comprehensively – both its Islamic traditions and elements of the colonial and modern experiences. In the process, they are attempting to transcend the 'Occidentalized' label in ways that do not place themselves in another category: 'Islamized.'

The Islamized Other

The nineteenth century and the first half of the twentieth century brought a wave of transformation upon the Islamic world. The vast majority of Muslim lands were directly subjected to colonialism, and those which were not (Turkey, Iran, and Afghanistan) were nonetheless confronted with imperial power and the challenges of defensive modernization. The pervasiveness of Western influences brought about significant cultural and intellectual changes, including the emergence of secular ideologies and liberal (or reformist) Islamic thinking.

Significantly, this movement toward cultural and intellectual liberalization – often at the behest of nationalist movements or the state – was not the only significant reaction of Muslim societies to European imperialism. Along with the liberal trends supported by modern educational institutions (patterned on European models) came a counter-movement seeking to reassert Islamic authenticity and 're-Islamize' cultural life. This current of Islamism – referred to in Chapter 3 as 'revivalism' – challenged all parties that were seen as having compromised the identity, vitality, and strength of Islamic societies. Even as new Islamic states emerged on the international stage, new Islamic movements arose to protest the legitimacy of political entities that in their view compromised the ideal of pan-Islamic unity, co-opted the traditional clergy, permitted penetration by Western culture, and practiced corruption.

As stated in Chapter 3, contemporary Islamic revival movements are not necessarily opposed to modernity. They do, however, actively seek to 'Islamize' contemporary Islamic cultures – to reassert what they see as fundamental Islamic precepts, and ensure the primacy of Islamic symbolism in all spheres of life, including public dress and gender relations, as well as education and knowledge creation. Intellectuals and activists associated with these movements are not necessarily on good terms with Muslim traditionalists, whom many revivalists regard as compromisers who are passive and to some degree complicit with domestic tyranny and foreign domination. Their relations with liberal and secular Muslims, as well as with the state, have often been highly antagonistic. One of the more divisive issues in debates between revivalists and their adversaries has been the status and public comportment of women.

Until the late 1960s, secular nationalist movements had the political upper hand throughout the Islamic world. More recent decades, however, have witnessed a shift in relations between secular and neo-Islamic movements, with secular nationalism (especially but not exclusively Arab and Persian nationalisms) declining and Islamic revivalism in the ascendance. It is this rise of Islamic revivalism that is implicated in the 'return of the veil' ('reveiling') that has drawn so much attention from those who write on the status of Muslim women.

Though the 'return of Islam' and the 'return of the veil' have brought about a reinforcement of conservative social norms on such matters as dress and gender relations, some Muslim women have sought to integrate the *Weltanschauung* of Islamic revivalism with discourse about women's rights. Effectively embracing both the re-emphasis on Islamic identity and their own identity as women, these activists have sought to 'reclaim Islam' and promote ideas such as 'Islamic feminism' (Badran, 2002).[18] Like Islamic revivalism itself, 'Islamic' or 'Muslim' feminism is a contested concept, associated with widely varying pronouncements on the rights of women, and raising more than a few eyebrows among secularists and Islamists alike (Karam, 1998).[19] What is clear, however, is that Islamization campaigns have by no means ended debate on these issues; rather, the debates are continuing within new discursive parameters. Some women are finding that 'homegrown' notions such as 'Islamic feminism' or 'Muslim feminism' – though suspect in the eyes of secularists – have greater popular resonance in society than Western feminism, and are arguing that it is possible to achieve genuine improvements in the lives of women while operating within an Islamic frame of reference. Umaima Abu-Bakr, Professor of Comparative Literature at Cairo University, offered the following commentary:

> Muslim women scholars are bolder now in their approaches to religious texts. There was the old school of the secular problem where women would avoid religion altogether feeling it was too complicated and messy – men will win out … [because it is] difficult to [win] at their own game. Then there are the anti-secularists who are not shying away [from Islamic discourse], rather they are engaging in critique of the Qur'an.[20]

Though she would not necessarily claim the title of 'Islamic feminist,' Abu-Bakr views the return of Islam to the women's rights discussion as a positive development. Referring to the Arab-Islamic concept of *niyyah* (intention), she expressed sympathy for the intention behind Islamic reformist thinking. 'You want to save [Islam] … reform it not destroy it. One must remain committed to Islam but need it without injustice.' She also noted that recent years have brought about more 'visible'

---

18   In Badran's 2002 article, she begins by stating the following:
The term Islamic feminism began to be visible in the 1990s in various global locations. It was from the writings of Muslims that I discovered the term. Iranian scholars Afsaneh Najmabadah and Ziba Mir-Hosseini explained the rise and use of the term Islamic feminism in Iran by women writing in the Tehran women's journal *Zanan* that Shala Sherkat founded in 1992.

19   Karam develops the term 'Islamic feminism' in relation to two other feminisms, 'secular feminism' and 'Muslim feminism.'

20   Umaima Abu-Bakr, interview by author, 2 October 2003, via phone in Cairo, Egypt.

engagement between Muslim scholars and such mainstream Islamic institutions as al-Azhar, including public dialogues on local television channels: 'There are more Muslim scholars, both women and men, from the periphery having an impact on debate.'

Just as Mona Zulficar felt that her perspective had been misrepresented as merely 'secular' or 'Western,' some Muslim women are quite uncomfortable with being associated too closely with Islamic revival movements. Like the 'secular' label, the 'Islamist' or 'Islamized' label has social consequences.

On the same day that I interviewed Mona Zulficar, I also interviewed Heba Rauf Ezzat, a Professor of Political Science and co-founder (with Shaykh Yusuf Qardawi) of IslamOnLine.com (one the largest Muslim cyberspace websites).[21] In our discussion, Rauf Ezzat stated that she has often felt that secular counterparts dismiss her discourse by mistakenly underscoring her association with the Muslim Brotherhood. By viewing her merely as a voice of Egypt's Islamic movement, secular feminists find an excuse to avoid engaging with her discourse – even though she is equally conversant with Islamic interpretation and Western social theorists such as Habermas. She wanted to underscore her intellectual qualifications and ability to engage in high-level debate with secular feminists and the *'ulama* alike.

The distinctiveness of Heba Rauf Ezzat's views as an Islamic thinker came out at several points during our conversation. For example, at the beginning of my encounter with Rauf Ezzat, I asked the question: 'What is your strategy for empowering Muslim women – textually and/or contextually?' At first Rauf Ezzat was quite cautious with the word 'empowerment':

> What do you mean by the word empowerment? Do you mean a distancing or modernizing of the Muslim woman to be 'better'? ... Modernity is a flagword which indicates a disintegration of culture and a sense of identity that is detached from the community.

For Rauf Ezzat, terms such as 'modernity' and 'empowerment' are related to a Western, Occidental project that is fundamentally individualist – and hence anti-communal – in character. She was also critical of Western formulations of 'development,' which she regarded as a 'disembedded process' that does not 'reconcile culture with tradition' but rather imposes external normative standards. It has to be 'measure[ed] from a Western framework.' These views contrasted quite markedly with Mona Zulficar's; Zulficar responded quite readily to the 'empowerment' question, and defined the term as 'having the basic ingredients for effective participation: economic, legal, legislative, and cultural.'

Heba Rauf Ezzat is not alone, however, in her reservations about the conventional Western terminology for improving the status of women. An American Muslim interviewee, Amina Wadud, stated that in her view 'enabling' is a more appropriate concept for Muslim women who are committed to processes of personal and social transformation.[22] Whereas the word 'empowerment' can be construed as carrying

---

21 Heba Rauf Ezzat, interview by author, 7 October 2003, at the Marriott Hotel lobby in Cairo, Egypt.

22 I have interviewed Amina Wadud on two occasions, both via phone. This quote was stated in our first encounter on 20 October 1999.

patriarchal as well as Western connotations associated with the word 'power,' the term 'enabling' carries less cultural and conceptual baggage. Wadud asserted that such distinctions have genuine practical significance, and defended what she sees as a trend toward a discourse of enablement. In defense of this contention, she shared details of her 'hands-on' experience of 'enabling' while working with Sisters in Islam (SIS) in Malaysia.[23]

As 'Islamic' or 'Muslim' feminists, both Rauf Ezzat and Wadud agreed that Muslim women confront two divergent and yet impinging forces: Western feminism, and learned religious men who insist on maintaining or tightening traditional norms affecting the status of women. Though Western feminists may find it difficult to understand how their emancipatory discourse might be viewed as an 'impinging force,' Yvonne Seng, a scholar of Middle Eastern and Islamic history, offered an explanation:[24] 'Western feminism seems to divide women into two categories: social and legal. In the legal aspect you see women wanting equal rights, such as the right to bear arms, whereas in the social aspect women focus on their needs.' Seng continued by observing that the legalistic aspect of Western feminism is associated with a more 'atomistic' or individualistic way of viewing society, in which relations between people are governed by formal legal norms associated with the state rather than by relationships of trust and cultural values. Legal change can easily become an end in itself, and cultural and social contexts are largely ignored.

In Seng's judgment, the practices of Western feminists are actually somewhat similar to those of the *'ulama*, who limit Islamic values to legal norms derived from specific historical practices of Muslim communities – practices which may or may not correspond with contemporary social needs and realities. Muslim women who take a more context-sensitive approach to the definition and advancement of values are therefore departing from the practices of 'Occidentalized' feminists and the *'ulama* alike. Seng therefore argued that women are most effective when they focus their attention on the holistic, social approach in order to 'begin to look at the texts from their own eyes,' rather than bypass them or subsume them to norms derived from another context. Then, and only then, can women stimulate a redefinition of Islamic values and social needs. The 'awakening' of Muslim women, then, could provide a culturally legitimate avenue for injecting women's voices into 'official' Muslim discourse, leading to greater respect for women's experiences and to dialogue with religious authorities.

As a political theorist, Rauf Ezzat believes that the most appropriate pathway to 'empowerment' for Muslim women is knowledge. Such empowerment is not a zero-sum game. Gains for women are also gains for the *'ulama*, and women should seek to 'empower' the *'ulama* by sharing the women's perspective. By making such points, it was clear that Rauf Ezzat believes in the importance of underscoring loyalty to Islamic culture and community, despite the risks such a position entails: becoming a mere symbol of religious and cultural authenticity for traditionalists and

---

23   For more about SIS, see Chapter 5.

24   Yvonne Seng, interview by author, 2 October 1999, at the American University in Washington, DC.

revivialists, or an icon of Islamic 'backwardness' for a Western media that represents non-Westerners as 'outcasts.'

Self-consciousness in the face of Western media portrayals was a common theme in my encounters. Many interviewees expressed frustration with decontextualized Western media images of veiled women, which have served (and still serve) to depict Islam in general and Islamic fundamentalism in particular as the enemy of Muslim women. They felt that such images projected a distorted and misleading image, and were politically dangerous as well: was not the 'liberation of Muslim women' being used to justify the American 'War on Terror'? And does not the global media environment created by such images privilege the Western perspective, rendering the 'unveiled' Muslim woman normal and the veiled Muslim woman 'backward' or 'aberrant'? Cannot Islamic culture and Islamic feminism provide a culturally valid alternative to Eurocentric liberal humanism and Western feminist models? Such questions were commonplace.

In addition to these concerns about becoming an 'other' for clinging to Islamic culture and identity, some of my interviewees were also concerned about the danger of isolating themselves from emergent global conversations. In Iran, Homeira Moshirzadeh, a Professor of International Relations at Tehran University, expressed ambivalence about current trends of globalization, which can lead to loss of historical identity *or* to a distorted reassertion of provincialism that interferes with genuine possibilities for dialogue. Muslims have a right to feel uneasy about globalization, because '[t]here is no tradition in the globalized world.' Yet there is a danger of overreaction:

> As Muslims we consume nostalgia for the golden era and as it increases so too does the lack of curiosity as well as creative thinking … We consume ideas from outside, but we do not produce ideas … [We] over-emphasize the traditional as the absolute self. Isolation [becomes] a mindset: [the] only way to preserve identity is through retreat or rejection.[25]

As examples of overreaction in the name of authenticity, Moshirzadeh cited Jalal al-Ahmed and Ahmad Fardid, both of whom had 'influenced today's thinking' in Iran by pioneering the notion of Westoxification (in Farsi '*gharbzadigi*').[26] She believed that such constructions of 'East' and 'West' are unsustainable, however, and focused

---

25 Homeira Moshirzadeh, interview by author, 16 May 2004, during a conference entitled 'A Gathering of Women on Socio-Cultural Issues and Globalization' at Tehran University, Iran.

26 In the Khomeini era of Iranian politics, many Iranians were (and still are) influenced by the populist discourse of *gharbzadigi*, also known as 'Westoxification.' Two prominent figures who wrote about Westoxification were Jalal al-Ahmed and Ahmad Fardid. Afsaneh Najmabadi, in Deniz Kandiyoti's *Women, Islam and the State*, offers some analysis on this concept:

Perhaps nowhere has this total rejection touched popular as well as intellectual imagination more acutely than in its rejection of the *gharbzadeh* woman. The *gharbzadeh* woman came to embody at once all social ills: she was a super-consumer of imperialist/dependent-capitalist/ foreign goods; she was a propagator of the corrupt culture of the West; she was undermining the moral fabric of society; she was a parasite, beyond any type of redemption (Najmabadi, in Kandiyoti, 1991, 65).

on a trend toward 'fractalization' of tradition and of the 'revolutionizing spirit' in reformist thought: each carries elements of the 'other' within itself, as traditionalists accept elements of reform and reformists develop their own traditions. Whether they like it or not, tradition and reform are in conversation with each other, and trends toward 'fractalization' are inevitable.

Another Iranian interviewee, Seyed Kazem Sajjadpour,[27] shared this concern. Troubled intercultural relations could easily lead to a retreat into a troubled notion of authenticity:

> The more 'the other' crosses a boundary aggressively, the more 'other' they become and the more defensive 'self' I become. I do not create the others in the beginning, the others are defined in the interaction of thinking and doing.

> [He then gave an example.] When Iraq under Saddam and the Baath regime constructed an identity that was anti-Iranian. In other words, it was [an] integral part of their regime's identity to be anti-Iranian. I did not like [the] Baathist identity because it constructed itself to be against me. I know it is wrong, but I have to be defensive … This kind of relationship has been very damaging for human beings, especially for Iran.

In other words, the existence of tendencies to caricature the 'Islamic' or 'Islamized' other should not cause Muslims to become defensive, or to distort and polarize their own identities.

Muslim Woman as Self: The Constructed Composite

The Rise of Women's Agency: A Question of Subjectivity and Intersubjectivity

As the interviews cited above attest, the topic of 'women and Islam' evokes a great deal of fragmentation and identity polarization. To raise the subject is to provoke a

---

Another example of overreaction as a result of 'othering' the Western world as well as non-Muslims is the formation of 'radical Islamist women's groups.' The most well-known Islamist women's group produces a magazine entitled *al-Khansaa*, which 'provides fitness tips for female holy warriors, information on treating injuries and advice on raising children to fight non-believers.' For more about *al-Khansaa*, see Usher, 2004.

27   Seyed Kazem Sajjadpour, interview by author, 30 May 2004, at the Institute for Political and International Studies in Tehran, Iran. In my interview with Sajjadpour, he responded to my question of 'How would you define self and other?' with the statement 'That is a very postmodern question.' He was not the only interviewee to respond to this question in that way. In another encounter, a focus group from al-Zahra University started the interview by asking me if I was a modernist or postmodernist. In addition to the question of self/other, there were other words/questions (for example, 'feminism,' 'modernity,' 'development') which also triggered similar reactions with many interviewees. Such experiences remind me of how, when language becomes appropriated/associated with the 'other' (whoever the other may be), it disconnects, creates a border between self and other. This thought was echoed in a statement made by Mouchine Ayouche, the Director the Halaqua Movement in Morocco, at the Annual Caravane Civique Conference: 'Language should never be a border; it should be traversed over and over again, every time anew.'

series of questions: 'Who are *you*? Whose side are you on? Where do you stand? What is *your* identity?' Indeed, the 'women and Islam' issue is a locus of complex cultural and ideological conflicts; even those who share an interest in organizing efforts to improve women's well-being cannot always communicate effectively with one another.

Despite the polarization and fragmentation to which my encounters attested, there were also many voices expressing optimism that women were indeed finding new ways to communicate with one another across cultural and interpretive boundaries. A number of interviewees went so far as to state that constructive dialogue and even reconciliation among secular and religious advocates of women's rights is 'inevitable.'

A question therefore arises: What grounds are there for hope in the potential for dialogue and integration? When I sought answers to this question during interviews, a frequent theme was the need for women to see themselves as active *agents* – as subjects within the public sphere, and not merely as objects. Many women perceived genuine advancements in their capacities to engage one another and their societies as activists and interpreters: they were no longer intimidated by revivalist Islamic discourse, nor were they in need of an exclusively secular framework for social action. In other words, they were beginning to feel more integrated and flexible in their advocacy efforts, able to negotiate among the different ideological tendencies within their society in the service of values that might potentially be shared across different intellectual camps. They were becoming more confident in their abilities to deal with complexity, and with apparent contradictions in ontology and epistemology.

Zainah Anwar articulated the new confidence of women's rights activists vis-à-vis Islamic culture in the following terms:

> I am not a Muslim scholar, but I *am* a Muslim, and I have something to say about Islam. I am also the citizen of a democratic country. I have the right to hold my government accountable. ... I will not let someone take away *my* Islam.[28]

Like Anwar, an increasing number of activists are claiming a *right* to engage themselves in debates about Islamic interpretation – to participate in public discussions and act in ways that occupy and reconstitute space for women in Muslim societies. By claiming this right to interpretive agency, they also assume new responsibilities – responsibilities to speak in their own cultural language and discuss the same authoritative texts that traditional authorities have utilized in the past (see Chapter 6 for further elaboration on Muslim women's roles in civic activism).

For some interviewees, this courage to engage in public discourse was associated with a distinctively 'modern' discovery of subjectivity. Azam Khatam, an Iranian urban sociologist who works on women's projects, emphasized the need for women 'both secular and religious to work with each other and do collective work' – to claim their agency as reflective subjects:

---

28 Zainah Anwar, keynote speech at the CSID conference, where I had an informal conversation with Anwar and then a more formal interview in Cairo, Egypt. See Chapters 5 and 6.

I have participated in many different regional dialogues and at each one, I noticed that sociological thinking is focused more on the agency than on the structure, objective forces. And I was trained in the tradition that emphasized more on the structures. So, something is different now … [Q]ualitative research and methods are more accepted. Such methods as I [took] to these conferences seemed not so abstract any more.[29]

The self and other is rapidly changing in the Muslim world … Subjectivity is the most important sign of being modern for me. Subjectivity is the value of thinking and valuing through the self autonomy of the mind. Being independent and thinking independent. [She then gave some examples of what she called 'signs of autonomy'] Girls going to school and divorce.

For Khatam, the other is 'a catalyst.' This notion was also shared by Neelam Hussain, Director of Simorgh Women's Resource and Publication Centre:[30] 'The stranger/other is an unknown entity who has an element of mystery and represents the possibility of something happening.' She added: 'He/she also creates fear/apprehension, which can be a vehicle for change and an instigator for action.' Having been influenced by the Qadri Sufi Order, Hussain understands 'the self as a non-static entity that is merging within shifting worlds.' What fascinated me about these interviews was not only the affirmation of subjective agency, but also the creative (as opposed to obstructive or irrelevant) role of the 'other.' On the one hand there was a confident claim to agency, and on the other hand an expressed intent to seek intersubjectivity through dialogue and encounter.

Mariam Hussain, an artist and daughter of Neelam Hussain, offered a compelling comment that mirrors contemporary academic discourse on intersubjectivity.[31] She described the self and other as 'co-habiting within oneself,' creating a sort of internal 'collage.' She was not blind to barriers, however, as not all borders are equally permeable, nor are all identities easily assimilated. Others such as 'the Islamic fundamentalist and US foreign policy' are difficult to assimilate.

Salima Hashmi[32] spoke about the other as 'the one who brings the ominous.' 'Searching for the other,' she stated, 'is one of the most embracing aspects of life. It is in searching that we become whole.' When I asked her how she would define dialogue she stated the following:

Living in between self and other is dialogue. Dialogue is crucial for every moment … As a teacher, it is second nature to be dialogical, for between the teacher and student there is a process of mutual learning.

29　Azam Khatam, interview by author, 29 May 2004, at her home in Tehran, Iran. She also mentioned that before her experiences at such conferences, she had only read such methods in books.

30　Neelam Hussain, interview by author, 24 May 2004, at the Simorgh office in Lahore, Pakistan.

31　Mariam Hussain, interview by author, 24 May 2004, via phone in Lahore, Pakistan.

32　Salima Hashmi, interview by author, 23 May 2004, at her home in Lahore, Pakistan. See Chapter 4, note 15.

Not all interviewees, of course, engaged these questions in such an unconventional (some would say postmodern) manner. Saideh Lotfian[33] was direct:

> Self is the closest person to one and other is anybody but you ... The stranger is someone whom you have not met before, a person whom you are meeting for the first time ... Difference makes the other. This brings both opportunity and limitation.

Other interviewees noted that my questions about 'self' and 'other' could be answered in multiple ways, depending on the manner in which the terms were translated. Hoda Rouhana, Program Officer for Middle East and North Africa networks for Women Living Under Muslim Laws (WLUML),[34] for example, noted the difference between two Arabic translations: *nafs* and *huwiya*. Whereas *nafs* is deeply personal and carries spiritual connotations ('the soul'), *huwiya* is less personal, connoting collective identity and social status. She went on:

> I am having difficulty answering the question, because I feel that my identity is constantly shifting. This question of identity is difficult because it can change in the context that it is asked. For instance, being asked it in England I will answer differently than if I am asked it in Palestine. The context matters. You feel different in different cases because you are positioned differently.[35]

Questions concerning the other or the stranger elicited answers that diverged and converged at the same time. The stranger was either no-one (meaning all people are somehow akin to ourselves) or everyone (meaning that all 'others' carry secrets and distinguish traits that make them unique as human beings). Jamila Hassoune highlighted the former theme: 'There is no stranger in the world.'[36] For Hassoune, the guiding principle for encountering the other should be *'Ahlan wa Sahlan'* – an Arabic phrase of welcome and hospitality which simultaneously invites the guest to feel at ease and to consider herself or himself as a member of the family.

This ideal of openness and dialogue was a common theme of my interviews, and at a Caravane Civique event I attended in Morocco. At this event, the former President of Spain, a keynote speaker, offered a view that complemented Hassoune's:

---

33   Saideh Lotfian, interview by author, 29 May 2004, at University of Tehran's Department of Law and Political Science.

34   Hoda Rouhana, interview by author, 8 July 2004, at WLUML London Office, England. This interview was part of a larger group interview with Cassandra Balchin and Anissa Helie. Rouhana had been working with BAOBAB since 1998 and had just recently started to work at the London headquarters for WLUML.

35   During this interview, Anissa Helie, another staff member of WLUML, added:

The question of self/other can be seen in the 'personal and political.' In our work (WLUML) at the political level, people try to construct identity in fixed and immutable ways. However, our personal experience tells us that it is shifting depending on context (i.e., what locality are we living in). The contrast how we feel as transnational activists and what fundamentalist ('religious extreme right') transnational activists feel (about what is a Muslim woman) is based in this difference of identity: is it fluid or fixed?

36   See Chapter 5, note 27.

The stranger is the one who we don't know about. Everyone is a stranger. The unknown is self ... When we travel over borders are we strangers?

This assertion of a fundamental paradox – the other is unknown, and yet also somehow a part of ourselves – recurred with remarkable frequency, as the following testimony from participants at the Caravane Civique conference suggests:

Ana fi al-akhr wa al-akhr fi ana. [Literal English translation: 'I am in the other and the other is in me.'] (Amina from Zagora, Morocco)

The other is the one who becomes an extension of self. (Yasmina from Casablanca, Morocco)

To know the other is a base for knowing self. (Fatna el-Bouih)[37]

Each individual has truth. Ibn Sina said: '*Al-wahid min al-ithnan wa al-ithnan min al-wahid.*' [The one is from the two and the two is from the one.] (Abdel Aziz, a former political prisoner in Morocco)

The commonplace nature of such discourse in my encounters would seem to demand explanation. Why was there so much emphasis on the need to cross boundaries, to know the 'other'? To be sure, my sample of interviewees was not representative of entire populations: it was representative of individuals who were seeking to cultivate networks and to confront obstacles to the advancement and well-being of women. Yet the subtlety of the comments was often provocative. Behind many of these philosophical statements I often found considerable depth of personal reflection and experience. For some, the commitment to cross boundaries arose from the pain of having been treated as a 'stranger' or 'other.'

This was the case for Homeira Moshirzadeh, a Professor of International Relations at Tehran University. Having been born into a non-religious family before the Iranian Revolution, Moshirzadeh had direct experience with secular, 'unveiled' life prior to the ousting of the Shah. At the time of the revolution, however, she began to wear the *hijab* voluntarily, before it became a requirement. Reflecting on this experience, she now recognizes that she has seen Iran from both sides of the veil, and known something about what it means to be on both sides of a major cultural and intellectual fault line. This has strengthened her belief in tolerance for the other, whoever the 'other' may be. It has also impelled her to seek a 'medium point, in-between' opposites. This, then, is the context of experience from which her testimony arose:

The stranger is the one who we do not know about (*al-ghayb*) ... Everyone, including the self, is a stranger. There is the unknown in everyone ... We can never know absolutely being. Therefore the stranger is present in every new moment.

 The world today, Moshirzadeh suggested, is afflicted by 'a problem of labeling without engaging,' and this non-engagement leads to 'the perception of the other as

---

37   See this chapter, note 6.

judged by outer appearance.' In response to this problem, she reasserted the limits to knowing others, especially from a distance and in the absence of engagement. Such remarks differ quite profoundly from the tone and tenor of the mutual denunciations between Iranian traditionalists and sympathizers with the late Shah, not to mention the cultural politics of demonization – in which the stranger is a definitively *known* and unconditionally despised *enemy* – that define relations between Iran and the United States. For Moshirzadeh, otherness means difference, but difference is not automatically a matter of mutual opposition. Awareness of self leads to the awareness of the other, and of the relationship that binds them. It prepares the way for dialogical engagement and understanding, regardless of outer forms such as the veil (see Chapter 4 and her definition for dialogue).

Conclusions

The constructions of 'self-' and 'other-' identities offered by my interviewees can be interpreted as acts of resistance against rigid, stereotypical dichotomies explored in the first section of this chapter. For so many of the women whom I interviewed, identity is a matter of ongoing negotiation rather than categorical certainties; self-knowledge, other-knowledge and dialogue evolve together. Though a sense of integration or wholeness seemed to evade many interviewees, each person's narrative suggested an identity that cannot easily be 'boxed' – an identity that is a complex composite of multiple social elements and currents, including aspects of the traditional as well as the modern, the secular as well as the religious (see Figure 7.2).

Although much more research will be necessary to shed light on the trends suggested by my encounters, it would appear that agents of social change on behalf of Muslim women are increasingly dissatisfied with the polarities that once defined and constrained their efforts. They are not finding that activism and freedom of expression must come at the expense of sacred meaning and religious belief, nor are they satisfied with attitudes that oppose political participation and autonomy to collective loyalty and historical memory.

In the process of negotiating for agency, many Muslim women are connecting to larger social, religious, national, and transnational communities. In light of this new development, 'Muslim women are becoming more cosmopolitan.'[38] Such spatial extensions of the self appear to be founded upon shifting habits of self-identification that allow Muslim activists to engage at local and global levels, and to embrace pluralism. Many of my interviewees emphasized the inescapability of change, and the challenges of reconciling multiple cultural values and visions. Elahe Kolaei, a Professor of Political Science at Tehran University, had spent decades of her life as a university professor and educator and also had experience as a parliamentarian in the Iranian Consultative Assembly – a parliamentarian who had recently been dismissed for insisting on wearing a light headscarf rather than the required chador (a traditional Iranian garment that covers the woman from head to foot). Her commentary focused

---

38 Azam Khatam, interview by author, 29 May 2004, at her residence in Tehran, Iran. See Chapter 5, note 33.

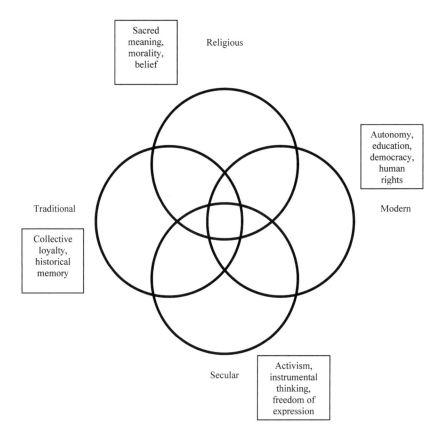

Figure 7.2 Dimensions of identity and value: the composite self

on the need to balance contending values in a search for coherence, progress, and integrity:

> We as a transitional society are in the mid-way of keeping traditions and accepting the achievements of a modern society … We can combine them together. This is a very serious question in all transitional societies and especially in all Islamic societies … We have to make a balance between what we can do and what we have to accept … Being a traditional society we must pass through what all transitional societies pass through … This is a very challenging stage, for many societies go through many critical crises: crisis of identity, cohesion, etc … As an ideological system that is based on Islamic values and norms, it is very important to make [a] balanced relationship between these values and the necessities of modern living and modern relationship within the society … We must make linkages amongst the traditional and the modern.[39]

---

39 Elahe Kolaei, interview by author, 30 May 2004, at the Department of Law and Political Science, Tehran University, Iran. In response to my question 'What is modernity?',

Another Iranian interviewee, Jaleh Shaditalab[40] spoke quite eloquently about her own efforts to preserve that which is valuable in the traditional and the modern while also making space for new developments – developments that would be desirable in many respects, yet not without costs. Her flexibility, openness, and honesty provide a compelling example of the type of cosmopolitan, pluralistic identity that is characteristic of many women whom I encountered, and which is arguably necessary for sincere efforts to maintain dialogical connections amidst diversity:

> Self is defined by 50 years of experience in living in different cultures (US, Europe, Iran). So, my definition of self is a definition of all my experiences and ideologies. My definition of self is an individual who has certain goals and who is trying to find the best means to achieve those goals.

> My definition of self is different and more complicated than others because of my encounter with complexity. There is a paradox in which I am in the middle of the whole thing [the cultural debate] because I do not want to look like a non-Iranian yet at the same time I want to be an Iranian which is civilized in her everyday life experience. I do not want to be defined as a backwards human being. I have read books, I have my PhD, I know what it means to be developed and being in the process of development. I have my own pride in being Iranian.

> The most difficult thing facing Iranians is the process of defining our identity, our selves, which is consistent with Iranian way of life and not going backward.

> [She then gave an example.] As a professor, my students have told me that sometimes I speak and I sound like their grandmother and at other times I sound like I come from the twenty-second century. I cannot ignore our history, the traditions, and our Iranian identity (this is when I sound like a grandmother) and yet at the same time I cannot forget what is happening in the world: how fast change is coming. If we do not think ahead and try hard, we will be backward (this is when I am living in the twenty-second century). I get nervous that we are not moving and that our identity is not mobile.

> These two sides create many emotions: sometimes happy, sometimes angry … We do not want the destruction of the traditional family and yet at the same time we want the social movements of women. There are inconsistencies within our different roles. But the more that we can come to embrace our complexity as Muslim women, ironically the more we will be upholding the tradition and the change that we feel so loyal to. In a way, all Muslim women throughout history have been such mediators.

Kolaei said the following: '[Modernity] can have different meanings. It does not have a fixed meaning because of the different changes in different societies. Even though there are differences, I think there are [also] commonalities: urbanization, education (literacy) … Modernity is different for each society (for example, rural and urban) …'

At the end of the interview, Kolaei also pointed out that: 'We [Iranians] as a nation are very idealistic because of our background: we have a rich history and because of it we feel that we have to play a very influential role in the region and in the world. This is a major component for understanding Iranians.' For more about Kolaei, see Boustany, 2004.

40   See Chapter 4, note 20.

As Muslim women consider their relations with one another and with the complex currents that constitute their societies, they are faced with the challenge of revisiting the theme of 'self' and 'other.' When taken to a deep level, this means reassessing competing value priorities and identity conflicts. Among the women I encountered, there was a surprisingly consistent response to the dilemmas posed by this exercise: women must transcend cultural dichotomies to engage the other and seek a larger context for action and identification. They wanted to retain a distinctively Muslim identity, without being constrained by traditional Islamic or stereotypically Western assumptions.

The patterns that emerged from my interviews raise important questions for academic researchers. Given the strong resistance of Muslim women activists to categories that have often been used to aid analysis (for example, secularist, Islamist, traditionalist), how can scholars generalize about processes of social change and advocacy without imposing foreign terms of reference or misconstruing the dynamics inherent in Islamic contexts? To what extent were the 'negative' identity characterizations ('not *x*' or 'not *y*') indicative of strategic considerations imposed by a conflicted social and international milieu, and to what extent do they reflect a genuine desire for new forms of identity that transcend existing dichotomies? Do Muslim women resist self-categorization at least partially on pragmatic grounds – to avoid being cast into the same lot as radical Islamists or Western imperialists? Or are they themselves searching for an integrative self-identity and worldview ('both/and') in a time of great transformations that demand new syntheses?

Many of these questions are difficult to answer definitively, yet researchers who are sensitive to the identity dilemmas and negotiations of Muslim women activists have the potential to shed light on issues that have grave import for the future direction of Islamic societies. By eliciting the narratives and identity claims of Muslim women, researchers can generate new insight into social forces and political tensions that shape our world, and gain inspiring glimpses of how courageous social agents are seeking to transcend deep polarizations and initiate secular–religious dialogues that integrate rather than fragment crucial human values.

Chapter 8

Conclusion: A Space for Connectivity and Dynamism

For several decades contemporary women's activism in the Islamic world was perceived as a largely secular phenomenon. Women generally relied upon secular nationalist discourse to advance claims to equality in the public and private spheres. Although at times women formed transnational networks of solidarity, expectations of improvement in status were closely linked to specific national projects. The resurgence of transnational Islamic revivalism and reformism – and the accompanying eclipse of secular nationalist ideologies – has prompted changes in the character of women's activism. Muslim women are adapting by forming their own transnational women's networks and many are taking a 'hermeneutic turn,' re-engaging with Islamic texts and identities.

Scholars who study women's movements, as well as scholars of Islam and transnationalism, have recently begun to analyze this development. Some have noted the utility of Islamic discourse to social activism, in particular national and cultural contexts, without a broader approach to comparative or transnational analysis. Others have relied primarily on socioeconomic categories when assessing the status of women, largely avoiding the subject of Islamic interpretation. Those scholars who are most preoccupied with reinterpreting Islamic texts tend to do so without specific reference to particular contexts of interpretation or to the past work of secular women's movements. Scholars who make claims about the transnational, in turn, demonstrate a similar preoccupation with the general rather than the particular: they offer analysis of organizations and activities without directly *encountering* the women involved to examine the texture of formal and informal networks and the ideas that animate them. Knowledge of Muslim women's lives, then, is fragmented and compartmentalized, revealing a need for frameworks of analysis that aspire to integrate the personal, the religious, the national/cultural, and the transnational.

In exploring identity constructions and meanings among Muslim women engaged in transnational dialogue, this book has sought to amplify the voices of women who are both creating transnational space and being changed by it through an interplay of structure and agency. On the one hand, they bring their own unique personal and national/cultural perspectives to the transnational, thereby helping to *constitute* transnational women's networks through secular as well as religious ideas and experiences. On the other hand, these women are also profoundly affected by their encounters within transnational networks, which allow them to enter into what we have characterized as a new (or emergent) hermeneutic field. In this book, I wanted to know how women are *experiencing* this emergent field: what it means to them, how it is affecting them, and how it shapes the ways they perceive their roles in society. To do so I sought to encounter a range of intellectuals and activists, to discuss their engagement with the transnational, with reference to their own primary vocabularies – including religion and religious interpretation.

While encountering these women, I sought to understand how the transnational influences the ways they perceive their identities as women, as Muslims, as citizens, and as activists. Deeming it presumptuous to test a preconceived hypothesis, I approached my study of this phenomenon in an inductive and exploratory manner, which accounts for the fact that many Muslim women – especially those who are not embedded in the uppermost strata of their societies – are just beginning to enter the transnational and/or just starting to realize how it affects them. I wanted to hear *their* voices with as little filtration as possible, and with less emphasis on pre-existing categories. In the preceding chapters, I have sought to convey their experiences and identify problems as they perceive them, with special reference to issues of identity and encounters with otherness. I also wanted to understand how these women – whose struggles remain culturally rooted – are embracing the complexity of their own identities.

This exploratory approach is also a way of studying transnational encounters without prematurely imposing a formula on a social process that may change and develop significantly over time. By accepting indeterminacy, this research rejects 'simple' modernist and secularist teleologies (that is, the proposition that Muslim women are becoming more 'Western') and tries to trace what the transnational means to these women *now*, as they emerge into and out of the transnational. In doing so, I try to understand the complexity of their experiences, while identifying cross-cutting themes and some tentative conclusions.

Key Findings

The rich data produced by this research are open to more than one interpretation, yet there is substantial support for a number of key findings. First, dialogue is providing those Muslim women who practice networking with a constructive means for opening lines of communication – not only to achieve short-term results in the domain of advocacy, but also to foster deeper levels of reflection on the competing normative paradigms which have in the past dichotomized and fragmented Muslim identity. Second, Muslim dialogue networks addressing 'the status of women' are becoming increasingly transnational in character, resulting in an increase in 'connectivity' among diverse practitioners as well as in greater ideational and practical dynamism. Third, experiences of transnational dialogue foster a sense of empowerment, in ways that encourage a reimagination of national 'public spheres' and the role of the self within them. Finally, Muslim women are perceiving that their personal understanding of 'selfhood' – as reflective social agents – can be expanded through dialogue, and that it need not be defined in ways that require a religious or Western 'other.'

Dialogue: Opening Lines of Communication

As described in Chapter 4, many interviewees experienced dialogue as a way to engage in the construction of Muslim meaning without feeling caught in an either/or world of dichotomies – 'traditional vs. modern,' 'religious vs. secular,' 'Western vs. authentically Islamic' – that fragment their societies. Those who participate in dialogue often perceive themselves as Muslims who dwell 'in between' the various terms of these polarities. As many interviewees noted, there are going to be some very important but also sensitive debates about Muslim identity in the years to come, and an inclusive approach to dialogue will become increasingly essential.

A number of interviewees described dialogue not only as a means of transcending conflict between normative systems, but also as a basis for building a sense of open identity – identity that is open to diverse relationships. They believed that increased participation in dialogue networks would be highly valuable, and that the ideational outcomes of dialogue should be disseminated more widely.

The Transnational: A Space for Connectivity and Dynamism

As was emphasized in Chapter 5, discussions about the status of women in Muslim societies are becoming increasingly transnational in character. Even though Islam has always been a 'transnational phenomenon,' new conditions are compressing time and space, making it easier for Muslim scholars and activists to reach across borders, engage people with overlapping interests, and form action networks. Ideas are moving across greater distances in much less time than in classical Islamic culture. Technological innovations such as the internet are having a particularly dramatic impact. As many scholars of Islam have noted, the internet is not only a vehicle for militant forces, but also for groups committed to peaceful change and democratic values. For many women it is a forum of connectivity, helping them to overcome feelings of isolation and marginalization within their own national and local contexts. As increasing numbers of intellectuals and activists are being drawn into a common set of conversations, the ideational dynamism and activist potential of their interactions increases.

From my interviews, it was clear that most of the interviewees had been thinking about 'the transnational' quite consciously – even though they sometimes differed on how to define it. Many interviewees had very articulate ideas about the transnational and were able to illustrate these ideas with examples. It was clear that, despite their widely varying national contexts, these interviewees were involved in shared *transnational conversations* about the practical and normative meanings of Islam in our times and the role of women in Muslim societies. Although their networks did not always intersect and participants were diverse in their ideological and cultural orientations, they were very much engaged in border-spanning discussions of issues with great contemporary significance.

One significant development noted by a wide variety of interviewees was that transnational dialogue is encouraging many activists to move beyond what might be described as the 'ideological comfort zones' and habituated positioning that surrounded their work in a national context. Transnational dialogue was creating new opportunities for engagement with pluralism, and encouraging participation within an emergent hermeneutic field. Many saw a pluralistic attitude as integral to their experiences of transnationalism, which in their view led to enhanced acceptance of diversity and to new 'bridging discourses.' Significantly, most interviewees drew a sharp distinction between transnationalism, which they viewed as empowering, and globalization, which they equated with Western economic and cultural hegemony.

Reimagining the Public

Throughout my travels, it was evident that Muslim women's activism is taking Islamic identity and the interpretation of religious sources much more seriously than in the past. Women from different camps – from revivalist to putatively 'secular' – are talking more with one another than in previous decades, and 'new camps' appear to be emerging, particularly among those who perceive a need to compromise, seek greater consensus, and engage both with secular critical discourse and with religious texts.

In response to the rise of fundamentalist and revivalist movements and the decline in secular nationalism, many interviewees reflected on the need to reconcile the religious with the secular. Entering into transnational dialogue prompts a reimagination of such competing paradigms and offers new insights into the national society and the role of the self in it. Concomitantly, as Muslim societies and Islamic public spheres are being reimagined to accommodate greater civic activism, so too are women gaining in agency. Despite the contentiousness of contemporary politics in many Muslim-majority countries, transnationalism appears to be strengthening 'civic Islam' at national and local levels, and vice versa: energized national and local spheres of activism are creating the basis for more assertive transnational activism. In the past, this was not necessarily the case.

This civic as well as critical engagement reflects how women are entering new roles in Muslim public spheres, in ways that may bring significant changes in the future. In some cases, women are challenging gender-segregated worship spaces, organizing religious groups, and even building mosques. The new transnational conversations are supporting these trends. Muslim women are increasingly networking to generate common hermeneutic attitudes and modes of activism.

Reclaiming Selfhood

The women engaged in transnational dialogue and advocacy are a diverse group about which few generalizations can be made. Indeed, many of the standard labels, such as 'traditional' or 'secular,' serve more to misrepresent the outlooks of these women than to clarify them. Moreover, many of the women are finding that the experience of dialogue challenges them to rethink some of their prior assumptions, as they seek to do greater justice to the diversity masked by labels. Dialogue, for example, makes it difficult to misrepresent contemporary traditionalist interpreters as being all of one opinion about the status of women, even though their reliance upon established juristic opinions predisposes them toward basically conservative outlooks. Likewise, sustained conversation reveals that some 'reactive' interpreters are willing to give at least verbal support to surprisingly 'progressive' positions on the status of Muslim women, even as seemingly 'secular' women reveal strong attachment to their identities as Muslims.

With surprising regularity, participants noted that dialogue had encouraged them to perceive their identities in more complex ways – to grapple with the difficulty of defining and claiming one's own self-identity rather than to rely on authoritative categories defined by others. They challenged existing social labels as far too constricting. Many interviewees expressed a preference for a more 'open' Islamic identity, which they had come to see as a viable cultural and intellectual possibility. This attitude of openness allowed them to reimagine Islamic authenticity and authority, to claim the status of authentic 'selfhood' as dynamic social agents, without becoming 'other' to their religiocultural communities, or defining themselves in a narrowly oppositional role vis-à-vis Western culture and foreign policies. Through dialogical encounters with complexity, they experienced a form of empowerment and in many cases transformation.

Transformation among Muslim women is happening in new ways, as individual Muslim women find themselves enabled to 'plug in' directly to transnational conversations – to experience themselves as part of an emergent, common experience of diverse Muslim women struggling to make sense of and respond to common issues and problems. United by a shared desire to overcome marginalization, the women rediscover themselves within a diverse context of similar and differing experiences. Through a process of reflection they develop shared meaning, particularly with reference to the importance of participation by women in civil society – women who are comfortable operating within a framework of Islamic discourse, yet not constrained by authoritative patriarchal interpretations, be they political or religious in nature.

Retrospect and Prospect

Limitations

This study has sought to provide an overview of cross-cutting themes in what appears to be an increasingly coherent, albeit still emergent, trend in contemporary Islamic thought – a trend in which the major protagonists are women. Through encounters with interviewees from localities throughout the Muslim world, I have provided first-hand testimony about why women are engaging in transnational dialogue, and have offered an interpretation of the significance of such dialogue for the identity and agency of Muslim women.

In assessing the nature of what has been learned, it is important to acknowledge limitations. First, this study has sought to offer an account of emergent transnational tendencies, seeking cross-cutting themes in ways that sometimes came at the expense of detailed attention to context, cultural particularism, and the specific social pressures (for example, economic necessities) that define localized experiences. As a group, Muslim women are tremendously diverse, and a project such as this cannot possibly do justice to their unique and widely varying experiences. The diversity of context-particular experiences, however, should not impede efforts to investigate genuinely *transnational* phenomena, or to elucidate how these phenomena are experienced by individual human beings who are actively engaged with them.

Second, this project has been exploratory in nature, and cannot offer a precise or global assessment of trends experienced by Muslim women. The judgments offered here, though based on concrete encounters and recurrent patterns, cannot be taken to represent all women engaged in transnational dialogue, let alone all Muslim women. Due to limited time and resources, the sample of interviewees utilized by this study cannot be assumed to represent the entire Muslim world. Further research, based on encounters in different localities and countries, is needed to substantiate the findings offered here (see suggestions for further research in the next section).

Responding to Potential Critiques

Studies of activism among Muslim women are subject to many potential critiques, but three lines of criticism are particularly commonplace: first, that women's activism in the Muslim world is a narrowly based, elite, and largely secular phenomenon; second, that this activism will inevitably be dominated by external agendas and a politicized 'Westernization vs. Islamic authenticity' debate, making genuine and sustained dialogue among diverse Muslim women activists highly improbable; and third, that transnational *conservative* activities – for example, male-dominated revivalist networking – are far more significant and influential.

Despite the limitations noted previously, this study provides evidence that challenges these preconceptions. As for the first criticism, it is true that many traditional feminist movements in Muslim societies have been strongly influenced by Western ideas, and have taken root first among the middle and upper classes. The networks I investigated, however, did not fit this stereotype. Most of the women I interviewed were not members of elite social classes, and only a few of them were educated in Western universities. Many had roots in working-class families, and had become involved in transnational activism only after a great deal of educational or activist effort. Some relied on high school educations and formative life experiences within contexts of largely 'oral' culture. Admittedly, many had indeed experienced a degree of social and political 'privilege' in their lives and most did not fit stereotypes of 'Muslim women' that are remarkably similar in both Western and revivalist Muslim contexts. When asked for their views on the subject of women and Islam, their answers were often remarkable more for their complexity (mixing diverse cultural, religious, and philosophical influences) than for their 'Islamicity' (insofar as this is typically related to scriptural references and religious narratives). Nonetheless, my interviewees consistently insisted on their Muslim identity, raising profound questions about essentialized understandings of 'Muslimness' and of standard typologies that posit clear boundaries between secular and religious forms of activism.

Rather than conforming to stereotypes, Muslim women involved in transnational networking were dialogically engaged not only with women from different national contexts, but also with different normative systems that interactively constitute contemporary Muslim women's identities. The inclusiveness of dialogue in women's networks was often quite impressive, as were the efforts of a number of leading women to empower those who would not otherwise have had access to transnational women's networks. Most of these women were also quite insistent about the cultural and political autonomy of their vision – they did *not* wish to be perceived as appendages of a Western (especially American) foreign policy to promote 'moderate Islam.'

Many of my interviewees were highly aware of how politicized the 'women and Islam' subject has become, and this relates to a second potential criticism of this research: that it is driven (and therefore predetermined in outcome) by an external political agenda, be it the agenda of the Bush administration, an agenda of Islamic reformation, or an agenda of Islamic revival. I will not deal extensively with this criticism, beyond noting that I have sought to fully and transparently present my assumptions, methods of inquiry, and findings. I will concede, however, that an enthusiasm for dialogue among competing camps played a significant role in motivating this research.

Finally, there are many who would argue that transnational women's activism 'doesn't have a chance' in contemporary Islamic cultures – that revivalism, particularly reactionary revivalism, is a far more potent ideological force. My primary response to this criticism can be found in the data related in previous chapters. While it is true that a strong current of cultural conservatism has swept the Muslim world in recent decades, claims that 'fundamentalism' always prevails (or, worse still, is characteristic of the religion itself) are misinformed. It is arguable that the Western media and even academic studies give insufficient attention to the diversity of Islamic voices, while focusing much more intently on revivalism and those tendencies that present a conceivable 'security threat' to the West. As the data of this study reveal, many Muslim women and men are offering new ways for expressing Muslim identity, and are actively involved in efforts to define contemporary social norms.

The Need for Further Exploration

Transnational networking among Muslim women is a new phenomenon in international affairs. The oldest formal network, Women Living Under Muslim Laws, was officially founded in 1987, and most other networks – formal as well as informal – are more recent in origin. Because transnational networking among Muslim women is such a novel and dynamic phenomenon, a number of avenues for further research are open for future exploration.

First, no systematic effort has yet been made to trace informal as well as formal women's networks. As mentioned previously, the goals of the present project were modest, and I was not able to comprehensively map formally organized projects and networks and their prior links to more informal forms of communication and collaboration. Consequently, there is a need for more detailed analyses of these emerging dialogues and networks. Such studies might usefully take an approach that is more structural in orientation (in contrast to the present study), giving particular attention to recent efforts, which have seen a marked increase in transnational networking. Research teams might conceivably work to engage some of the many worthy activists who remain to be interviewed, and to explore the impact of collaborative projects that have developed through transnational efforts. Attention might also be given to the impact of the internet on Muslim women's networks, and to other factors which 'enable' their activism.

Second, there needs to be further analysis of the more formal networks, like Women Living Under Muslim Laws, and their relationships with more localized organizations that are gaining transnational notoriety (for example, Sisters in Islam, Malaysia). How have these networks and organizations influenced one another? What are their perceptions of each other? How have they changed over the course of their existence – in methods as well as in outlook and discourse? Researchers can make a significant contribution by exploring such forms of shared activism, and describing them in more detail.

Third, further research should also be devoted to the efforts of Muslim women to acquire 'authoritative' status as religious interpreters, taking into consideration both broad trends in Muslim societies toward gender equality in higher education and more recent events in North America, in which women have begun aspiring to fulfill roles in the Muslim community that have previously been the exclusive prerogative of men (for example, the appointment of Ingrid Mattison as the Executive Director of the Islamic Society of North America, and Amina Wadud and Asra Nomani's more 'controversial' efforts to act as female imams for mixed Muslim congregations). Such research could address the following questions: How are major sociological shifts, such as the growth of literacy and professional engagement among Muslim women, affecting perceptions concerning the role of women in public religious life? What is the impact of women's religious empowerment on specific Muslim communities, on transnational Muslim identity, and on political dynamics in particular contexts? What are some of the most important substantive issues that are currently 'under negotiation' in mosques, Muslim community centers, and Muslim voluntary associations, in diaspora communities as well as in Muslim-majority contexts?

Learning from the Encounters

This study has provided an introduction to the role of transnational activism in identity formation among Muslim women. Rather than focus exclusively on the activities of a single organization or network, it has utilized an exploratory research design to provide insight into developing trends that connect diverse contexts of Muslim social life. Research has been conducted in an investigative manner, with exposition of cross-cutting themes, and a review of implications for social change and the status of Muslim women. The encounters through which data was gathered provided vivid evidence of emergent tendencies toward new forms of transnational identification. Such tendencies have only begun to be identified and analyzed. They need to be noticed, traced, and interpreted by scholars of women and Islam.

Although there is a growing literature on women and Islam as well as on Islam and the transnational (as well as on the 'transcultural' and 'translocal'), there has thus far been an absence of attention to the impact of transnational Muslim politics *on* and *for* women. This study attempts to help fill this gap, by formulating an understanding of how transnational dialogue has challenged those Muslim women who have been engaging in it to rethink assumptions – about themselves, about their cultural conditioning, and about the range of humane, moral, and religiously legitimate options that are available to them. It has also encouraged them to generate a greater awareness of ways in which the cultural and religious norms that they experience are the result of *interpretive practices*, and are therefore open to reinterpretation. This insight into the importance of hermeneutics is helping women to work with secular/ religious divides in new ways, and is resulting in a great deal of new thinking about what Islamic ethics prescribes for gender relations in the Muslim world.

At a time of tremendous international tension and of intellectual ferment within predominantly Muslim societies, there is a profound need for research that allows the voices of Muslim women to be heard – with minimal filtration and without efforts to subordinate their concerns to grand political designs, such as the 'imposition of democracy' or the reassertion of 'Islamic authenticity.' The issues of filtration and co-optation are very real, particularly since the tragic events of 11 September 2001 and ensuing American efforts to cultivate a 'moderate Islam.' While such efforts have brought increased attention to Muslim women in the West, they have also increased the sensitivity of women's activism in Muslim societies. Many women feel that their cause has been undermined by this unprecedented external attention, alloyed as it is with geopolitical agendas – yet some are also eager to seize opportunities to raise awareness about their fundamental concerns. If they persist in their efforts to build bridges of understanding across the many divides that fragment their realities – divides among Muslims, as well as between Islam and the West – their chances of becoming agents of transformation will significantly increase.

Appendix

List of Key Interviewees and Some Focus Group Participants

Key Interviewees

Mahboubeh Abbas-Ghulizadeh, Convenor of the Muslim women workshop, *Forum for Dialogue: Learning from Each Other* at Tehran's Institute for Women's Studies and Research, Iran.

Umaima Abu-Bakr, Professor of Comparative Literature at Cairo University, Egypt.

Jamila Afghani, Director of the Noor Educational Center, Kabul, Afghanistan.

Meltam Agduk, Project Coordinator for the United Nations Population Fund (UNFPA), Ankara, Turkey.

Manzooruddin Ahmad, former Professor of Political Science and Philosophy as well as Vice Chancellor at the University of Karachi, and currently the Chairman of the Executive Board for the Usman-Institute of Technology in Karachi, Pakistan.

Seyed Jaffar Ahmed, Acting Director of the Pakistan Study Centre at the University of Karachi, Pakistan.

Monir Amadi Qomi, Managing Director, Institute for Women's Studies and Research (IWSR), Tehran, Iran.

Zainah Anwar, Executive Director of the Sisters in Islam organization based in Kuala Lumpur, Malaysia.

Mohammed Arkoun, Emeritus Professor of the History of Islamic Thought at the Sorbonne Nouvelle in Paris, France.

Gholam Reza A'wani, Director of the Iranian Institute of Philosophy (IRIP), Tehran, Iran.

Cassandra Balchin, Deputy Office Coordinator, Women Living Under Muslim Laws Network, London, England.

Hamid Bashiriyeh, Director of International Affairs at the International Center for Dialogue Among Civilizations (ICDAC) in Tehran, Iran.

Rachida ben Faida, Professor of Humanities at the Université Cadi Ayyad in Marrekech, Morocco.

Ayatollah Borjnurdi, Professor of Islamic Law, Tehran, Iran.

Salima Hashmi, Dean of Beaconhouse National University in Lahore, Pakistan.

Jamila Hassoune, Manager of Hassoune's Bookshop and co-founder of Caravane Civique and Club du Livre et de Lecture Marrakech, Morocco.

Anissa Helie, Program Officer, Women Living Under Muslim Laws Network, London, England.

Mariam Hussain, Artist and activist, Lahore, Pakistan.

Neelam Hussain, Director of Simorgh Organization, Lahore, Pakistan.

Hauwa Ibrahim, first Muslim woman lawyer in Nigeria.

Suroosh Irfani, Professor of Humanities, National College of Arts, Lahore, Pakistan.

Shehnaz Ismail, Director of the Indus Valley School of Art and Architecture in Karachi, Pakistan.

Laya Joneydi, Attorney at Law and Professor of Law, Tehran University, Iran.

Azam Khatam, Urban Sociologist, Urban Planning and Architecture Research Center, Tehran, Iran.

Elahe Kolaei, Professor of Political Science, Tehran University, Iran.

Saideh Lotfian, Professor of Political Science at Tehran University, Iran.

N. Mosaffar, Professor of Political Science, Tehran University, Iran.

Homeira Moshirzadeh, Professor of International Relations, Tehran University, Iran.

Halima Oulami, Co-founder of Club du Livre et de Lecture Marrakech, Morocco.

Farhat Naz Rahman, General Secretary, RAHM Women's Research Organization, Karachi, Pakistan.

Heba Rauf Ezzat, Professor of Political Science, Cairo University, and co-founder of IslamOnLine.com.

Hoda Rouhana, Program Officer for networking in the Middle East and North Africa, Women Living Under Muslim Laws Network, London, England.

Seyed Kazem Sajjadpour, Director General of the Institute for Political and International Studies, Tehran, Iran.

Yvonne Seng, Author and scholar of Middle Eastern and Islamic History.

Jaleh Shaditalab, Director of the Center for Women's Studies at Tehran University, Iran.

Farida Shaheed, Co-director of Shirkat Gah and Women Living Under Muslim Laws (WLUML), Lahore, Pakistan.

Muhammad Ali Siddiqui, Dean of Humanities and Social Sciences, Hamdard University, Karachi, Pakistan.

Bine Bine Touria, Founding President of the First Soroptimist Club in Marrakech, Morocco.

Amina Wadud, Professor of Religious Studies, Virginia Commonwealth University, USA.

Mona Zulficar, Lawyer and key activist in the Personal Status Law coalition and a founding member of the National Council for Women, Egypt.

Some Focus Group Participants

8th Caravane Civique conference in Casablanca, Morocco: focus group participants included a group of grassroots activists from Zagora, Morocco; an activist group from Marrakech, Morocco (members of the Club du Livre et de Lecture Marrackech: *Halima Oulami, Samira Elouargi*, and *Rachid Ouled Housseine*); Moroccan and international coordinators of the conference (that is, *Jamila Hassoune, Houda Hassoune, Fatna El-Bouih, Najia El-Boudali, Neama Ouazzani, Wafae Guessous, Aziz Al Ouadi*, and *Mouhcine Ayouche*).

The Center for Women's Studies, University of Tehran, Iran. This focus group consisted of five women who were working on different projects for the center. One project is the creation of a regional transnational dialogue with participants from Iran, Iraq, Afghanistan, and Pakistan, as well as Uzbekistan.

Forum for Dialogue: Learning from Each Other (a Muslim women's workshop at Tehran's Institute for Women's Studies and Research, Iran): some of the focus group participants were *Susan Rakhsh*, *Meltam Agduk*, *Roja Fazaeli*, and *Maasum Parvi*.

Sisters in Islam, main headquarters, Kuala Lumpur, Malaysia. The author interviewed *Zainah Anwar*, the Executive Director of SIS, and communicated with different members via the internet.

Women Living Under Muslim Laws at the London headquarters: some of the focus group participants were *Cassandra Balchin*, *Anissa Helie*, and *Hoda Rouhana*.

Women's Research Center, al-Zahra University, Tehran, Iran: some of the focus group participants were *Ali-Reza Ahmadi*, *Akram Khamseh*, and *A. Pakniam*.

Women's Research Centre, University of Karachi, Karachi, Pakistan. The focus group consisted of eight women who were working on different projects for the centre. One project is the production of the *Pakistan Journal of Women's Studies*.

Bibliography

Abdul Rauf, Feisal (2005), *What's Right with Islam is What's Right with America*, NY: HarperCollins Publishers.

Abizadeh, Arash (2005), 'Does Collective Identity Presuppose an Other? On the Alleged Incoherence of Global Solidarity,' *American Political Science Review*, vol. 99(1), February, pp. 45–59.

Abou El-Fadl, Khaled (2001a), *And God Knows His Soldiers: The Authoritative and Authoritarian in Islamic Discourses*, Lanham, MD: University Press of America.

_____ (2001b), *Speaking in God's Name: Islamic Law, Authority, and Women*, Oxford, England: Oneworld Publications.

Abu-Lughod, Lila (ed.) (1998), *Remaking Women: Feminism and Modernity in the Middle East*, Princeton, NJ: Princeton University Press.

_____ (2000), *Veiled Sentiments: Honor and Poetry in Bedouin Society*, CA: University of California Press.

Afkhami, Mahnaz (ed.) (1995), *Faith and Freedom: Women's Human Rights in the Muslim World*, New York: Syracuse University Press.

Afsaruddin, Asma (ed.) (1999), *Hermeneutics and Honor: Negotiating Female 'Public' Space in Islamic/ate Societies*, Cambridge, MA: Harvard University Press.

Afshari, Reza (2002), 'Egalitarian Islam and Misogynist Islamic Tradition: A Critique of the Feminist Reinterpretation of Islamic History and Heritage,' *Institute for the Secularization of Islamic Society* [website], <http://www.secularisalm.org/women/afshari.htm> (accessed 11 April 2002).

Afzal-Khan, Fawzia (ed.) (2005), *Shattering the Stereotypes: Muslim Women Speak Out*, Northampton, MA: Olive Branch Press.

Ahmed, Leila (1992), *Women and Gender in Islam: Historical Roots of a Modern Debate*, CT: Yale University Press.

_____ (1999), *A Border Passage: From Cairo to America – A Woman's Journey*, New York: Penguin Books Ltd.

_____ (2000), 'Open Letter to President Khatami,' *The New York Review of Books*, vol. 47(5), 23 March.

Al-Ali, Nadje (2007a), 'Iraqi Women: Four Years After the Invasion,' in *Foreign Policy in Focus*, Silver City, NM and Washington, DC, March, 14.

_____ (2007b), *Iraqi Women: Untold Stories from 1948 to the Present*, NY: Zed Books.

Al-Hibri, Azizah (ed.) (1982), *Women and Islam*, Oxford: Pergamon Press.

_____ (2005), 'Dr. Azizah Al-Hibri Explores What it Means To Be an American Muslim,' *The American Arab Dialogue: English Supplement of Al-Hewar Magazine*, vol. 16(2), Winter/Spring.

Aljazeera.net (2003), 'Indian Women Build Own Mosque,' <http://www.english.

aljazeera.net/english/DialogBox/> (accessed 18 December 2003).

Amanuallah, Shahed (2005), 'The Lilith Prayer: Female Imam Sparks Global Controversy,' <http://www.alt.muslim.com/> (accessed 28 March 2005).

Ambah, Faiza Saleh (2004a), 'Saudi Round-Up Reformers,' *The Christian Science Monitor*, 18 March, pp. 1 and 7.

_____ (2004b), 'Saudi Reformers Recoup After Blow,' *The Christian Science Monitor*, 22 March, p. 6.

Amir-Ibrahimi, Massaret (2004), 'Performance in Everyday Life and the Rediscovery of the "Self" in Iranian Weblogs,' *Bad Jens: Iranian Feminist Newsletter*, seventh edition, September, <http://www.badjens.com/rediscovery.html> (accessed 30 September 2004).

Anderson, Benedict (1991), *Imagined Communities: Reflections on the Origins and Spread of Nationalism*, New York: Verso Publishers.

Anderson, Jon W. (1997), 'Is the Internet Islam's "Third Wave" or the "End of Civilization"?' unpublished paper for United States Institute of Peace's conference, *Virtual Diplomacy*, 1–2 April 1997.

_____ (2001), 'Muslim Networks, Muslim Selves in Cyberspace: Islam in the Post-Modern Public Sphere,' paper for the conference, *The Dynamism of Muslim Societies*, in Tokyo, Japan, 5–8 October 2001, available at <http://nmit.georgetown.edu/papers/jwanderson2.htm> (accessed 28 March 2005).

An-Naim, Abdullahi (1996), *Toward an Islamic Reformation: Civil Liberties, Human Rights, and International Law*, NY: Syracuse University Press.

_____ (2002), 'Religion and Global Civil Society: Inherent Incompatibility or Synergy and Interdependence,' in Marlies Glasius, Mary Kaldor and Helmut Anheier (eds), *Global Civil Society 2002*, Oxford: Oxford University Press, pp. 55–73.

Arkoun, Mohammed (1999), 'Islam, Europe, the West: Rethinking the Mediterranean Space,' unpublished paper for the international conference, *The Frontiers of the Mind in the 21st Century*, at the Library of Congress in June 1999.

_____ (2002), *The Unthought in Contemporary Islamic Thought*, London: Saqi Books.

Armajani, Jon (2004), *Dynamic Islam: Liberal Muslim Perspectives in a Transnational Age*, Lanham, MD: University Press of America.

Armario, Christine (2004), 'US Latinas Seek Answers in Islam,' *The Christian Science Monitor*, 27 December.

Aslan, Reza (2005), *No god but God: The Origins, Evolution, and Future of Islam*, New York: Random House Publishing Group.

ASMA [website] (2006), 'Muslim Women Leaders Launch Global Movement to Empower Muslim Women,' *ASMA Press Release*, <http://www.asmasociety.org/wise/news.html> (accessed 8 November 2006).

Azimi, Negar (2007), 'Hard Realities of Soft Power,' *The New York Times Magazine*, 24 June, pp. 50–55.

Azirhi, Abderrazzak (1996), 'Necessity of Dialogue,' *Islamic Culture*, vol. LXX(2), April pp. 19–26.

Badran, Margot (2002), 'Islamic Feminism: What's in a Name?' *Al-Ahram Weekly On-Line*, issue no. 569, <http://www.weekly.ahram.org.eg/2002/569/cu1.htm>

(accessed 23 January 2002).

Bakhtin, M. (1981), *The Dialogic Imagination: Four Essays*, translated by Caryl Emerson and Michael Holquist, Austin, TX: University of Texas Press.

Balchin, Cassandra (2003), 'With Her Feet on the Ground: Women, Religion and Development in Muslim Communities,' *Society for International Development*, vol. 46(4), December, pp. 40–47.

Banerjee, Neela (2004), 'Iraqi Women's Window of Opportunity for Political Gains is Closing,' *The New York Times*, 26 February p. A12.

Baobobconnections.org (2003), <http://www.baobabconnections.org/artikel. php?id=345/> (accessed 28 November 2003).

Barazangi, Nimat Hafez (2000), 'Muslim Women's Islamic Higher Learning as a Human Right,' in Gisela Webb (ed.), *Windows of Faith: Muslim Women Scholar-Activists in North America*, New York: Syracuse University Press, pp. 22–47.

Barlas, Asma (2002), *'Believing Women' in Islam: Unreading Patriarchal Interpretations of the Qur'an*, Austin: University of Texas Press.

_____ (2004), 'Amina Wadud's Hermeneutics of the Qur'an: Women Rereading Sacred Texts,' in Suha Taji-Farouki (ed.), *Modern Muslim Intellectuals and the Qur'an*, Oxford: Oxford University Press, pp. 97–123.

_____ (2005), 'The Excesses of Moderation,' *The American Journal of Islamic Social Sciences*, vol. 22(3), Summer, pp. 158–65.

_____ (2007), 'Un-reading Patriarchal Interpretations of the Qur'an: Beyond the Binaries of Tradition and Modernity,' *American Journal of Islamic Social Sciences*, vol. 24(2), Spring, pp. 129–35.

Bavikatte, Sanjay (2003), 'Allah is in the Details: Towards a Theory of Progressive Islam,' *Qalandar On-line Journal*, <http://www.islaminterfaith.org/issue.html> (accessed 1 July 2003).

_____ (2004), 'Promises of a Brave New World,' *CHOWK On-Line* [website], <http://www.chowk.com/show_article.cgi?aid=00001418&channel=university% 20ave&start=0&end=9&chapter=1&page=1> (accessed 20 December 2004).

Bayes, Jane H. and Nayereh Tohidi, (eds) (2001), *Globalization, Gender, and Religion: The Politics of Women's Rights in Catholic and Muslim Contexts*, New York: Palgrave.

Berger, Peter L. and Thomas Luckmann (1966), *The Social Construction of Reality: A Treatise in the Sociology of Knowledge*, New York: Doubleday Publishers.

Berkey, Jonathan P. (2002), *The Formation of Islam: Religion and Society in the Near East, 600–1800*, Cambridge: Cambridge University Press.

Bernal, Victoria (1994), 'Gender, Culture, and Capitalism: Women and the Remaking of Islamic "Tradition" in a Sudanese Village,' *Comparative Studies in Society and History*, vol. 36(1), January, pp. 36–67.

Bernstein, Richard J. (1976), *The Restructuring of Social and Political Theory*, PA: University of Pennsylvania Press.

Blaney, David and Naeem Inayatullah (2003), *International Relations and the Problems of Difference*, New York: Routledge Publishers.

Bodman, Herbert L. and Nayereh Tohidi (eds) (1998), *Women in Muslim Societies:*

Diversity Within Unity, Boulder, CO: Lynne Reinner Publishers.

Bohm, David (1990), *On Dialogue*, CA: David Bohm Seminars.

Bonino, Emma (2005), 'Women: Revolutionaries in the Arab World,' *The Globalist* [website], <http://www.theglobalist.com/DBWeb/printStoryId.aspx?StoryId=4493> (accessed 14 April 2005).

Boroujerdi, Mehrzad (1996), *Iranian Intellectuals and the West: The Tormented Triumph of Nativism*, New York: Syracuse University Press.

Boustany, Nora (2004), 'A Beacon, Even in the Darkest Hours,' *The Washington Post*, 20 February, p. A21.

Bowen, John R. (2007), *Why the French Don't Like Headscarves: Islam, the State, and Public Space*, Princeton, NJ: Princeton University Press.

Brown, L. Carl (2000), *Religion and State: The Muslim Approach to Politics*, New York: Columbia University Press.

Brown, Claudia (2001), 'Morocco's Survivors: Activists Shed Light on "Dark Years,"' *San Francisco Chronicle*, 13 April.

Brown, DeNeen L. (2004), '"Muslim Refusenik" Incites Furor with Critique of Faith,' *The Washington Post*, 19 January, p. A14.

Bunt, Gary (2000), *Virtually Islamic: Computer-Mediated Communication and Cyber Islamic Environments*, Cardiff, United Kingdom: University of Wales Press.

Carter, Erqun Mehmet (2003), *Voices Behind the Veil:* The World of Islam through the Eyes of Women, MI: Kregel Publications.

Castelli, Elizabeth A. (ed.) (2001), *Women, Gender, Religion: A Reader*, New York: Palgrave Publishers.

Chatty, Dawn and Annika Rabo (eds) (1997), *Organizing Women: Formal and Informal Women's Groups in the Middle East*, Oxford: Berg Publishing.

Chittick, William C. (1994), *Imaginal Worlds: Ibn al-'Arabi and the Problem of Religious Diversity*, Albany, New York: SUNY Press.

Clark, Rosemary (2000), *The Sacred Tradition in Ancient Egypt: The Esoteric Wisdom Revealed*, St Paul, MN: Llewellyn Publications.

Cochran, Molly (1999), *Normative Theory in International Relations: A Pragmatic Approach*, Cambridge: Cambridge University Press.

Cohen, Anthony P. (1985), *The Symbolic Construction of Community*, London: Routledge Publishers.

Constable, Pamela (2006), 'Afghan Girls: Back in the Shadows,' *The Washington Post*, 23 September, p. A10.

Cooke, Miriam (2001), *Women Claim Islam: Creating Islamic Feminism through Literature*, New York: Routledge.

Cooke, Miriam and Bruce B. Lawrence (eds) (2005), *Muslim Networks: From Hajj to Hip Hop*, NC: The University of North Carolina Press.

Cowan, J. Milton (ed.) (1980), *Hans Wehr: A Dictionary of Modern Written Arabic*, Beirut, Lebanon: Librairie Du Liban.

Daftary, Farhad (ed.) (2000), *Intellectual Traditions in Islam*, London: I.B. Tauris Publishers.

Dahlen, Ashk P. (2003), *Islamic Law, Epistemology and Modernity: Legal Philosophy in Contemporary Iran*, New York: Routledge Publishers.

Daily Times/Reuters (2006), 'Women's Council to Interpret Qur'an,' *WLUML and Shirkat Gah Newsheet*, vol. XVIII(4), December, p. 8.

Dallmayr, Fred (ed.) (1999), *Border Crossings: Toward a Comparative Political Theory*, Lanham, MD: Lexington Books.

_____ (2002), *Dialogue Among Civilizations: Some Exemplary Voices*, New York: Palgrave.

Davies, Merryl Wyn (1988), *Knowing One Another: Shaping an Islamic Anthropology*, New York: Mansell Publishing Limited.

Davutoglu, Ahmet (1994), *Alternative Paradigms: The Impact of Islamic and Western Weltanschauungs on Political Theory*, Lanham, MD: University Press of America.

al-Dawalibi, Muhammad Ma'ruf (1998), 'The Emancipation of Women: A Continuing Priority,' in A. Bouhdiba and M. Ma'ruf al-Dawalibi (eds), *The Different Aspects of Islamic Culture: The Individual and Society in Islam*, New York: UNESCO Publishing, pp. 185–202.

Der Derian, James and Michael J. Shapiro (eds) (1989), *International/Intertextual Relations: Postmodern Readings of World Politics*, New York: Lexington Books.

Donnelly, Paul (2004), 'The Ban on a Muslim Scholar,' *The Washington Post*, 28 August, p. A25.

Doyle, John (2007), 'Little Mosque is Gloriously Canadian,' *The Globe and Mail*, 9 January, pp. R1 and R2.

Ebadi, Shirin (2004), 'Bound but Gagged,' *The New York Times*, 16 November.

Eck, Diana L. (2004), 'Why Exclude a Muslim Voice?' *The Boston Globe*, 4 September.

Eickelman, Dale F. (1999), 'The Coming Transformation of the Muslim World,' *Middle East Review of International Affairs (On-Line)*, vol. 3(3), September, <http://www.biu.ac.il/SOC/besa/meria/journal/1999/issue3/jv3n3a8.html> (accessed 20 November 2001).

Eickelman, Dale F. and Jon W. Anderson (1999), 'Redefining Muslim Publics,' in Dale F. Eickelman and Jon W. Anderson (eds), *New Media in the Muslim World: The Emerging Public Sphere*, Bloomington, IN: Indiana University Press, pp. 1–17.

Eickelman, Dale F. and James Piscatori (1996), *Muslim Politics*, Princeton, NJ: Princeton University Press.

Eisenberg, Carol (2004), 'Toward a New Muslim Moment,' *Newsday On-Line*, <www.newsday.com/features/ny> (accessed 20 October 2004).

Eisenstadt, Shmuel N. (2002), 'Concluding Remarks: Public Sphere, Civil Society, and Political Dynamics in Islamic Societies,' in Miriam Hoexter, Shmuel N. Eisenstadt and Nehemia Levtzion (eds), *The Public Sphere in Muslim Societies*, New York: State University of New York Press, pp. 139–61.

El-Tablawy, Tarek (2005), 'Woman Leads Muslim Prayer Service in NYC,' *Guardian Unlimited*, 19 March.

Emirbayer, Mustafa (1997), 'Manifesto for a Relational Sociology,' *American*

Journal of Sociology, vol. 1103(2), pp. 281–317.

Engineer, Asghar Ali (2004), 'Book Review: Modern Muslim Intellectuals and the Qur'an,' *Institute for Islamic Studies* [website], <http://www.csss-isla.com/IIS/archive/archive.php?article=http%3A//www.csss-isla.com/IIS/archive/2004/october.htm> (accessed 28 March 2005).

Esack, Farid (1997a), 'Gender Justice,' *As-Salamu 'Alaykum: Muslim Peace Fellowship Newsletter*, vol. 2(7), September, pp. 12–14.

_____ (1997b), *Qur'an Liberation and Pluralism: An Islamic Perspective of Interreligious Solidarity Against Oppression*, Oxford: Oneworld Publications.

_____ (2002), *The Qur'an: A Short Introduction*, Oxford, England: Oneworld Publications.

_____ (2003), 'Religio-Cultural Diversity: For What and with Whom? Muslim Reflections from a Postapartheid South Africa in the Throes of Globalization,' in Abdul Aziz Said and Meena Sharify-Funk (eds), *Cultural Diversity and Islam*, MD: University Press of America, pp. 165–85.

Falah, Ghazi-Walid and Caroline Nagel (eds) (2005), *Geographies of Muslim Women: Gender, Religion, and Space*, New York: The Guilford Press.

al-Faruqi, Lois Lamya, 'Women in a Qur'anic Society,' *al-Tawhid, vol. 1* [website], <http://www.al-islam.org/al-tawhid/women-society.htm> (accessed 30 September 2001).

Fawzi El-Solh, Camillia and Judy Mabro (eds) (1994), *Muslim Women's Choices: Religious Belief and Social Reality*, Oxford: Berg Publishers Ltd.

Feminist Daily News Wire (2007), 'Iranian Women's Rights Activists Released, NGOs Closed,' in *WLUML and Shirkat Gah Newsheet*, vol. XIX(1), April, p. 1.

Ferdinand, Klaus and Mehdi Mozaffari (eds) (1988), *Islam: State and Society*, United Kingdom: Curzon Press.

Fernea, Elizabeth Warnock (1998), *In Search of Islamic Feminism: One Woman's Global Journey*, NY: Knopf Publishing Group.

Fischer, Michael M.J. and Mehdi Abedi (1990), 'Qur'anic Dialogics: Islamic Poetics and Politics for Muslims and for Us,' in Tullio Maranhao (ed.), *The Interpretation of Dialogue*, Chicago: University of Chicago Press, pp. 120–53.

Flyvbjerg, Bent (2001), *Making Social Science Matter: Why Social Inquiry Fails and How it Can Succeed Again*, Cambridge: Cambridge University Press.

Ford, Peter (2005), 'Europe's Rising Class of Believers: Muslims,' *The Christian Science Monitor*, 24 February.

Frey, Jennifer (2001), 'Thinking Outside the Burqa,' *The Washington Post*, 30 November, pp. C1 and C4.

Friedman, Thomas L. (2005), 'Brave, Young and Muslim,' *The New York Times*, 3 March.

Frost, Mervyn (1996), *Ethics in International Relations: A Constitutive Theory*, Cambridge: Cambridge University Press.

Fulbright, William J. (1966), *The Arrogance of Power*, New York: Random House.

Gadamer, Hans Georg (1976), *Philosophical Hermeneutics*, translated and edited by David E. Linge, Los Angeles, CA: University of California Press.

_____ (1998), *Truth and Method*, translated by Joel Weinsheimer and Donald G.

Marshall, New York: Doubleday Publishers.

Gauch, Sarah (2005), 'Political Gains for Mideast Women,' *The Christian Science Monitor*, 3 May.

Gedda, George (2004), 'Islamic Countries Commit to Reforms,' *YahooNews (Associated Press)*: <http://news.yahoo.com/news?tmpl=story&cid=535&u=/ap/20041211/> (accessed 12 December 2004).

Geertz, Clifford (1968), *Islam Observed: Religious Development in Morocco and Indonesia*, Chicago: University of Chicago Press.

_____ (1973), *The Interpretation of Cultures*, New York: HarperCollins Publishers.

Gellner, Ernest (1983), *Nations and Nationalism*, Ithaca, NY: Cornell University Press.

Geuss, Raymond (1981), *The Idea of a Critical Theory: Habermas and the Frankfurt School*, New York: Cambridge University Press.

Al-Ghazali (2000), *Tahafut al-Falasifah: The Incoherence of the Philosophers*, translated by Michael E. Marmura, Provo, Utah: Brigham Young University Press.

Giddons, Anthony (1986), *The Constitution of Society: An Outline of the Theory of Structuration*, Berkeley, CA: University of California Press.

Glasse, Cyril (1989), *The Concise Encyclopedia of Islam*, New York: HarperCollins Publishers.

Gocek, Fatma Muge and Shiva Balaghi (eds) (1994), *Reconstructing Gender in the Middle East: Tradition, Identity, and Power*, New York: Columbia University Press.

Gramsci, Antonio (1971), *Selections from the Prison Notebooks*, translated and edited by Quintin Hoare and Geoffrey Nowell Smith, New York: International Publishers.

Greenwood, Davydd James and Morten Levin (1998), *Introduction to Action Research: Social Research for Social Change*, CA: SAGE Publications.

Grewal, Inderpal and Caren Kaplan (eds) (1994), *Scattered Hegemonies: Postmodernity and Transnational Feminist Practices*, MN: University of Minnesota Press.

Guillaume, Xavier (2002a), 'Foreign Policy and the Politics of Alterity: A Dialogical Understanding of International Relations,' *Millennium: Journal of International Studies*, vol. 31(1), pp. 1–26.

_____ (2002b), 'Reflexivity and Subjectivity: A Dialogical Perspective for and on International Relations Theory,' *In Forum: Qualitative Social Research* [On-Line Journal], vol. 3(3), September, <http://www.qualitative-reserach.net/fqs-eng.htm>.

_____ (2003), 'A Dialogical Perspective for and on IR Theory,' paper for 2003 ISA Convention in Portland, Oregon.

Haddad, Yvonne (2004), 'The Quest for a "Moderate Islam,"' *Al-Hewar Magazine*, vol. 115(2), Winter–Spring, pp. 8–12.

Haddad, Yvonne Yazbeck and John L. Esposito (eds) (1998), *Islam, Gender, and Social Change*, Oxford: Oxford University Press.

Haddad, Yvonne Yazbeck, Jane I. Smith and Kathleen M. Moore (2006), *Muslim*

Women in America: The Challenge of Islamic Identity Today, Oxford: Oxford University Press.

Hasan, Asma Gull (2001), *American Muslims: The New Generation*, New York: The Continuum International Publishing Group, Inc.

Hasan, Zoya (ed.) (1994), *Forging Identities: Gender, Communities and the State in India*, Boulder, CO: Westview Press.

Hashmi, Salima (2002), *Unveiling the Visible: Lives and Works of Women Artists of Pakistan*, Pakistan: ACT, ONAID.

Hashmi, Sohail H. (ed.) (2002), *Islamic Political Ethics: Civil Society, Pluralism, and Conflict*, Princeton, NJ: Princeton University Press.

Hassan, Farzana (2006), *Islam, Women, and the Challenges of Today*, Toronto: White Knight Books.

Heidegger, Martin (1996), *Being and Time*, translated by Joan Stambaugh, Albany, NY: State University of New York Press.

Hirsi Ali, Ayaan (2006), *The Caged Virgin: An Emancipation Proclamation for Women and Islam*, New York: Free Press.

_____ (2007), *Infidel*, New York: Free Press.

Hoagland, Jim (2003), 'A King's Appeal,' *The Washington Post*, 16 October.

Hobbes, Thomas (1985), *Leviathan*, NY: Penguin Books.

Hobsbawm, Eric (1990), *Nations and Nationalism Since 1780: Programme, Myth, Reality*, Cambridge: Cambridge University Press.

Hodgson, Marshall G.S. (1974), *The Venture of Islam: Conscience and History in a World Civilization, Vol. 1: The Classical Age of Islam*, Chicago: The University of Chicago Press.

Hoexter, Miriam, Shmuel N. Eisenstadt and Nehemia Levtzion (eds) (2002), *The Public Sphere in Muslim Societies*, Albany, NY: SUNY Press.

Holstein, James A. and Jaber F. Gubrium (1995), *The Active Interview*, CA: SAGE Publications.

Hughes, John (2004), 'Turbulent Indonesia, Moderate Islam,' *The Christian Science Monitor*, 14 April, p. 10.

Hunt, Krista (2006), '"Embedded Feminism" in the War on Terror,' in Krista Hunt and Kim Rygiel (eds), *(En)Gendering the War on Terror: War Stories and Camouflaged Politics*, New York: Ashgate Publishers.

Hunt, Krista and Kim Rygiel (eds) (2006), *(En)Gendering the War on Terror: War Stories and Camouflaged Politics*, New York: Ashgate Publishers.

Hussain, Neelam and Maha Malik (1985), *Reinventing Women: Representation of Women in the Media During the Zia Years*, Lahore, Pakistan: Simorgh Women's Resource and Publication Centre.

Hutchinson, John and Anthony D. Smith (eds) (1994), *Nationalism*, Oxford: Oxford University Press.

Ibn Rushd (1954), *Tahafut al-Tahafut (The Incoherence of the Incoherence) Vols. I and II*, translated by Simon Van Den Bergh, Cambridge, England: EJW Gibb Memorial Trust.

Iriye, Akira (2002), *Global Community: The Role of International Organizations in the Making of the Contemporary World*, Berkeley, CA: University of California

Press.

Jackson, Patrick Thaddeus (2002), 'Rethinking Weber: Towards a Non-Individualist Sociology of World Politics,' *International Review of Sociology*, vol. 12(3), pp. 439–68.

Jung, Hwa Yol (1999), 'Postmodernity, Eurocentrism, and the Future of Political Philosophy,' in Fred Dallmayr (ed.), *Border Crossings: Toward a Comparative Political Theory*, MD: Lexington Books, pp. 277–96.

Kandiyoti, Deniz (1991a), 'Identity and Its Discontents: Women and the Nation,' *Millennium: Journal of International Studies*, London: London School of Economics, vol. 20(3) pp. 429–43.

_____ (ed.) (1991b), *Women, Islam, and the State*, Philadelphia, PA: Temple University Press.

_____ (ed.) (1996), *Gendering the Middle East: Emerging Perspectives*, New York: Syracuse University Press, 1996.

Karam, Azza M. (1998), *Women, Islamisms, and the State: Contemporary Feminisms in Egypt*, New York: St. Martin's Press.

_____ (2002), 'Muslim Feminists in Western Academia,' in Johan Meuleman (ed.), *Islam in the Era of Globalization: Muslim Attitudes towards Modernity and Identity*, New York: Routledge Publishers, pp. 171–87.

Kazem, Halima (2005), 'In Afghanistan, Laura Bush Focuses on Roles of Women,' *The Christian Science Monitor*, 31 March.

Keddie, Nikki R. (1999a), 'Women and Religious Politics in the Contemporary World,' *ISIM Newsletter*, no. 3, July, p. 6.

_____ (1999b), 'Women and Twentieth Century Religious Politics,' in Nikki R. Keddie and Jasamin Rostam-Kolayi (eds), *The Journal of Women's History*, vol. 10 (Winter).

_____ (2000 and 2001), Women in Iran Since 1979,' *Social Research*, vol. 67(2), Summer, and reproduced on-line for *WLUML Dossier 23–24*, July, [WLUML website], <http://www.wluml.org/english/pubsfulltxt.shtml?cmd%5B87%5D=i-87-2793> (accessed 25 April 2004).

Kelsay, John (2002), 'Civil Society and Government in Islam,' in Sohail H. Hashmi (ed.), *Islamic Political Ethics: Civil Society, Pluralism, and Conflict*, Princeton, NJ: Princeton University Press, pp. 3–37.

Kennicott, Philip (2004), 'Shirin Ebadi's Moral Bookkeeping,' *The Washington Post*, 4 May, pp. C1 and C4.

Kent, Jonathan (2003), 'Scholars Debate Future of Islam,' *BBC Online News*: <http://www.news.bbc.co.uk/go/pr/fr/-/2/hi/asia-pacific/3058041.stm> (accessed 7 July 2003).

Keohane, Robert O. (1984), *After Hegemony: Cooperation and Discord in the World Political Economy*, Princeton , NJ: Princeton University Press.

Khalid, Asma (2007), 'Why I am not a Moderate Muslim,' *The Christian Science Monitor*, 23 April.

Khalil, Ashraf (2003), 'Egypt's First Female Judge May Remain "The Only,"' *Women's eNews*, <http://www.womensenews.org/article.cfm/dyn/aid/1536> (accessed 23 September 2003).

Khan, Muqtedar (2002), *American Muslims: Bridging Faith and Freedom*, VA:

Amana Publications.

Khan, Sarfraz (2003), *Muslim Reformist Political Thought: Revivalists, Modernists and Free Will*, London: Routledge Publishers.

Khan, Shahnaz (2007a), 'Saving Afghan Women and the Limits of Colonial Feminism,' paper presented for discussion panel on *Dialogue with Muslims after 9/11?* at the annual American Academy of Religion's Eastern International Region Conference, Renison College, University of Waterloo, 4 May 2007.

_____ (2007b), *Zina, Transnational Feminism, and the Moral Regulation of Pakistani Women,* Vancouver: UBC Press.

Khan, Sheema (2004), 'Such Arrogance: You Can't Pigeonhole 1.2 Billion Muslims,' *The Globe and Mail*, 30 July.

_____ (2007a), 'Can We Put the Racism Genie Back in Bottle?' *The Globe and Mail*, 17 April, p. A21.

_____ (2007b), 'There Really is a Canadian Way,' *The Globe and Mail*, February 6, p. A19.

Kian, Azadeh (1997), 'Women and Politics in Post-Islamist Iran: The Gender Conscious Drive to Change,' *British Journal of Middle Eastern Studies*, vol. 24(1), pp. 75–96.

Kogler, Hans Herbert (1996), *The Power of Dialogue: Critical Hermeneutics after Gadamer and Foucault*, translated by Paul Hendrickson, MA: MIT Press.

Kremmer, Janaki (2004), 'Taking a Stand for Moderate Islam,' *The Christian Science Monitor*, 21 July, pp. 15–16.

Kristof, Nicholas D. (2002), 'Women's Rights: Why Not?' *The New York Times*, 18 June.

Kurzman, Charles (ed.) (1998), *Liberal Islam: A Sourcebook*, Oxford: Oxford University Press.

_____ (1999), 'Liberal Islam: Prospects and Challenges,' *Middle East Review of International Affairs*, vol. 3(3), September.

_____ (2002), *Modernist Islam, 1840–1940: A Sourcebook*, Oxford: Oxford University Press.

Lampman, Jane (2004), 'Muslim Scholar Barred from US Preaches Tolerance,' *The Christian Science Monitor*, 21 September, p. 16.

_____ (2005), 'Muslims Split Over Gender Role,' *The Christian Science Monitor*, 28 March.

Lancaster, John (2003), 'In India, Rulings for Women, by Women: Muslims Turn to Female Scholars on Varied Matters of Faith and Femininity,' *The Washington Post*, 5 October.

Lapid, Yosef and Friedrich Kratochwil (eds) (1996), *The Return of Culture and Identity in IR Theory*, Boulder, CO: Lynne Rienner Publishers, Inc.

Lapidus, Ira (1983), *Contemporary Islamic Movements in Historical Perspective*, CA: University of California Press.

_____ (1988), *A History of Islamic Societies*, Cambridge: Cambridge University Press.

MacDonald, Gayle (2007), 'Little Mosque on the Champs Elysees,' *The Globe and Mail*, 9 May, p. R1.

Macfarquhar, Neil (2004), 'Wrestling Faith from the Extremists,' *Toronto Star*, 11

December, pp. A29–A30.

_____ (2007), 'Iran Cracks Down on Dissent, Parading Examples in Street,' *The New York Times*, 24 June, A01 and A09.

Machiavelli, Niccolo (1950), *The Prince and the Discourses*, NY: Random House.

Mack, Arien (ed.) (2003), 'Islam: The Public and Private Spheres,' *Social Research: An International Quarterly of the Social Sciences*, vol. 70(3), Fall.

Mackinnon, Mark (2005), 'We're Bored. Go Away!: After Five Decades of Repression, Younger Egyptians are Fed Up,' *The Globe and Mail*, 4 June, p. F8.

Mahmood, Saba (2005), *Politics of Piety: The Islamic Revival and the Feminist Subject*, Princeton, NJ: Princeton University Press.

Majid, Anouar (2000), *Unveiling Traditions: Postcolonial Islam in a Polycentric World*, Durham: Duke University Press.

Malik, Aftab Ahmad (2006), *With God on Our Side: Politics and Theology of the War on Terrorism*, Columbia, MD: Amal Press.

Malinowski, Tom (2004), 'Absent Moral Authority,' *The Washington Post*, 2 February, p. A17.

Mandaville, Peter (2001), *Transnational Muslim Politics: Reimagining the Umma*, London: Routledge Publishers.

Mandaville, Peter G. and Andrew J. Williams (eds) (2003), *Meaning and International Relations*, London: Routledge Publishers.

Manji, Irshad (2004), *The Trouble with Islam: A Wake-Up Call for Honesty and Change*, New York: St. Martin's Press.

Marotte, Bertrand (2007), 'Quebec Tae Kwon Do Team Knocked Out for Wearing Hijab,' *The Globe and Mail*, 16 April, pp. A1 and A6.

Masmoudi, Radwan (2003), 'The Silenced Majority,' *Journal of Democracy*, vol. 14(2), April, pp. 40–44.

_____ (2004), 'Why the US Should Engage Moderate Muslims Everywhere,' *The Daily Star*, 26 October.

Maso, I., P.A. Atkinson, S. Delamont and J.C. Verhoeven (eds) (1995), *Openness in Research: The Tension Between Self and Other*, The Netherlands: Van Gorcum & Comp.

Melucci, Alberto (1985), 'The Symbolic Challenge of Contemporary Movements,' *Social Research*, vol. 52(4), Winter, pp. 789–816.

Mernissi, Fatima (1990), *Beyond the Veil: Male–Female Dynamics in Modern Muslim Society*, IN: Indiana University Press.

_____ (1991), *The Veil and the Male Elite: A Feminist Interpretation of Women's Rights in Islam*, translated by Mary Jo Lakeland, Reading, MA: Addison-Wesley Publishing Company, Inc.

_____ (1992), *Islam and Democracy: Fear of the Modern World*, translated by Mary Jo Lakeland, Reading, MA: Addison-Wesley Publishing Company.

_____ (1993), *The Forgotten Queens of Islam*, translated by Mary Jo Lakeland, MN: University of Minnesota Press.

_____ (1994), *Dreams of Trespass: Tales of a Harem Girlhood*, Reading, MA: Perseus Books.

_____ (1996), *Women's Rebellion and Islamic Memory*, NJ: Zed Books Ltd.

_____ (2000), *The New Cheherazads: Women and Civil Society in Digital Islam*, (booklet).

_____ (2001), *Scheherazade Goes West: Different Cultures, Different Harems*, New York: Washington Square Press.

_____ (2005), 'The Satellite, the Prince, and Shaherazad: Women as Communicators in Digital Islam,' in Fereshteh Nouraie-Simone (ed.), *On Shifting Ground: Muslim Women in the Global Era*, New York: Feminist Press, pp. 3–16.

_____ *Vanishing Orient: Papa's Harem is Shifting to Mama's Civil Society*, Personal Document.

Meuleman, Johan (ed.), (2002), *Islam in the Era of Globalization: Muslim Attitudes towards Modernity and Identity*, New York: Routledge Publishers.

Michelfelder, Diane P. and Richard E. Palmer (eds) (1989), *Dialogue and Deconstruction: The Gadamer–Derrida Encounter*, New York: SUNY Press.

Milani, Farzaneh (2004), 'Silencing a Modern Scheherazade,' *CSID Email Bulletin*, <www.islam-democracy.org> (accessed 3 December 2004).

Mir-Hosseini, Ziba (1999), *Islam and Gender: The Religious Debate in Contemporary Iran*, Princeton, NJ: Princeton University Press.

Moaddel, Mansoor and Kamran Talattof (eds) (2000), *Contemporary Debates in Islam: An Anthology of Modernist and Fundamentalist Thought*, New York: St. Martin's Press.

Moallem, Minoo (2001), 'Transnationalism, Feminism, and Fundamentalism,' in Elizabeth A. Castelli (ed.), *Women, Gender, Religion: A Reader*, New York: Palgrave Publishers, pp. 119–45.

Moghadam, Valentine (2002), 'Violence and Terrorism: Feminist Observations on Islamist Movements, States, and the International System,' *Alternatives: Turkish Journal of International Relations*, vol. 1(2), <http://www.alternativesjournal.net/volume1/number2/valentine.htm> (accessed 15 June 2002).

_____ (2003), 'Globalizing the Local: Transnational Feminism and Afghan Women's Rights,' *Femmes & Mondialisation*, <http://www.peuplesmonde.com/article.php3?id_article=20> (accessed 26 December 2003).

_____ (2004), 'Islamic Feminism and its Discontents: Notes on a Debate,' *Iran Bulletin On-Line*, <http://www.iran-bullentin.org/women/Islamic_feminism_IB.html> (accessed 30 September 2004).

_____ (2005), 'Feminists versus Fundamentalists: Women Living under Muslim Laws and the Sisterhood is Global Institute,' in *Globalizing Women: Transnational Feminist Networks*, Baltimore, MD: John Hopkins University Press, pp. 142–72.

_____ 'From International to Transnational Organizing: A Century Feminist Journey,' unpublished paper.

Moghissi, Haideh (1999), *Feminism and Islamic Fundamentalism: The Limits of Postmodern Analysis*, New York: Zed Books Ltd.

Mohammadi, Ali (ed.) (2002), *Islam Encountering Globalization*, London: Routledge Publishers.

Mohanty, Chandra Talpade, Anne Russo and Lourdes Torres (eds) (1991), *Third World Women and the Politics of Feminism*, IN: Indiana University Press.

Moosa, Ebrahim (2003), 'The Debts and Burdens of Critical Islam,' in Omid Safi (ed.), *Progressive Muslims: On Justice, Gender and Pluralism*, Oxford: Oneworld

Publications, pp. 111–27.

Morgenthau, Hans J. (1973), *Politics Among Nations: The Struggle for Power and Peace*, New York: Alfred A. Knopf, Inc.

Mueller-Vollmer, Kurt (ed.) (2000), *The Hermeneutics Reader: Texts of the German Tradition from the Enlightenment to the Present*, New York: Continuum Publishing Co.

Mumtaz Ali, Muhammad (2007), 'Liberal Islam: An Analysis,' *American Journal of Islamic Social Sciences*, vol. 24(2), Spring, pp. 44–70.

Munch, Richard (2001), *Nation and Citizenship in the Global Age: From National to Transnational Ties and Identities*, New York: Palgrave.

Murata, Sachiko (1992), *The Tao of Islam: A Sourcebook on Gender Relationships in Islamic Thought*, New York: SUNY Press.

Murphy, Caryle (2003), 'Islam and Feminism: Are the Barriers Coming Down?' *Carnegie Reporter*, vol. 2(3), Fall.

_____ (2006), 'For Conservative Muslims, Goal of Isolation a Challenge,' *The Washington Post*, 5 September, p. A01.

Muzaffar, Chandra (2002), *Rights, Religion, and Reform: Enhancing Human Dignity through Spiritual and Moral Transformation*, London: RoutledgeCurzon.

Nafisi, Azar (2003), *Reading Lolita in Tehran*, New York: Random House, Inc.

Najmabadi, Afsaneh (1991), 'Hazards of Modernity and Morality: Women, State and Ideology in Contemporary Iran,' in Deniz Kandiyoti (ed.), *Women, Islam, and the State*, Philadelphia, PA: Temple University Press, pp. 48–76.

Nasr, Seyyed Hossein (1966), *Ideals and Realities of Islam*, Boston: Beacon Press.

_____ (1987), *Traditional Islam in the Modern World*, New York: Metjuen Inc., Routledge & Kegan Paul.

_____ (2004), *The Heart of Islam: Enduring Values For Humanity*, NY: HarperCollins Publishers.

Nasrawi, Salah (1998), 'Women's Pursuit of Judgeship Sparks Heated Debate in Egypt,' *The Grand Rapids Press*, 26 July, p. A14.

Nassef, Ahmed (2004), 'Listen to Muslim Silent Majority in US,' *The Christian Science Monitor*, 12 April, p. 10.

Neumann, Iver B. (1999), *Uses of the Other: 'The East' in European Identity Formation*, Minneapolis: University of Minnesota Press.

Nomani, Asra Q. (2003), 'She Shouldn't Be Stoned to Death. None of Us Should,' *The Washington Post*, 1 June, pp. B1 and B4.

_____ (2005), *Standing Alone in Mecca:* An American Woman's Struggle for the Soul of Islam, New York: HarperCollins Publishers.

Noor, Farish A. (2002), *The New Voices of Islam*, Leiden, Netherlands: ISIM Publications.

Nouraie-Simone, Fereshteh (ed.) (2005), *On Shifting Ground: Muslim Women in the Global Era*, New York: Feminist Press.

Nourallah, Riad (ed.) (2002), *The Future of Islam: Wilrid Scawen Blunt*, London: RoutledgeCurzon Publishers.

Ommaya, Ayub K. (1995), 'Requirements for a Renaissance of Science in Islamic Polity: A Muslim Neuroscientist's Perspective,' *Islamic Thought and Scientific*

Creativity, vol. 6(4), pp. 7–46.

Othman, Norani (1997), 'Shari'a and the Citizenship Rights of Women in a Modern Nation-State,' *IKMAS Working Paper, No. 10*, Bangi, Malaysia: Institut Kajian Malaysia dan Antarabangsa.

Panikkar, Raimon (1996), *Cultural Disarmament: The Way to Peace*, NY: Westminister John Knox Press.

Pasha, Mustapha K. and Ahmed I. Samatar (1994), 'Globalization and New Social Movements: The Resurgence of Islam,' paper for the workshop, *Globalization: Opportunities and Challenges*, at the American University, 26–27 March 1994.

Prabhu, Joseph (ed.) (1996), *The Intercultural Challenge of Raimon Panikkar*, Maryknoll, New York: Orbis Books.

Peletz, Michael G. (2002), *Islamic Modern: Religious Courts and Cultural Politics in Malaysia*, Princeton, NJ: Princeton University Press.

Petito, Fabio and Pavlos Hatzopoulos (eds) (2003), *Religion in International Relations: The Return from Exile*, New York: Palgrave Macmillan.

Plato (1993), *Symposium and Phaedrus*, translated by Benjamin Jowett, Toronto: Dover Publications.

Pollitt, Katha (2007), 'After Iraq and Afghanistan, Muslim Feminists are Leery of Seeming Close to the West,' *AlterNet* [website], <http://www.alternet.org/story/53209> (accessed 27 June 2007).

Power, Carla (2007), 'A Secret History,' *The New York Times Magazine*, 25 February, p. 22.

Prus, Robert (1999), *Beyond the Power Mystique: Power as Intersubjective Accomplishment*, Albany, NY: SUNY Press.

Qureshi, Emran and Michael A. Sells (eds) (2003), *The New Crusades: Constructing the Muslim Enemy*, New York: Columbia University Press.

Rahman, Fazlur (1965), *Islamic Methodology in History*, Karachi, Pakistan: Central Institute of Islamic Research.

_____ (1982), *Islam and Modernity: Transformation of an Intellectual Tradition*, Chicago, IL: The University of Chicago Press.

_____ (2000), *Revival and Reform in Islam: A Study of Islamic Fundamentalism*, Oxford, England: Oneworld Publications.

Ramadan, Tariq (2002), *To Be a European Muslim*, London: Islamic Foundation Limited.

_____ (2004a) *Western Muslims and the Future of Islam*, NY: Oxford University Press.

_____ (2004b), 'Too Scary for the Classroom?' *The New York Times*, 1 September.

_____ (2005), 'Muslims Need Creative Pluralism,' *The Globe and Mail*, 19 February, p. A23.

Rasian, Karim (2002), 'Indonesia's Moderate Islamists,' *Foreign Policy*, July–August.

Raza, Raheel (2005), *Their Jihad ... Not My Jihad!* Ingersoll, ON: Basileia Books.

Reynolds, Paul (2005), 'Preventing a Clash of Civilizations,' *BBC News Online, World Affairs*, <http://news.bbc.co.uk/1/hi/world/americas/3578429.stm>

(accessed 28 March 2005).

Ricoeur, Paul (1974), *The Conflict of Interpretations: Essays in Hermeneutics*, Evanston, IL: Northwestern University Press.

Risse-Kappen, Thomas (ed.) (1995), *Bringing Transnational Relations Back In: Non-State Actors, Domestic Structures, and International Institutions*, Cambridge: Cambridge University Press.

Rosenau, James (1990), *Turbulence in World Politics: A Theory of Change and Continuity*, Princeton, NJ: Princeton University Press.

Rosenau, Pauline Marie (1992), *Post-Modernism and the Social Sciences: Insights, Inroads, and Intrusions*, Princeton, NJ: Princeton University Press.

Rubin, Herbert J. and Irene S. Rubin (1995), *Qualitative Interviewing: The Art of Hearing Data*, CA: SAGE Publications.

Sabra, Martina (2004), 'Women's Rights by the Grace of the King,' *D + C (A Magazine for Development and Cooperation)*, February.

Sacirbey, Omar (2006), 'Muslim Extremists Target Moderates,' *Toronto Star*, 6 May, p. L11.

Sadri, Ahmad (2003), 'Nobel for Shirin Ebadi,' *The Daily Star On-Line*, <www.dailystar.com.lb/opinion/14_10_03_b.asp> (accessed 14 October 2003).

Safi, Omid (ed.) (2003), *Progressive Muslims: On Justice, Gender and Pluralism*, Oxford: Oneworld Publications.

Said, Abdul Aziz (2001), 'Islam and the West Today: "Blessed are the Strangers,"' paper for United States Institute of Peace Workshop on *The Role of Faith in Peacemaking: An Islamic Perspective*, 7 November.

_____ (2003), 'Toward a Contemporary Islamic Synthesis,' opening speech for the international conference *Contemporary Islamic Synthesis*, at the Library of Alexandria in Egypt, 4–5 October 2003.

Said, Abdul Aziz and Nathan C. Funk (2001), 'Understanding Revivalism: The Case of Islam in Global Perspective,' in Patricia M. Mische and Melissa Merkling (eds), *Toward a Global Civilization? The Contribution of Religions*, New York: Peter Lang Publishing, pp. 308–30.

Said, Abdul Aziz, Charles O. Lerche III and Charles O. Lerche Jr (1979), *Concepts of International Politics in Global Perspective*, NJ: Prentice Hall.

Said, Edward W. (1978), *Orientalism*, New York: Random House Inc.

_____ (1994), *Representations of the Intellectual: 1993 Reith Lectures*, New York: Pantheon Books.

Sakamoto, Yoshikazu (1997), 'Civil Society and Democratic World Order,' in Stephen Gill and James H. Mittelman (eds), *Innovation and Transformation in International Studies*, Cambridge: Cambridge University Press, pp. 207–19.

Saktanber, Ayse (1994), 'Becoming the "Other" as a Muslim in Turkey: Turkish Women vs. Islamist Women,' *New Perspectives on Turkey*, Fall, vol. 11, pp. 99–134.

_____ (2002), *Living Islam: Women, Religion and the Politicization of Culture in Turkey*, London: I.B. Tauris & Co. Ltd.

Saliba, Therese, Carolyn Allen and Judith A. Howard (eds) (2002), *Gender, Politics, and Islam*, Chicago, University of Chicago Press.

Salih, Ruba (2003), *Gender in Transnationalism: Home, Longing and Belonging among Moroccan Migrant Women*, London: Routledge Publishers.

Salvatore, Armando (1997), *Islam and the Political Discourse of Modernity*, London: Ithaca Press.

Salvatore, Armando and Almut Hofert (eds) (2000), *Between Europe and Islam: Shaping Modernity in a Transcultural Space*, Brussels: P.I.E.-Peter Lang.

Saunders, Doug (2007), 'Muslims Find Their Voice Outside Religion: Secular Movement Stirring Controversy Across Europe,' *The Globe and Mail*, 10 March, pp. A01 and A20.

Schemm, Paul (2004), 'Book Banning in Egypt targets a Muslim Moderate,' *The Christian Science Monitor*, 22 September, p. 11.

Schleifer, Yigal (2005), 'In Turkey, Muslim Women Gain Expanded Religious Authority,' *The Christian Science Monitor*, 27 April.

Schmidt, Garbi (2003), 'The Formation of Transnational Identities among Young Muslims in Denmark,' paper for the international seminar, *The Impact of Information and Communication Technologies on Religious, Ethnic, and Cultural Diaspora Communities in the West*, Gothenberg University, 27–29 October 2003.

Schneider, Howard (2000), 'Women in Egypt Gain Broader Divorce Rights,' *The Washington Post*, 14 April, pp. A01 and A17.

Schorr, Daniel (2004), 'Serious US Image Problem Abroad,' *The Christian Science Monitor*, 1 October, p. 9.

Scrivener, Leslie (2004a), 'Progressive Muslims Challenge Tradition,' *Toronto Star*, 16 October, pp. A1 and A26.

_____ (2004b), 'Progressive Muslims Responding to Very Narrow Version of Islam,' *Toronto Star*, 14 November, p. F7.

Seguin, Rheal and Heather Scoffield (2007), 'Quebec Leaders Seize Hijab Issue,' *The Globe and Mail*, 28 February, p. A11.

Senturk, Recep (2001), 'Toward an Open Science and Society: Multiplex Relations in Language, Religion, and Society,' *Islam: Arastirmalari Dergisi (Turkish Journal of Islamic Studies*, Sayi 6, pp. 93–129.

Shaaban, Bouthaina (1988), *Both Right and Left Handed: Arab Women Talk about Their Lives*, Bloomington, IN: Bloomington University Press.

_____ (1995), 'The Muted Voices of Women Interpreters,' in Mahnaz Afkhami (ed.), *Faith and Freedom: Women's Human Rights in the Muslim World*, Syracuse, NY: Syracuse University Press, pp. 61–77.

Shadid, Anthony (2005), 'Syria's Voices of Change,' *The Washington Post*, 25 May, p. A1.

Shaheed, Farida (1994), 'Controlled or Autonomous: Identity and the Experience of the Network Women Living Under Muslim Laws,' *SIGNS: A Journal of Women in Culture and Society*, vol. 19(4), Summer.

_____ (2001), 'Constructing Identities, Culture, Women's Agency and the Muslim World,' in *WLUML Dossier 23–24* (July 2001), <http://www.wluml.org/english/pubsfulltxt.shtml?cmd%5B87%5D=i-87-2788> (accessed 20 September 2004).

Shami, Seteney (1997), 'Domesticity Reconfigured: Women in Squatter Areas of Amman,' in Dawn Chatty and Annika Rabo (eds), *Organizing Women: Formal and Informal Women's Groups in the Middle East*, New York: Oxford International Publishers Ltd., pp. 81–99.

Sharify-Funk, Meena (2000), *Women and Islam: The Role of Holistic Interpretation*, Masters thesis, American University, August.

Sharify-Funk, Meena and Nathan C. Funk (forthcoming), 'Realpolitik, Authority, and the (Re)Construction of Boundaries: Challenges for Inter-Contextual Peacemaking between "Islam" and "the West,"' in Danielle Poe and Eddy Souffrant (eds), *Parceling the Globe: Philosophical Exploration in Globalization, Global Behavior, and Peace*.

Sharify-Funk, Meena and Abdul Aziz Said (eds) (2003), *Cultural Diversity and Islam*, Lanham, MD: University Press of America.

Sharify-Funk, Meena, Abdul Aziz Said and Mohammed Abu-Nimer (eds) (2006), *Contemporary Islam: Dynamic, not Static*, London: Routledge Publishers.

Shatz, Adam (2002), 'An Arab Poet Who Dares,' *The New York Times*, 13 July.

Shotter, John (1993), *Conversational Realities*, London: Sage Publications.

_____ (1999), 'Dialogue, Depth, and Life Inside Responsive Orders: From External Observation to Participatory Understanding,' in Bo Goranzon and Ingalill Holmberg (eds), *Dialogues on Performing Knowledge*, Stockholm, Sweden.

Singerman, Diane (forthcoming), *Rewriting Divorce in Egypt: Reclaiming Islam, Legal Activism, and Coalition Politics*, Princeton, NJ: Princeton University Press.

Sisters in Islam Organization, Internet website, <http://www.sistersinislam.org>.

_____ (1991), *Are All Women and Men Equal Before Allah?* SIS booklet.

_____ *Letters to the Editor and SIS brochure* (personal documents).

_____ (2001), *Report on Regional Workshop and Justice for Muslim Women*, June 8–10, found on the following website: <http://www.muslimtents.com/sistersinislam/resources/1report_workshop2001.html>, (accessed 20 October 2001).

Sjoberg, Gideon (1997), 'Reflective Methodology: The Foundations of Social Inquiry,' in *A Methodology of Social Research*, Prospect Heights, IL: Waveland Press, Inc.

Smith, Anthony D. (1991), *National Identity*, London: University of Nevada Press.

Smith, Craig S. (2004), 'Europe's Muslims May Be Headed Where Marxists Went Before,' *The New York Times*, 26 December.

Smith, Jackie, Charles Chatfield and Ron Pagnucco (eds) (1997), *Transnational Social Movements and Global Politics: Solidarity Beyond the State*, New York: Syracuse University Press.

Smith, Jane I. (ed.) (1980), *Women in Contemporary Muslim Societies*, NJ: Associated University Press.

Smock, David (2005), 'Ijtihad: Reinterpreting Islamic Principles for the Twenty-First Century,' USIP Special Report 125 on the USIP's website, <www.usip.org/pubs/specialreports/sr125.html> (accessed 26 February 2005).

Stowasser, Barbara Freyer (1994), *Women in the Qur'an, Traditions, and Interpretation*, Oxford: Oxford University Press.

Surber, Jere Paul (1998), *Culture and Critique: An Introduction to the Critical*

Discourses of Cultural Studies, Boulder, CO: Westview Press.

Sylvester, Christine (2002), *Feminist International Relations: An Unfinished Journey*, Cambridge: Cambridge University Press.

Taji-Farouki, Suha (ed.) (2004), *Modern Muslim Intellectuals and the Qur'an*, Oxford: Oxford University Press.

Teotonio, Isabel (2005), 'Women Leads Mixed-Gender Prayers for City Muslims,' *Toronto Star*, 25 April, p. A20.

Thanh Ha, Tu (2007), 'Muslim Woman Wears Her Hijab and a Black Belt with Pride,' *The Globe and Mail*, 17 April, p. A3.

Thompson, Michael J. (ed.) (2003), *Islam and the West: Critical Perspectives on Modernity*, MD: Rowman & Littlefield Publishers, Inc.

Tickner, Ann J. (2001), *Gendering World Politics: Issues and Approaches in the Post-Cold War Era*, New York: Columbia University Press.

Tilly, Charles (2002), *Stories, Identities, and Political Change*, MD: Rowman & Littlefield Publishers.

Tohidi, Nayerah (2002), 'The Global–Local Intersection of Feminism in Muslim Societies: the Cases of Iran and Azerbaijan,' *Social Research*, Fall.

United States Department of State's Bureau of Democracy, Human Rights and Labor, (2001), 'The Taliban's War Against Women,' Special Report, November.

Usher, Sebastian (2004), '"Jihad" Magazine for Women on Web,' *BBC Online News*, <http://news.bbc.co.uk/go/pr/fr/-1/hi/world/middle_east/3594982.stm>, (accessed 8 August 2004).

VandeHei, Jim (2005), 'First Lady Lobbies for Women's Rights in Mideast,' *The Washington Post*, 22 May, p. A20.

Vick, Karl (2003), 'Big Prize, Little Change: Iran's Nobel Winner Renews Rights Push,' *The Washington Post*, 4 November, pp. A19 and A22.

_____ (2004), 'Wrong Chador: In Tehran, "Reading Lolita" Translates as Ancient History,' *The Washington Post*, 19 July, pp. C1 and C5.

Voll, John O. (1983), 'Renewal and Reform in Islamic History: *Tajdid* and *Islah*,' in John Esposito (ed.), *Voices of Resurgent Islam*, Oxford: Oxford University Press, pp. 32–47.

Wadud, Amina (1999), *Qur'an and Woman: Rereading the Sacred Text from a Woman's Perspective*, Oxford: Oxford University Press.

_____ (2000), 'Muslim Women as Citizens?' in Nissim Rejwan (ed.), *The Many Faces of Islam: Perspectives on a Resurgent Civilization*, FL: University Press of Florida, pp. 206–9.

_____ (2002), 'A'isha's Legacy,' *The New Internationalist*, vol. 345, May.

_____ (2006), *Inside the Gender Jihad: Women's Reform in Islam*, Oxford: Oneworld Publications.

Wadud-Muhsin, Amina (1992a), *Qur'an and Woman*, Kuala Lumpur, Malaysia: Penerbit Fajar Bakti Sdn. Bhd.

_____ (1992b), 'Understanding the Implicit Qur'anic Parameters to the Role of Woman in the Modern Context,' *Islamic Quarterly*, vol. 36(2), pp. 125–30.

Walker, R.B.J. (1992), *Inside/Outside: International Relations as Political Theory*,

Cambridge: Cambridge University Press.

Wallerstein, Immanuel (1996), *Open the Social Sciences*, CA: Stanford University Press.

Waltz, Kenneth N. (1956), *Man, the State, and War: A Theoretical Analysis*, New York: Columbia University Press.

Warnock Fernea, Elizabeth (1998), *In Search of Islamic Feminism: One Woman's Global Journey*, New York: Anchor Books, Doubleday.

Weber, Max (1949), '"Objectivity" in Social Science and Social Policy,' in Edward A. Shils and Henry Finch (eds), *Max Weber on the Methodology of the Social Sciences*, IL: Free Press, pp. 49–112.

Wesselius, Janet Catherina (1998), 'Gender Identity Without Gender Prescriptions: Dealing with Essentialism and Constructionism in Feminist Politics,' *Symposium: Journal of Canadian Society for Hermeneutics and Postmodern Thought*, vol. II(2), Fall, pp. 223–35.

Whitehouse.gov (2001), 'Radio Address by Laura Bush to the Nation,' 17 November, <http://www.whitehouse.gov/news/releases/2001/11/print/20011117.html>, (accessed 2 March 2007).

Williams, Daniel (2004), '"Modern Muslims" Forge Hybrid Culture,' *The Washington Post*, 24 July, p. A15.

Wiltz, Teresa (2005), 'The Woman Who Went to the Front of the Mosque,' *The Washington Post*, 5 June, p. D1.

Wolfowitz, Paul (2004), 'Women in the New Iraq,' *The Washington Post*, 1 February, p. B07.

Wright, Robin (2007), 'Iran Curtails Freedom in Throwback to 1979: Repression Seen as Cultural Revolution,' *The Washington Post*, 16 June, p. A10.

Yacoob, Saadia (2004), 'Developing Identities: What is Progressive Islam and Who are Progressive Muslims?' unpublished paper for the 33rd Annual AMSS Conference, 24–26 September 2004.

Yamani, Mai (ed.) (1996), *Feminism and Islam: Legal and Literary Perspectives*, New York: New York University Press.

Yankelovich, Daniel (2004), 'To Defeat Al-Qaeda, US Must Build Trust of Moderate Muslims,' *The Christian Science Monitor*, 20 September, p. 9.

Yusuf, Hamza (2001), 'If You Hate the West, Emigrate to a Muslim Country,' *The Guardian*, 8 October.

Zaman, Muhammad Qasim (2002), *The Ulama in Contemporary Islam*, Princeton, NJ: Princeton University Press.

Zine, Jasmin (2004), 'Creating a Critical Faith-Centered Space for Antiracist Feminism: Reflections of a Muslim Scholar-Activist,' *Journal of Feminist Studies in Religion*, vol. 20(2), Fall, pp. 167–87.

_____ (2006), 'Between Orientalism and Fundamentalism: Muslim Woman and Feminist Engagement,' in Krista Hunt and Kim Rygiel (eds), *(En)Gendering the War on Terror: War Stories and Camouflaged Politics*, New York: Ashgate Publishers, pp. 27–49.

Zuhur, Sherifa (1992), *Revealing Reveiling: Islamist Gender Ideology in Contemporary Egypt*, Albany, NY: SUNY Press.

Index

Notes: Italic page numbers denote diagrams; numbers in brackets preceded by *n* are footnote numbers.

Gender in a Global/Local World